THE MANSION OF HISTORY

Carl G. Gustavson

"The mansion of history
has enough rooms to accommodate all of us"
(C. V. Wedgwood).

McGraw-Hill Book Company

New York • St. Louis • San Francisco • Auckland • Düsseldorf • Johannesburg
Kuala Lumpur • London • Mexico • Montreal • New Delhi • Panama • Paris
São Paulo • Singapore • Sydney • Tokyo • Toronto

123456789MUMU79876

Library of Congress Cataloging in Publication Data

Gustavson, Carl G
   The Mansion of History

   (McGraw-Hill Paperbacks)
   1. History—Philosophy. I. Title
D16.8.G867   901   76-197 Sept 27, 1976
ISBN 0-07-025276-9

To Ruth and Edwin Kennedy,
Patrons of Learning

Preface

Books, too, have their own histories. That *A Preface to History* should have a successor first occurred to me while involved in a University of Georgia summer federal institute at the invitation of Professor Lester D. Stephens. It was outlined during a two-week January passage of the North Atlantic on a Moore-McCormick freighter, and a preliminary draft was prepared in the evenings at the Wenner-Gren Center in Stockholm while I was otherwise engaged in a Fulbright research project at the Royal Library. The manuscript was substantially completed three years later during an eight-month stay at the Chalet les Quartre Saisons in Leysin, Switzerland.

Events at our state university, during the five-year period of student unrest throughout the country, reinforced my conviction that the specific teaching of historical-mindedness, in addition to the standard frame of reference, is an essential educational function of the profession. The incessant display, especially in the student newspaper, of rudimentary historical concepts by persons innocently unaware that they also live in the time dimension made the approach used in this book imperative. The most suitable recourse when beginning this teaching process would seem to be to identify and describe the elementary concepts that form the common tools used by those unfamiliar with history. It also seemed appropriate to illustrate these concepts by showing how they were used before the relatively recent development of history as a mode of thought. Then follows, in Parts III and IV, an exposition of what are here called basic historical processes, the current conventional ideas of social forces, change and continuity, and how things usually happen. Part V describes the more sophisticated tools of professional historical-mindedness, their origins and continued contemporary development.

The successive sections are designed to dovetail broadly with the customary sequence in a general survey course: Part II centers on the ancient era; Part III draws most of its illustrative material from the medieval period and on into the Reformation; Part IV runs up to the end of the eighteenth century; Part V roughly parallels the nineteenth century. For courses not covering the entire span of world history, the first parts are sufficiently short to serve as preliminary material. In order to simplify matters somewhat for those not versed in the customary outline of historical information—as, for instance, in certain kinds of interdisciplinary courses—certain topics recur repeatedly over a number of chapters.

An effort has also been made to weave into the text the spirit and traditions of the guild of historians, the names of famous historians, celebrated sayings, and well-known ways of expressing profound insights that have become the common property of the craft. In so doing, I am only striving to serve, in a summary fashion, as a reporter of professional wisdom, contradictions, and dilemmas.

I am indebted, for answers to questions or other assistance, to the following colleagues: Harry Stevens, Phillip Bebb, Alan Booth, James Chastain, Gifford Doxsee, Richard Harvey, William Kaldis, Roy Rauschenberg, and Willard Elsbree; and to Carl Denbow for his helpful interest and stimulating conversations over the years; Sheppard Black of Logan's Book Store; Deborah Klein of Creative Book Services; and Caryl, who puts up with it all. To the staff of the Ohio University library, a belated expression of gratitude for their patience with my impatience during the writing of several books.

The Mansion of History is respectfully dedicated to Ruth and Edwin Kennedy in appreciation for their long financial support of faculty scholarship at Ohio University through the John C. Baker Research Grants and the Distinguished Professor Awards.

C.G.

At BredaBlick
Kenora, Ontario

Contents

I

PAST AND PRESENT

A Most Dangerous Product: History

The scene: the government palace in Futureville. The year: 20—. The occasion: a cabinet meeting, presided over by Dictator Won Ahl de Marbles. The minister of propaganda, Dr. Boeggels, is speaking:

". . . and now that the Future has arrived and the Splootch Telepather has given us control of the world, we must take further measures to ensure our mastery. Among our more urgent priorities, we must make the people forget the past, we must abolish history.

"We are now the masters of 178 former countries, each with its own history. As long as they remember their past achievements as separate peoples, the Americans, the Russians, the Chinese and all the others are not going to be loyal subjects of our global empire. We must obliterate these divisive memories permanently."

The minister of culture spoke up: "I quite agree. The memories of the past also help to keep the various religions alive. If we abolish history, Islam, Christianity, Judaism, Shintoism, and the other religions will be easier to destroy. Marxism, too, depends upon history and will be snipped at the roots."

"If we can abolish their recollections of past struggles, the labor organizations will be much easier to quash," contributed the minister of labor.

The dictator turned to Dr. Splootch, inventor of the Splootch machine. "Well, then, have all the preparations been made?"

Splootch responded, "All is in readiness, Your Excellency, for a trial run. It will be limited, at first, to the capital city, where we have already carried on intensive indoctrination. The public has been repeatedly warned that thinking historically is a heresy and that those guilty of it will be splootched—vaporized— without further warning. The telepather has been programmed, for the time being, to the telepathic waves of the inhabitants of this city. It will work exactly as when we splootched everyone in Washington, the American capital, which—ah—persuaded all other governments to capitulate immediately."

"Good," said the dictator, "turn it on." Splootch walked over to the huge panel blinking with many lights on one side of the room and pushed a button. A faint whirring sound pervaded the room.

"And now to the next item on the agenda," began Won Ahl, after a brief admiring pause, but a door burst open, and an excited attendant gestured urgently to the dictator. "Your Excellency, those architects in the anteroom have vanished, just disappeared into thin air."

"What? Heretics so close at hand! Good to have found them out. Now back to the agenda. Mr. Precedence, as minister of justice, what do you . . ." He stopped. A trail of vapor curled where Mr. Precedence had sat. The ministers looked hastily about—four other seats were also empty.

"Traitors! In the cabinet itself! . . . What do *you* want?" This was directed to an attendant looking out the window who had started muttering incoherently to himself. He swung around, a terrified look on his face, "Your Excellency, the people in the Great Square, the people, the . . . they . . ."

The telephone started ringing. The chief of police answered it, then turned to the cabinet. "Someone is calling from the war department. It seems that the chiefs of staff were having lunch together and have suddenly all disappeared."

The phone was already ringing again. A moment of listening, then "There's an emergency at the hospital. Some of the doctors cannot be located." He hung up, whereupon the phone started clamoring again. "It's from the university. They claim something mysterious is going on down there, professors disappearing from in front of classes and most of the students also. Only some environmentalists and a couple behaviorists still seem to be teaching."

A cabinet minister rose, shouting at Dr. Splootch: "How is that contraption hooked up? Turn off . . ." Even as he spoke, he vanished. So did three other ministers. The attendant at the window was yammering, "The Square, the Square! All that's left is a boy and girl standing there smooching."

Dr. Splootch snarled defensively, "I am a technician, not an ideologue. I do what I am told—program the machine to vaporize anyone thinking about the past!" The telephone was ringing incessantly, an attendant rushed into the room, started to shout, and vanished. Only three cabinet ministers were now left. Dr. Boeggels roared: "You idiot, couldn't you tell the difference between . . ." and became a cloud of vapor.

"Turn it off!" ordered the dictator. Splootch started for the machine, saying, "I don't see what's wrong. When I hooked it up to vaporize Washington . . ." and vanished. So did everyone else in the room except the dictator, who was now screaming too loudly to hear anyone else: "Turn it off! Turn it off!"

The dictator stopped for breath, stared at the vapor clouds with unbelieving eyes, and went into hysterics: "I am Emperor of the World! I am the greatest conqueror in hist . . ."

The room was empty.

Preposterous? In a sense, it actually did happen once. The Emperor Shih Huang Ti (246–210 B.C.), forcefully reorganizing

China after the end of the Chou dynasty, tried to obliterate the traditions of the past by ordering all works of history and literature destroyed. Hundreds of manuscripts were burned and numerous scholars executed. He survived for a few more years, but after his death Chinese history was at least partially restored from hidden books and the memories of surviving scholars.

Dr. Splootch seems to have received faulty instructions. The intent must have been to eliminate the history of countries and groups as it is taught in formal classes or as it may be used to inculcate loyalty. Apparently these people did not understand that history is inextricably woven into the context of many areas of knowledge. Lawyers work with precedences; a long legacy out of the past guides the varied skills of architects, generals, and physicians, while geologists and professors of literature may be as much involved in the past as historians themselves.

Equally distressing, the cabinet evidently overlooked that everyone is his or her own historian, that our daily life is cluttered with our personal past, and that we rely upon our own experiences in facing today's happenings. Where is the dividing line between now and the past? Many times a day we all encounter the past, last week or ancient, in such forms as living memory, personal records, published allusions, habitual group conduct, and artifacts in our material environment.

"History" is most often defined as "the remembered past" or as "the memory of things said and done." One more precise version suggests that it is "the story of the deeds and achievements of men living in societies." It is the story of the past, the memory of human beings recollected, usually, in the form of narrative. We often refer to the past itself as "history," and the technician in Futureville, obviously confused over usage, hooked up his machine to this, rather than to any organized body of knowledge about it. That is, when we allude to history, we may be thinking of the happenings themselves or of the *recorded* memories of these events. There is also a third kind, the inchoate public memory of the past, full of myths and half-truths, which politicians often invoke while trying to win elections; in its more mystic, rather sacerdotal, form, the losers are apt to appeal to it, to posterity, for a more just judgment of themselves and their deeds.

These people in Futureville also made a very common error by regarding history as a burden, as an obstacle to their future. This is being much too selective, forgetting that the good things and the dynamic forces that power our age have also come out of the past.

Many have condemned history. Everyone knows that Napoleon Bonaparte once said that history is a "lie agreed upon." The historians, Thomas Carlyle and Edward Gibbon, declared, respectively, that it was a "great dust-heap" and an account of the "crimes, follies, and misfortunes of mankind." Voltaire called it a pack of tricks played upon the dead. Henry Ford swept the whole business aside with the simple declaration that history was "bunk."

For sheer power of invective, however, one must particularly admire the denunciation by Paul Valéry, the French poet: "History is the most dangerous product evolved from the chemistry of the intellect. Its properties are well known. It causes dreams, it intoxicates whole peoples, gives them false memories, quickens their reflexes, keeps their old wounds open, torments them in their repose, leads them into delusions of grandeur or persecution, and makes nations bitter, arrogant, insufferable, and vain."

Whatever its merits or demerits, history must be of extraordinary importance in order to earn such sweeping broadsides. Furthermore, Napoleon's opinion did not prevent him from creating more of it, nor did Carlyle or Gibbon stop writing about the past. And apparently the bunk did not extend to the history of automobiles, for Ford's museum at Dearborn Village contains a magnificent collection of vehicles illustrating the evolution of modern transportation.

History comes in many varieties and has many uses. It can be exciting or tedious, instructive or misleading, an intellectual discipline or blatant superstition. Properly practiced and reflective of the diversities of human experience, "the mansion of history," in the words of Cicely V. Wedgwood, "has enough rooms to accommodate all of us."

History's oldest and persistent service has been for entertainment, the enjoyment of stories of actual happenings as a pastime. Customarily regarded as a branch of literature until the middle of the nineteenth century, it still usually retains the form of a narrative and continues to provide material for cinema, television, and books of fiction. Vicarious experiences of the past invite us to partake of adventures in which we cannot ourselves adventure and to view broadening human panoramas otherwise unseen. For those too despondent over the trials of the present, the past may offer healing surcease. The future we cannot visit, but journeys to other peoples in other times are readily available.

Posterity, through history, memorializes those who have gone before, confers an earthly immortality as recognition of individual achievement. History is not for those who may accept the work of a hundred generations without acknowledging any debt to their predecessors; perhaps, they, too, will have descendants who will regard us as too benighted to be worth remembering and for whom the past will also be such a shadowy limbo that only *their* Now will seem imperishable.

Nations, institutions, and social groups use it to inspire loyalty to themselves and to create a sense of shared community by the telling of stories about past struggles, victories and defeats, and the sacrifices made for the benefit of posterity. Heroes are held up for emulation, and villains paraded as warnings. Lacking earlier traditions, American writers soon after their country's independence created their own versions of their country's past and have continued to do so. The growth of European nationalism in the nineteenth century inspired a long series of historians to write about the past in terms of their respective peoples' glories and destinies. Clearly subject to extreme abuse, this was the kind of history denounced so vehemently by Paul Valéry. Newly independent countries in Asia, Africa, and the West Indies quickly began to produce their own histories in order to give themselves a separate identity, a sense of mission, and to engender pride in their nationhood. Ghana and Mali, formerly the Gold Coast and the French Sudan, adopted proud historical names of earlier empires when they became independent. American blacks, seeking self-awareness and a fair place in society, demanded their own history and a more just description of their past role in the community.

Though the past is often, much too often, depicted as a struggle between the Good Guys (ourselves, naturally) and those Bad Guys in the Outer Darkness, history, in more objective forms, also describes the origins of things. The more background we know, the better we comprehend our contemporary world and our own place in it. As these lines are being written, a small child is running up the path of our little Canadian island; for her, the path that we hacked out and everything that was recently built are "given," they simply exist, the island has no past. Cicero commented, a couple thousand years ago, that a person who does not know what happened before he was born will remain forever a child. Each generation in turn, like explorers arriving in a strange land, must familiarize itself with the world of the living, and history, the collective memory of the community, serves as one guide for learning the contours of reality and how they came to be there.

Are the "lessons of history," beloved of political orators, useful? Back in 1934 and 1937, groups of German mountain climbers, full of the reckless zeal of Nazi Germany, staged onslaughts on Mount Nangi Parbat in the Himalayas for the greater glory of the Third Reich. Both expeditions met grim fates, eleven dying in 1934 and sixteen being buried in an avalanche in 1937. Mountain climbers, like all groups, have their own history, the stories of their achievements and tragedies, a collective memory of experiences helpful in confronting problems inherent in such endeavors. Those two groups ignored the lessons of mountaineering history, and they "met the fate they deserved." Shortly thereafter, Adolf Hitler led the Nazis in a greater onslaught, the military and political conquest of Europe, and for a few years the Fuehrer seemed to be a magically successful wizard of history. After spectacular early successes, however, the venture suffered total disaster. Had Hitler, like the mountain climbers, failed to consult history properly?

Although the answer to that particular question may seem easy, the factors involved are usually so diverse and interrelated that using lessons of history is about like trying to figure the trajectory of a space rocket to Jupiter with only elementary arithmetic. A prefatory "History teaches that . . ." should generally be taken as a signal that the speaker or writer is about to peddle his or her pet nostrum. Perhaps Sir Lewis Namier summed up a sensible answer best by saying that history gives an "intuitive understanding of how things do *not* happen." John H. Plumb put it another way, suggesting that history reveals what may be prudent.

History's importance often looms the most starkly in episodes in which it has been omitted from the calculations. This is exemplified, in two often-cited examples, by a Neville Chamberlain, bereft of much historical knowledge, thinking he could do business with Hitler, or a Colonel Edward House at the Paris peace conference in 1919 assuming that he could ignore the historical factors represented by the statesmen there and deal successfully with these men on a purely personal basis. History reveals the limitations of any one specific action by presenting the numerous factors that are involved in any current problem. It engenders a "feel" for the probabilities, on the basis of rather similar circumstances, and warns of simplistic solutions based on a too-limited selectivity of facts or excessive faith in one particular creed.

Is history actually relevant to our problems in an age of rapid change? Why study the past if, as some insist, it is obsolete? This argument could be reversed: if change is this rapid, then a student focusing only on the present will discover, a few years later, that *this* has also become obsolete, that he or she was concentrating on a transitory moment in history. When individual events follow in rapid sequence, the sensible procedure is to study the patterns, the direction of development over a period of time, in order to gain orientation. In horse and buggy days, we could watch the fence posts go by, but when we now drive on a highway, we must be aware of the contours of the road and the pattern of traffic.

Put another way, studying only the present is comparable to looking at a still picture from a stopped movie projector, seeing only the suspended animation of action that had begun much earlier, one moment only out of a continuing story on the reel of time. We live in a community whose social groups and institutions usually have much longer longevity than we do and whose habitual conduct can only be understood by watching their behavior over a lengthy period. Our Now is only one historical moment in the drama, an instant in an "infinity of present instants" (George Kubler). That child on the island path may live only in the Now, but she is also curious, fulfilling a natural need for explanations which usually must reach back to events that happened earlier.

Then, too, perhaps we are overly impressed by the rate of change because we happen to be participants. The synthetic rush of the news media contributes to this feeling, although the impression of fast-breaking events often reflects the imperatives of journalists' work rather than what really is out there. As a consequence, in our journey through life many of us keep watching the fence posts whiz by, not the broader panorama. Did immigrants traveling overseas from Europe perhaps face as much or more change? Or European peasants going to work in a factory town? Are recent technological developments actually more revolutionary in their impact than those of the nineteenth century?

Sometimes we delude ourselves about the nature of change itself. We may be deceived by old ideas masquerading under new labels or become excited about a new proposal to solve an old problem, not realizing that this proposal, in its essentials, has been tried before, perhaps many times. Our circumstances may seem novel if, lacking the collective memory of humanity, we do not often recognize basically similar circumstances that we share with our ancestors. Paradoxically, to be purely present-minded is to risk being entrapped in the past without even recognizing it as such.

History alleviates the fear of the unknown. The vicarious experience of history is good training for confronting the crises of our own age because, even though history does not repeat itself exactly, the happenings often have an evocative similarity. Community experiences do recur in various guises, and they can provide the perspective for seeing our own trials in the light of earlier crises and tribulations. In the midst of the brawling American scene at the beginning of the 1970s, the president of the American Historical Association told his fellow historians at their annual convention that they might "find some comfort" and perhaps also some enlightenment by looking at the crises of the fourth and fourteenth centuries. Others have pointed to the sixteenth century for similarities to the disorientation and mood of our own times. Knowing about the past makes not only the present but also the immediate future much less uncharted.

History, properly used, teaches respect for reality, an ability to discern and trace out the existing contours and the social forces at work in society. This is also a hard saying for those who either prefer to employ it as ammunition for special causes or who do not like recollections of the past because earlier experiences argue against their particular panacea. History is a good corrective for those who are constantly camped at the river Jordan, impatiently waiting to be led into the Promised Land. The historian's past does have a future, and we know what it is; we read about the American Revolution and are aware of what its future would bring. The historically minded know that the future is part of Time, part of our world, and that basically similar processes will still be at work. History soberly tells us the expectancy, the unlikelihood that we will suddenly encounter a secular Second Coming, either a sudden end of our world or an equally abrupt entry into a blessed Millennium. In the words of Jacques Barzun, history "molds minds strong enough to stand without flinching the terror and confusion of existence."

Beyond these specific uses, however, the most significant contribution of history to our contemporary world lies in its mode of thought, that is, in historical-mindedness. As one of the intellectual tools of the modern mind, it provides a dimension of human life, like the artistic or the spiritual, a way of enriching our perceptions of the environment. A virtually indispensable attribute of the civilized individual, a lack of historical-mindedness is comparable, in some ways, to being color-blind or tone-deaf. Not that all can be historically minded, any more than all of us can be musical or poetic, but the acquisition of its magical powers effectively transforms our perceived surroundings in depth and meaning.

A mature sense of historical-mindedness stimulates self-identity, enabling the individual to surmount, intellectually, his or her immediate environment and emancipating the individual, to some extent, from the pressures to conform to this year's vogues. He or she ceases to be a pawn of the social forces and their representatives. The words of C. V. Langlois and Charles Seignobos, in a history manual written at the end of the last century, still carry conviction: the "practice of the historical method . . . is very hygienic for the mind, which it cures of credulity."

We cannot escape history, which is as omnipresent as the air about us, and we are often no more aware of its presence. The only question is whether individuals use it in a rudimentary sense or develop it into a tool useful for themselves as human beings and citizens. Even the most adamant hillbillies, in the time sense, who are determined not to leave their own cherished parochial valley because it is manifestly the best valley, cannot abolish history; they can merely reduce it to superstitions. Like any other skill, whether cultural, technical, or athletic, historical-mindedness as a discipline requires a certain amount of training in order to be a useful, satisfying possession.

2

The Oxen of Sybaris: The Past in the Present

On our little vacation island in Canada the rocks are pre-Cambrian, which means that they are at least 1.2 billion years old. They were formed by a lava flow before anything more than microscopic life existed on this planet.

Up above, on a clear night, the sky is bright with stars. Directly overhead is our home galaxy, the Milky Way, over a 100,000 light years in diameter, and beyond it, if one knows where to look, the faint luminescence of far more distant galaxies. The light from the nearest sun (a triple star, actually) has been traveling through outer space for about four years, and the light from the others for progressively longer periods of time; beyond the vision of the naked eye, the light had already left those remote, gigantic caldrons of energy before these rocks were laid down.

Our eyes do not see the present universe, it is the past—from four years back to a billion and more—that flickers at us from outer space. We live in a physically three-dimensional world in which time is the fourth dimension and in which astronomers measure spatial distance by light years. Standing in our human present, on rocks laid down over a billion years ago, and looking at the cascade of cosmic lights from all of Time, mortals can more readily grasp that our reality is four-dimensional. In this cathedral of eternity, any portrayal of our world in terms of only the present seems as grossly incomplete and deceptive as insects thinking their few dozen square yards of territory the only reality.

Here on the planet Earth, this test tube in the laboratory of Creation, traces of the human past, often unbeknownst to us, constantly impinge upon us. Sometimes the past survives with astonishing tenacity. Take, for example, the following exotic instances, chosen at random during cursory reading: some white oxen grazing in a field near the Gulf of Taranto in Italy; a procession of girls going to a shrine on a treeless plain in the same area; a taboo against eating the carp in a pool at Urfa (Edessa) in Turkey; a mask worn in ritual dances on the Ivory Coast in Africa; and funeral processions at Pagan in Burma, which go the long way around by boat when a land route would be easier.

They are all glimpses of the distant human past. The sophisticated and luxurious Greek city of Sybaris was destroyed in 510 B.C. Its coins carried pictures of white oxen, and nearly 2,500 years later the same kind of oxen continue to graze in the meadows of the one-time city of Sybaris. The girls in a Roman Catholic procession duplicate processions of girls equally long ago going to a Greek temple in a sacred grove to offer sacrifices. Carp were sacred to the moon goddess a couple thousand years ago in Edessa, and they are still not allowed to be eaten. The masks worn by the Senufu people of the Ivory Coast seem virtually identical to masks portrayed on cliff walls in the Sahara of perhaps 5,000 years ago. As for the funeral processions, long ago these went out the west gate of Pagan and then on to the cemetery; the Irrawaddy River has washed away the gate and wall, so, rather than go out the south gate, the mourners get into boats and follow the exact route formerly followed on dry land.

Often the historical dimension, though there, remains unseen by most people. A photograph taken at the funeral of Charles de Gaulle happened to show Grand Duke Jean of Luxembourg sitting beside the president of the United States and the prime minister of Israel. Jean was the only reigning Bourbon, and, in his attendance, a thousand years of French history, through the male lineage of the Bourbon-Valois-Capetian dynasties, seemed present at the final ceremonies for the great Frenchman. Or consider the curious historical echo in the Israeli–Palestinian Arab struggle of the Old Testament feud between the Israelites and the Philistines, from whom originated the name of Palestine.

The habitual life of the Eastern Mediterranean farming community of 3,000 years ago would seem to have little relevance now. Nevertheless, Judaism has carried on a cycle of religious observances based on these early habits, even though most Jews have long lived where a very different natural cycle has prevailed. Before the first of a new year's harvest was ready, a period of abstinence and deprivation was usually necessary, and so originated the Passover, as well as, later, the Christian Lent. The first fruits of the harvest came in April, although this timing does not accord at all with harvests in Europe or North America. Seven more weeks of work, from the first reaping of barley to the end of the wheat harvest, was followed by the Feast of Weeks. Yom Kippur starts a new year, when the annual cycle started over again in the Eastern Mediterranean region.

Some fragments of the past are artificially maintained in museums. The burning of eternal fires at Arlington and the Arc de Triomphe in Paris carry on one of humanity's oldest traditions, the keeping of the sacred fire in the ancient temples (from whence extinguished household fires might be relit), which in turn goes back to the precious and mysterious fire that Paleolithic people learned to preserve and use. Statues of those who once dominated the scene, especially in European cities, stand as silent inhabitants in the midst of today's bustling crowds. They sustain the dimension of time, that in the sum total of the community the living remain the comrades of those who have departed and of those yet to come. The Roman church does the same with its saints, keeping them alive in the memories of those now living.

At a more prosaic level, the past survives in the kitchen, where every article of food and drink has its own history. Some ways of doing things may be amazingly persistent. Why do Americans hold their eating utensils differently than the Europeans? Why do Americans usually drink coffee, whereas the British prefer tea? How explain the prevalence in different cultures of wine, beer, Bourbon, Scotch, vodka, raki, or tequila?

History can be seen in almost anything, even the family dogs. Their presence reminds us of the military alliance, mutually beneficial, contracted by the dog with our ancestors in the hunting community many millenniums ago. Now, the canine soul incurably wedded to that of the human being, they think to earn their keep by loudly defending the family territory, while also assiduously boosting the human ego through cultivating the arts of excessive flattery. Having a dog is also a vestige of those thousands of years when we lived with domestic animals and knew them as individuals with personal traits and worthy of bearing their own names. Who has not, at a zoo, heard animal noises that stirred up an atavistic unease, a pang of recollection of jungles and savannahs before we were quite human?

A few stragglers out of the remote human past still survive: Stone Age peoples on Mindanao in the Philippines, small tribes in the Brazilian jungles, perhaps a few among the aborigines of Australia and the Bushmen of southern Africa. The Ainus of Japan have a bear cult, which, judging by evidence of bear skulls and thigh bones found in caves, could conceivably be traced all the way back to the Neanderthal. Until fairly recently, the Lapps preserved intact a reindeer culture very similar to that of the ancient Europeans who followed the receding glaciers at the end of the last Ice Age.

Enough, however, of these wisps of the past. Some elements out of more recent history are so pervasive that perspective may be lacking to see their full dimensions. The legacy in memories, attitudes, and political reflexes from the time of the American

Civil War remained a potent force in the South more than a century later. The psychic wounds of the American blacks, out of their past, are likely to be a long time healing. A great depression and World War II permanently molded the generation in Europe and North America that lived through them. Like some supernova in human affairs, the energies of the Industrial Revolution, started a couple centuries ago, are still spreading over the planet.

For those acquainted with geology, the survival of the historic past in the present offers numerous parallels to that of the geological past in the physical environment. In both, the present scene is the product of the past. Their respective processes are living, in the sense that they are always visibly at work and today's forces are basically similar to those of long ago. Both have time durations of such length that genuinely profound alterations may not be much perceptible over the lapse of a few years, though historical change has greatly accelerated recently. Agencies of erosion are always wearing away the creations of the past, while new features, deposits from our own time, gradually modify the environment. Some contours, more massive or resistant to forces of destruction than others, remain as prominent outcroppings of earlier ages. Certain areas may also be much more unstable than others, catastrophic earthquakes and eruptions suddenly altering the familiar lineaments of yesteryear.

These geological processes are largely the ordinary, well-known agencies such as wind or water erosion and deposits of sediments, which are familiar to the contemporary observer and whose results become effective in a cumulative way. Most of the historical processes consist of the cumulative effect of people living together, the results of the various motivations and needs of the human community, and these processes usually persist regardless of governmental planning and direction. Only occasionally, from the long-term perspective, are the processes of either catastrophic, and even these are explicable in natural terms.

Over long periods of time, the components in the processes may change; the disappearance of the last Ice Age in North America and Europe brought with it successively different climatic circumstances, altering in turn the kinds of flora and fauna which would thrive. In the human past, also, a sort of historical climate may be discerned, in which a given geographical area may have passed through successive eras characterized by a tribal Heroic Age, city-states, imperial domination, feudalism, and an urban, technological civilization.

Manifestly, the forces of erosion in the historical world, as in the geological, work more rapidly in some areas than in others. Nowhere, probably, do they function as swiftly as in the United States, under the impact of technological innovations. Americans, traveling in some parts of the world, feel themselves making a swift journey back several decades, or a century, or perhaps even a millennium. Tourists need go no further than neighboring Mexico to encounter another phenomenon, to walk in cities as modern as our own and then to go into a country village and be back, virtually, to the eighteenth century.

Historical processes in the past put together the jigsaw puzzle of the contemporary world. Much of the superficially visible environment is the product of the fairly recent past, but more careful scrutiny reveals the deposits left by earlier historical periods. Some contours betray episodes of more dramatic quality which distorted normal development. The basic lineaments of the world environment, however, loom like mountain ranges, long since created and long enduring. National communities and mountains alike may seem given, eternally rooted in the world for those not comprehending the processes whereby they have come into existence.

To understand the shapes of the pieces in the jigsaw puzzle requires a knowledge of the past. The existence of English-language communities in widely dispersed parts of the world and the prevalence of English in such other areas as the Indian subcontinent and parts of Africa is scarcely explicable except historically. Why is French spoken in Quebec, Louisiana, and Haiti, and also so widely in some other parts of Africa? Why the vast expanse of Spanish-speaking people in the Americas? Arabic is spoken from Morocco to the borders of Iran. Islam occupies the same regions but also penetrates deeply into Africa and further eastward, though not continuously, to Indonesia and Mindanao. Then, too, there is the persistence of Latin, the language of an empire long vanished from the Mediterranean, and the continued presence in Rome of a *Pontifex Maximus,* or Roman high priest.

With the exception of Judaism, the cultural strata laid down in the ancient Eastern Mediterranean region may seem part of the limbo of the distant human past. Hieroglyphics and cuneiforms, temple worship, and priestly invocation of the stars, surely these have long since vanished? On the contrary, the Chinese form of writing, the equivalent of hieroglyphics and cuneiforms and which seems to go back to about 1500 B.C., remains in use among a quarter of the world's population. The priesthoods of Mesopotamia and Canaan, with their city gods, reverent processions, and sacrifices, disappeared ages ago, but in Japan an outcropping of these religions survives in the temple worship of Shintoism.

Astrology, an underworld ideology based on past beliefs that the planets and other heavenly bodies represented gods and influenced the individual, still pokes its supernatural myths into our modern community. Fortune telling continues as a survival out of ancient Babylonia, from over 3,000 years ago, though the twelve signs of the zodiac, originally named for constellations conspicuous in the twelve locations of the heavens, no longer quite accord with their present locations. So much time has elapsed that the perspective from our planet of these remote stars has somewhat shifted, but the needs of some personalities apparently remain the same.

Ancient legacies may survive in the wellsprings of our own personalities. Citizens watching the killings on American television may not be all that superior to Romans enjoying the hungry lions feasting on Christians. There are those who insist that deep within our beings, never wholly tamed by civilizing influences, lurks the biological heritage of our ancestral, predatory hunting band—qualities of "old Adam" once necessary for survival and now an ever-present danger to the community.

But, still, does the past actually concern us personally? Is it not external book learning, something outside our own beings?

Here another perspective may be helpful. College students, after not living in their home neighborhoods for two or three years, may become aware of unwelcome changes there as friends and familiar faces disappear and they are greeted by stares or total indifference in the old hangouts. Going back to the high school, a student looks eagerly for the familiar and may feel an irrational twinge of resentment that others now fill his or her place. These others may even be a trifle patronizing about the intrusion of a has-been who, at most, survives in their present only as a name on a plaque in the trophy case. Discovering that they have become the past in a new present, visiting alumni nevertheless know that their past is still part of their living reality and may be vaguely disturbed that the personal property of their memories is being destroyed by these present-minded people. This is one of the reasons for the survival of history; we all soon become the past in someone else's present. Through history, in a larger sense, we survive where we once lived, the personal property of our memories is not totally obliterated, and we preserve our identity and being.

3

The Eyes of Agamemnon: Visiting the Past

One day, when our eldest son was about seven years old, he came home from school full of enthusiasm about Indian arrowheads and announced that he was going out into the newly plowed field in back of our home and find some more. We knew better, of course, and hoped that his disappointment would not be too great. After a while he returned, triumphantly clutching half a dozen excellent arrowheads and totally unaware of his luck. The unexpectedness of it contributed to the sudden sense of the nearness of the past, as though the Indians, waiting near the draw for the animals to come down to the river, had let fly those arrows only a year or two ago.

For many persons, the past exists as a sort of gray, lifeless limbo, unreal and impenetrable. This type of sudden confrontation with the past, as though shadowy redskin ghosts were still flitting about in the backyard, can be an inviting "open sesame" to the treasures of the past.

At the opposite extreme is Arnold Toynbee's famous description of the feeling that came over him one day in London after World War I. Toynbee wrote that suddenly he "found himself in communion . . . with all that had been, and was, and was to come." He was "directly aware of the passage of History gently flowing through him in a mighty current, and of his own life welling like a wave in the flow of this vast tide." Historians would probably consider this mysticism rather than historical-mindedness, and one of them, in a most uncharitable review, dubbed it "the day of Toynbee's Transfiguration." Nevertheless, most of them would surely recognize, in a milder form, Toynbee's feeling.

Though the future cannot be visited now, the past is accessible, often requiring only the choice of any one of a number of vehicles plus a certain amount of curiosity and imagination. A textbook in history serves the purpose, in this sense, of a road map. The possibilities of places in time to visit and of experiences to savor vicariously are virtually limitless; history is likely to be musty and dull only to those who do not know how to live in the present either.

Occasionally, the viewing of the so-called past on cinema or television can be an authentic experience. More often, the presentations are concoctions by present-minded people, in which little more than the stage props are genuine. We may, however, go back and visit the American Civil War in the books of Bruce Catton, living through it on an almost day-to-day basis, as virtual eyewitnesses, and seeing events more distinctly than was possible for the participants themselves. Here we can watch Ulysses S. Grant, his dispositions made at the Battle of the Wilderness, sitting against a tree and whittling at a stick while awaiting reports, or see the final scene at Appomattox. Anyone wishing to experience the opening month of World War I, as the Germans bore down upon Paris and then were halted at the First Battle of the Marne, should use Barbara Tuchman's *Guns of August* as a guide. The story of one of the most dramatic years in the history of the Anglo-Saxon peoples can be followed in Garrett Mattingly's *The Armada*. A quick glance at the library shelves reveals books through which one may watch the famous Six Hundred gallop to destruction in the Crimean War, see the Bolshevik Revolution in Russia taking place through the eyes of one who was there, share in the invasion of Normandy on D-Day in 1944, or observe Hitler in his Berlin bunker in 1945.

Literature is full of imaginative journeys to the past, their historical quality varying greatly according to the ability and willingness of the author to reconstruct the past. Because the novelist has greater latitude, the spirit of the times may come through with much more impact than in an authentic historical work, as it does in Kenneth Robert's *Northwest Passage* or in Lawrence Durrell's novels based on ancient Alexandria. Quite often, however, a literary work takes the reader on a double journey, one to the location of the story itself, and the other to the time of the writer. An author may reveal as much about the attitudes and values of his or her own era in the plot and characters as about the age he or she is ostensibly re-creating. Sir Walter Scott is still a nineteenth-century Romanticist when he writes about Richard the Lion-Hearted, and Schiller tells us more about the eighteenth-century outlook in his plays than he does about that of Mary Stuart or Don Carlos. Such purported visits to the past are not likely to reflect the genuine reality. However, a man writing novels about his own times, a William Faulkner, Sinclair Lewis, Scott Fitzgerald, or Marcel Proust, may convey to later generations an overpowering sense of intimacy with an era.

For those who have the opportunity and means, another way to enter the past is to visit places where it is deliberately preserved. Most tourists know about Williamsburg, Old Sturbridge Village, and Tombstone as examples of an earlier America, while those who visit Europe can scarcely escape the past in Granada, Avignon, Carcassonne, Siena, or Florence. Travelers delight in glimpses into the cities of our ancestors in Toledo, the Île de la Cité of Paris, or Gamla Stan in Stockholm. Anyone going to Pompeii should first spend a little time in an

Italian town, for its spirit has not changed all that much in two millenniums. Someone interested in the medieval can take a vehicle to the past by driving the "Romantic Road" in Germany from Würzburg in central Germany to Füssen down on the Austrian border. The route passes through Rothenburg, Dinkelsbühl, and Nördlingen, three towns whose city walls and narrow cobblestone streets are still there; and Nördlingen even maintains a night watchman who cries "all's well" in German at intervals. At Füssen, a fake castle may be visited, built in the nineteenth century by Mad King Ludwig of Bavaria.

John A. Lukacs says that we enter the past "through sudden mental 'jumps' of recognitions." We encounter individuals whose personalities, motivations, and responses are familiar because we know ourselves, or we happen upon situations with recognizable circumstances and, through empathy, begin to participate in the action.

Sometimes an arrested moment in the past can evoke a poignant sense of reality. It may be something as simple as a pressed flower in an old book. Sometimes the passage of the years seems wiped out with the abrupt sense of the immediacy of a moment when something happened. An account in *The National Geographic* mentions the discovery in northern Canada of a skin plate still containing leftovers, Eskimo food preserved in the permafrost for perhaps 800 years; something had happened, someone had scrambled out of his hut leaving a meal unfinished and never returned. In Transylvania (Romania) an immensely rich treasure trove was once discovered that was identified as Visigothic, a sacred hoard hurriedly hidden when the Visigoths were forced to flee the invading Huns; they never came back, and there it still lay undisturbed, as though the Goths had just left. Excavations at Pylos in Greece seemed to unveil its last day, the day of doom, when invaders sacked and destroyed it, some 3,200 years ago. An uncovered palace at Zakros in eastern Crete revealed cooking pots on the hearths, food partly prepared, tools in the workshops abruptly dropped, and preparations underway for propitiatory religious ceremonies as day turned into night; the whirlwind rose, the earth quaked, and the ash from Thera began to fall. Of which more in a later chapter.

Such a suspended moment can be incredibly long ago. At Olorgesaillie in Kenya where Louis and Mary Leakey excavated, a visitor may walk on raised catwalks and see, among other things, almond-shaped hand axes standing upright in clay as they were left about 400,000 years ago! The geologist, of course, penetrates into a much more remote past than even this. Loren Eiseley in *The Immense Journey* gives a classic description of venturing into a slit in the prairie, carved by running water, and descending through the rift in the sandstone to several million years ago. There he found a skull out of that "low, snuffling world" from which our ancestors came. He had "projected" himself "across a dimension" he could not travel in the flesh into an earlier world where our ancestral hominids were still—and would for a long time yet be—only animals among other animals.

Sometimes we can accompany the historians or archaeologists as they explore the past. Possibly the most famous discovery of them all was the tomb of Pharaoh Tutenkhamen in 1922 with much of its furnishings intact. James and Charles Breasted, father and son, tell, in *Pioneer to the Past,* of entering the tomb, of feeling hot air rushing out that had been cooped up for nearly 3,300 years, of seeing a dessicated bouquet of flowers that had been picked on the banks of the Nile on the day of the funeral and still sitting there, and of being astonished at a mature level of artistic skill comparable to any in world history.

Many other such books exist, two examples being Leo Deuel's *Testaments of Time* and Ernst Doblhofer's *Voices in Stone.* In the former, the reader accompanies Constantin von Tischendorf as he finds a fourth-century Bible, the *Codex Sinaiticus*, in a monastery in the Sinai peninsula and follows Sir Aurel Stein along the caravan routes to China across Central Asia, where, by rummaging in ancient garbage heaps, he unearths all kinds of manuscripts. Others discover valuable papyri in similar deposits in Egypt. A synagogue near Cairo is found to contain a storage room, a Geniza, full of discarded manuscripts untouched for a thousand years. Doblhofer describes how stone and clay writings were made to speak again, and the excitement, in an age of Bible readers, of Biblical names coming to life in them. The reader learns how George Smith of the British Museum exulted in the fact that he was the first person to read "this text after two thousand years of oblivion." This same explorer of the past also created a sensation by announcing that he had found a much older reference to the Deluge than the one in the Bible (1862).

Newspapers once reported that Heinrich Schliemann, finding a gold mask at Mycenae in the Peloponessus, wired the king of Greece that "I have just looked into the eyes of Agamemnon." It had not, however, been made for that hero of the Trojan War, and, alas, the story about the telegram is itself a dubious piece of journalism, but the very existence of the tale faithfully reflects the mood of such explorers regarding the past. We feel it again in a recent account of the uncovering of a Greek stone statue in Anatolia: the dirt being brushed away from the face, there appeared "the face of a fellow man whose memory lives still in this bit of stone . . . resurrected from centuries of darkness."

Leo Deuel, in another of his books, *Flights Into Yesterday,* describes a different approach to the past, observing ancient traces on the earth from the air, seeing contours not visible on the ground. Old fields, trails, ditches, ramparts, walls, and villas can be detected, often by slight variations in the color of the vegetation. He calls large tracts of England "palimpsests, partly effaced, twice written pages from Clio's notebook whose superimposed symbols can be deciphered." So, too, the "ghosts" of ancient towns become visible from an airplane. In Iraq may be seen the faint crisscross of former irrigation canals in the dry, deserted wilderness.

Much that is familiar can be encountered in the past. Occasionally, it strikes home with special impact, as in a letter, dug out of an Egyptian refuse heap, where a boy is writing to his father, trying to cozen him by both wheedling and threats into giving him something he wants. Again, a Sumerian father, some 4,000 years ago, writes despairingly to a son who prefers to roam the streets and loiter in the public square: "Night and day you waste in pleasures," and "Come now, be a man!" In still another letter, a wife writes to her soldier husband begging him not to get himself killed by trying to be a hero.

Nevertheless, once we have been reassured by such familiarity, we may assume too much. The hitherto unknown may go altogether unnoticed. The look of familiarity may be as deceptive as recognizing, while in a strange town, the faces of persons who in fact are strangers. Some who claim to visit the past are like those American tourists abroad who stay in American luxury hotels, order American food, casually look at the famous buildings, know no foreign languages, and then come home thinking they have seen Europe. A century and a half ago, Thomas Macaulay, in comparing history to foreign travel, complained that many a visitor had seen the famous sights and then left without knowing the real England. If students in a class are asked to evaluate the achievements of, say, Peter the Great, some will respond by judging him on the basis of our contemporary values, perhaps on his devotion to rule by the people or by his concern for the lower classes. Their historical road map may have been scrutinized most conscientiously, but they have not actually visited the past.

Nor should those figures encountered in the past be patronized. Finding few of our own cherished ideas and attitudes and not penetrating to the true matrix of their thought, we may see little more than ignorance and backwardness. This again is like those tourists who, too unsophisticated to appreciate other styles of life, expect American services overseas and look down on the local inhabitants. Dropped into any milieu of our ancestors, we would speedily discover the imperative necessity for their skills and knowledge in making clothes and tools, in their study of animals both domesticated and wild, and in their observations about weather, soil, and plants.

Wherever the evidence permits ample reconstruction, the past is anything but a gray, lifeless limbo. In an astoundingly busy scene, many impressive figures, tragic or triumphant, are encountered, energetically imprinting their deeds upon the scroll of time. Personalities and episodes that form only an indistinct background for the larger historical figures in textbooks crowd forth upon a stage seemingly as lively and well-populated as that of the present year. We must not measure the past by our own time or assume that ours is better, warns Sir Herbert Butterfield: "Their day [was] as full and as vital to them as our day is to us." In the words of Leopold von Ranke, all ages are equal in the sight of God.

A writer like Barbara Tuchman can make the decades before World War I come alive in *The Proud Tower*. However, try visiting the sixth century by reading *Beowulf*. Soon the reader is lost. What were the composers of *Beowulf* getting at? Why the circumlocutions, and why the odd, imaginative verbiage and figures of speech? Most of us will speedily become impatient, waiting for the action to begin. An alien mentality seems at work behind those words, though some readers are very probably directly descended in flesh and blood from those that composed or recited it long ago. Explanations are needed. Those able to give them may well have undergone a training as grueling and extensive in its own way as that of the astronauts, in order to journey successfully into the distant past. Though we may enjoy trips to the past in many instances with little effort or training, we often do so because historians and others have prepared themselves, with virtually a lifetime of effort, to serve as guides in a partially alien environment and among people not quite like ourselves.

Occasionally one may personally happen on a helpful perspective. *Beowulf* became more comprehensible to this writer on an all-day trip in a European bus when the travelers started passing the time by various forms of entertainment, much like Chaucer's Canterbury pilgrims. One man started declaiming long pieces of poetry. He spoke slowly, intoning the words; as in *Beowulf,* the words were vehicles for expressing subjective feelings rather than action, causing the audience to participate, to hear the wind in the pines, the lapping of water on the shore, the distant howl of a wolf in the forest. They were word pictures, common in the days before photography or television, the emphasis being on imagery and a slow, cadenced word-by-word building of the picture. This little episode briefly opened a door into the past, a glimpse into an older world where such entertainment formed a major pastime of life.

Understanding the physical environment, the kinds of buildings, the clothing they wore, and the weapons they used is much easier than entering into their mental world. We can scarcely avoid, without much training and experience in time travel, attributing our own ideas to earlier peoples. As Frederic W. Maitland once warned, if we commit this anachronism "we shall be doing worse than if we armed Hengest and Horsa with machine-guns or pictured the Venerable Bede correcting proofs for the press." To visit the past only to pick out the familiar, or the seemingly familiar, is not a very useful pursuit. Part of history's value lies in discerning the differences, making comparisons, acquiring new perspectives for viewing our own times, and treating the past as foreign country with exciting scenes, events, and ways of thought.

For most travels in time, a guide is needed, someone who has been there, who has the experience and expertise derived from long visits in a particular region. That guide is the historian or someone in another discipline who also makes it his or her life's work to colonize that specific area of the past.

4

Guide to the Past:
The Historian

An historian is a professional traveler to the past who usually becomes a specialist in some particular area and spends a lifetime in intellectual residence there. Those who have chosen to colonize a certain region of the past continue to enlarge their knowledge of it by successive expeditions into its various provinces. In a sense the historian plays God for that age, resurrecting episodes and personalities, conferring a terrestrial immortality on the departed, and perhaps finding meaning in their deeds. Unlike today's unfinished drama, the scroll of time can be unrolled at will; knowing their future, an historian discerns the historical patterns much more clearly than did the participants themselves.

For this generation, which happens to live on this planet near the end of the twentieth century, historians are ambassadors from the realms of the past. Many hundreds of these domains, overlapping and subdivided, exist, centering in some period of time and usually demarcated according to geographic and topical interests. Each domain has been colonized by specialists, who appraise each other's work, share their knowledge, and mature a rather similar cast of mind. As a group, historians are likely to have more in common with each other, regardless of nationality, than with their neighbors or fellow nationals.

Historians are by no means the only inhabitants of these colonies in the past. Beyond the range of history as commonly conceived, the dimension of the past provides an "indispensable common denominator" for many other disciplines. Other residents include experts from a number of fields, especially political scientists, economists, geographers, philologists, and writers on literary subjects and the fine arts. Though focusing on their own pursuits, they all contribute to their common knowledge and provide insights useful in disciplines other than their own.

How the historian penetrates into the past depends upon where he or she goes, different methods being required according to the milieu and problems. For some areas, especially the last couple centuries, written evidence is so overwhelming in volume that the problem becomes partially one of selection. Historians who work far back in time often encounter severe difficulties in even "detecting the traces." Evidence may also be lopsided in origin. Medieval accounts come largely from the clergy, who themselves were interested in some aspects of life and ignored others. Perhaps it is fitting that prehistoric peoples, absorbed by the hunt for food, should be identifiable mostly by evidence from their "kitchens," by pottery and a few other artifacts.

Historians call the actual traces *primary sources,* that is, eyewitness accounts or anything dating from the times, while, broadly speaking, accounts by later historians, using the primary materials, are considered *secondary sources.* Source materials can be actual writings, such as chronicles, from that period. They can be legends or folk tales, inscriptions on monuments, or the buildings themselves. Coins, sculpture, or even tapestries qualify, as do fortifications, weapons, furniture, and aqueducts. For more recent periods, government documents, newspapers, magazines, and surviving letters are especially important—

anything which permits observation through contemporary eyes.

Obviously a time traveler must be thoroughly competent in the languages of that area, including the vernacular then in use. He or she may need to be able to read the handwriting of that century, or, if earlier, decipher alphabetic, syllabic, or picture writing. Anyone who deals in official or business documents, such as medieval charters, requires training in "diplomatic" research, meaning official documents rather than diplomacy, and, depending upon area of concentration, it may be necessary to know about sigillography (seals), numismatics (coins), or epigraphy (usually inscriptions on monuments). Those who work in more recent periods must learn how to find their way about in archives. Archaeologists equip themselves with a series of separate skills, among them, knowing how to excavate properly, how to identify accurately successive stratifications, and how to do chemical analysis.

Historians possess their own scientific methodology, a form different from the experimental or statistical types now commonly associated with science, which is focused on the finding of relevant evidence, the validation of its information, and the achievement of maximum faithfulness to the reality being described. The "science of men in time" (Marc Bloch) is governed by its own canons and standards for accepting or rejecting statements about the past. Teaching historiography, the writing of history, is not, however, the purpose of this book; a number of such books exist, the best known being *The Modern Researcher,* by Jacques Barzun and Henry F. Graff.

Historians have plied their trade, not necessarily under that name, for virtually as long as organized communities have existed. Though they now work mostly with printed pages, history was recited or sung among many early peoples, usually in the form of a story of great persons and memorable deeds. The Jews, Greeks, Romans, and Chinese, however, produced narratives about the past, recognizably historical in the modern sense. Historians have fully shared in the explosion of knowledge during the past century; according to Boyd Shafer, a former secretary of the American Historical Association, more historians are alive today than in all of the preceding centuries put together. If historians still had to sing for a living, most of them would starve, though they do much reciting of lectures and quite possibly with less flair than in days of old.

The true test of the professional is that he or she sometimes reads the footnotes with more excitement than the textual presentation; footnotes contain the pedigrees of precise scholarly knowledge, as well as much of the shoptalk whereby historians all over the world communicate with one another. H. G. Wells once suggested that the world's problems be solved by creating a great depository of all knowledge, a "world brain." Perhaps all great libraries have, in effect, become such storehouses of learning, for, in the form of published books and articles, films and tapes, it is all there. Knowledge, however, consists of more than passive information; it also involves the living texture of the human mind at work. Without indulging in excessive fantasy, the international scholarly community of the historians may be conceived of as a sort of world brain in which, facilitated by rapid communications, the more active, gifted, and persistent scholars maintain an incessant interaction among themselves. The knowledge about the past being transmitted greatly transcends the mere information, interwoven as it is with qualities of the spirit, skilled thought processes, and a wisdom born of experiences in making journeys in Time.

Historians themselves tend to disagree over whether the past should be studied for its own sake or for its usefulness and relevance to the present. Those who emphasize the present stress the historical dimension in understanding the present as the principal contribution of the historian to his or her community. History should help us, they insist, in solving our current problems or, in the optimistic words of Lord Acton at the beginning of this century, be an instrument of action.

The others, however, emphasize the difference between former eras and our own; to explore the past, says V. H. Galbraith, "is to be . . . overwhelmed with the sense of difference." Looking for present phenomena in earlier times obscures the authentic past and blurs or destroys the comparative differences and similarities between them, thereby vitiating or dangerously distorting the utility of the past for understanding the present. An interpretation of an earlier era in terms of the present all too often confirms our preconceptions, teaching us only what we want it to teach. The adherents of the two points of view undoubtedly serve to provide a useful corrective for each other: while the former group keeps history updated in terms of the concerns and problems of the present generation, the latter group, the "pure" historians, perpetually check the others and, perhaps, prevent them from wandering too far from accurate reporting of the past.

Beyond the ranks of the professionals, history is all things to all men. Politicians, journalists, and clergymen, especially, plunder the past for purposes of their own. It is too often taught as book learning, as only information, and not much awareness of historical-mindedness is developed. On the secondary-school level, a crass caricature is sometimes presented by men who, far from journeying into the past, have their minds out on the football field.

The Mansion of History, which has always been located directly in the forum of the community, has many rooms. Some of the shops on the ground floor of the Mansion, selling goods on the busy thoroughfare, are the equivalent of the penny arcade. The mythmakers, using the materials of history for nonhistorical purposes, call out their wares, while hawkers push shoddy fakes hastily produced without fear and without research. Honest bookshops also exist, selling history oriented toward the problems of the age and high quality, popularized accounts about the past itself.

We may picture the historians who believe in relevance as working on the floors immediately above the shops, exposed to the crowd noises, often mingling with the populace, and focusing their own research and writing on the questions of the decade. Some, like the late Charles A. Beard, may even have "an air of the market place about him." In the higher stories live those who often think it necessary to escape the contemporary hubbub entirely in order to make successful journeys to the past.

More in empathy with their own era of work than with the present, they are likely to be as much transformed by their journeys in time as are world travelers by their experiences. These historians generally assume, not always correctly, that they dwell on a higher level of scholarship as well, while the ones closer to the street and the members of the crowd oftentimes suspect that the upper stories consist of ivory towers. The analogy may be completed by visualizing a number of wings to the Mansion, where members of other disciplines either live or lease space as a necessity for their own work. Finally, some people ostentatiously avoid the building and may even want it demolished.

Because the Mansion is located close to the crowd and because, unlike some other disciplines, the historian's use of ordinary language offers deceptively easy access, amateur "experts" proliferate. Authorities in other fields, with barely a rudimentary conception of what actually happens in historical processes, come crowding in to pronounce weighty judgments to a credulous populace. Others, adamantly ahistorical while themselves unknowingly trapped in the ongoing historical processes, produce stunted three-dimensional parodies of today's moment in history. It is the glory, and the despair, of historians that their area of work belongs to everyone. The historian knows that he or she is not an engineer, but the engineer may have no qualms about playing the historian.

Not explicable through universal propositions or formulas or complete as narrative information, today's versions of history are more subtle than the amateur realizes. Monographs are not as simple as their prosaic language may suggest; they also demand a wealth of prior knowledge on the part of the reader, intimate personal experience in dealing with the materials of history, and careful reading between the lines. Everyman's use of history, contrasted to the expert's, is comparable to the average person's common-sense perception of the physical world versus that of the scientist. Briefly put, the historians' narrative is preferable because they use verified evidence, understand the temptations of improper selectivity, and have a matured sense of how things usually happen.

Quite aside from the primary function of ensuring contemporaries a progressively better picture of foregoing ages, the historians contribute to their own generation a certain set of mental attributes. From the journeys to the past and the handling of historical phenomena, they develop certain ways of thinking, a mental discipline useful for today's world also. The purpose of the following chapters is to illustrate this historicalmindedness and to sketch out the shapes of the historical processes as historians usually visualize them.

II

ELEMENTARY HISTORICAL- MINDEDNESS

5

A Clean Sheet of Paper: This Horrid Ignorance

China's six hundred million people are first of all poor, and secondly "blank." That may seem like a bad thing, but it is really a good thing. . . . A clean sheet of paper has no blotches and so the newest and most beautiful words can be written on it, the newest and most beautiful pictures can be painted on it.

Mao Tse-tung's political version of David Hume's famous eighteenth-century *tabula rasa,* taken at face value, is incredibly naive. Unless Mao regarded any mind not trained in Marxism as blank, his peasants and workers undoubtedly possessed many political and historical words and pictures by no means new and not necessarily Marxist beautiful. No matter how disinterested, few individuals could possibly live in a social community for any length of time without developing a certain rudimentary set of notions about its politics and history.

Were this not so, the learning of history beyond the purely informational level would be much easier. By the time that a student is exposed to more advanced ideas, he or she already has acquired a series of assumptions and certain elemental ways of thinking about the past. Much of this must be *unlearned* before a mastery of basic history is attained. The Leningrad School of Ballet will not accept students who have already had some training in ballet. "It is too difficult to correct the harm of bad training." A teacher of history, however, constantly confronts this problem.

At least five important sources, other than the school, mold the individual's way of thinking about history and politics: the influence of family and community; the qualities of the story applied to history; the early logic of the child; the mass media; and our participatory role in that moment of history known as the present.

A child usually thinks of history as a series of stories that happened long ago in a past that has neither dimensions nor sequences. That they occurred in olden times is sufficient explanation for a children's fairyland. On a formal school level, a child then learns some of the traditions of the community, the names of national heroes, and some fragmentary information about memorable episodes, while family background perhaps contributes additional glimpses. History comes to him or her, or is understood, as a series of stories that need neither be sorted out nor arranged by lengths of time as yet totally incomprehensible. Later, more conventional history may be encountered somewhere between the ages of twelve and eighteen, often as pure book learning not absorbed into personal ways of looking at things.

That which is likely to be incorporated into the child's thought processes about the history of the community are the qualities of the story, which in themselves provide a certain rudimentary historical-mindedness. These ingredients involve heroes and villains, emotions enlisted on behalf of a righteous cause, and a problem solved or goal achieved by direct action. As the child lives with stories in school and from books and television, this, too, becomes the original conception of what happens in history. Some adults never do advance much beyond this level. Living in the complex modern community, such persons' capacity for understanding historical forces may not actually be higher than that of the citizens of Rome or Greece a couple thousand years ago.

Unless replaced by insights and concepts more adapted to dealing with historical materials, the elements at this level of thought engrave their own crude images upon the past. Thus, in the Great Man theory, history centers about the deeds and contributions of farsighted, courageous leaders, whose willful actions suffice as explanations for historical events or contemporary politics. Their good work, in turn, imperatively requires the counterpoise of talented black-hearted villains. Hence, the Good Queen Bess and the Bad King John kind of history, as well as the Plot theory, in which the Bad Guys conspire against us Good Guys. Politics on the mass level all too often functions on the level of this elementary type of historical-mindedness.

For the sake of the telling, the story reduces the skein of circumstances to a single, simple cause or even to praise or blame for an individual or group achievement. Action must be sustained through struggle between opposing forces, historical energies being unleashed largely or even exclusively through dramatic events. Applied to politics, this elementary thinking results in people being mobilized to march out on crusade on behalf of righteousness. The problem to be solved may be simplified to the level of Heroic Age barbarians, to the shape of a citadel or to a walled city that must be stormed and its evil defenders exterminated. Oftentimes the wrong culprit is identified. Presently, while still besieging the first victim, the bugles sound the attack upon an entirely different, still erroneous fort.

Psychologically, the maturation of personal historical-mindedness depends upon a sharpening apprehension of time and of time duration. History must begin for a child in the form of stories because he or she does not possess the means in his or her short life to visualize any true depth in time; the stories necessarily occur in a generalized past, lacking true dimension and sequences. An adult linear sense of time as Western society conceives it, in the form of a line along which time progresses regularly in one direction, may not fully manifest itself until the early teens. As this develops, historical events are first seen as being strung out in a static fashion along this line, like the dates in history, but eventually a sense of duration is added, thereby approaching a true conception of historical time. These two phases can be compared to a slide projector with its series of still pictures, which is then followed in the second stage by moving pictures in which the action flows through successive unbroken sequences.

The child may live on in us more than we realize; for those whose historical time dimension remains stunted, recourse must be sought in explanations lacking the time element. Our institutions must therefore be invented and great events result from the inspired moment, both explicable in the framework of Now. The growth process, the successive modifications, the past interplay of creative forces, these and other living factors are omitted from the static contours of the present, the entire process of change in the midst of persistent continuity being sheared off. A lack of time sense intensifies our impatience with the slow solution of problems, as though a miracle would be wrought immediately if only the right button could be pushed.

According to Jean Piaget, a child under six years of age experiences difficulty in separating his or her own dreams and imaginative schemes from the surrounding external world. Inanimate objects are believed to have consciousness and life, like human beings, and to make efforts analogous to our own muscular forces. Everything about the child has tendencies and intentions, focusing on himself or herself. The sun and moon are interested in us. To quote Dennis the Menace: "God turns the sun off at night 'cause it's too expensive to keep it runnin' when everybody's asleep." All happenings must have explanations, though miracles and exceptions abound. Then, between the ages of about six and ten, children start to disassociate their subjective selves from the outside world, begin to discern the differences between their own subjective visualizations of the world and the objective reality of the surroundings. However, some of them may still fumble around, perhaps for years, with explanations far wide of the scientific ones.

Social forces in the environment are difficult to observe realistically, the more so since human beings participate in them. Adults, often only aware of powerful but nebulous forces affecting their lives, may still handle them in the most simplistic terms. They may be attributed to the will of conspicuous personalities, clothed in the guise of demonologies, or ascribed to the element of the catastrophic or apocalyptic in a chaotic world. The child's belief in the miracle may survive in an adult's faith in miraculous solutions to social problems.

Children do not understand adult causality. Piaget says that small children are "completely confused" as to the difference between laws of the physical universe and moral laws, both of which govern their conduct, and only later do they learn to differentiate. Obviously an equivalent sort of confusion persists in adult perception of community moral laws and the actualities of historical processes. When an adult is unable to visualize the realities of social forces in the environment or to recognize the contours of regularities in social phenomena, this citizen's concept of social and political surroundings is likely to be powered, in lieu of causality, by an oversimplified moralism.

As with children whose environment seems dominated by both active benevolence and malevolence, many adults tend to attribute these qualities to social forces according to how the qualities affect them individually. This, of course, is not to reject a moral approach or to suggest that contemporary society not pursue policies in a humanitarian direction. The complaint is with gross oversimplifications of complex circumstances, the frequent moralizing on the basis of a misapprehension of the facts. Thinking primarily in terms of good and evil avoids coming to grips with the hard facts, the rough and often awkward contours of reality and the forces at work, and thereby makes effective solutions to specific problems more difficult. Most of us espouse a moralism convenient to ourselves, and misguided fanatics may shield themselves and their panaceas from criticism by manifest moral integrity.

Natural physical phenomena were long explained in terms of myths, of gods and goddesses or demons and spirits, for lack of the true reasons, and this approach, in effect, continues to prevail among those who view the social and political environment through the rudimentary tools of elementary history. Natural scientists learned respect for reality in the physical world, discovered the natural forces at work, by ceasing to believe in spirits and gods in water, wind, earth, and fire. Geologists abandoned catastrophism, the Hand of God, and a belief in a specific Creation when formulating modern geology. Myths may generate emotions and misplaced collective energy, but they rarely solve problems. Airplane pilots do not bring a plane to its destination by morally willing it there; they must learn to fly an airplane, and mankind did more than will to fly in outer space before achieving it.

The mass media—newspapers, television, and radio—often accentuate the characteristics of elementary history by their handling of today's stories. Dramatic action being the very essence of journalism, the account is present-minded and presented in a profile form stripped of nonessential circumstances. Rather than depicting the normal contours and functioning of society, the mass media tend to flourish on the Prodigious Fallacy, the exceptional, dramatic, and sensational.

Being participants in this year's cross section of continuing history may intensify our persistent adherence to elementary-level thinking. The plot of history culminates in a present drama in which we all are actors playing a role. Many citizens find it difficult to rise above the dreams, outlook, and imperatives of their own tribe to see that there are other groups whose conceptions of the world may be as close to ultimate reality and just as necessary for society as our own. We may never quite escape the feeling that out there beyond our tribal camp fire lurk shadowy enemies, known or unknown.

In summary, elementary historical-mindedness contains several ingredients, starting with the simplistic moralism of the good-evil dichotomy. Along with this goes the monocausal explanation, in which one cause does the work of many and happenings derive from the Great Man, the Plot, or antagonists in conflict. A stunted sense of time foreshortens the processes of change to the sensational episode and the willful acts of personalities. These are mental tools too crude to discern the shapes of historical processes or to recognize the compulsions and obstructions of their social forces.

Should readers perchance suspect that they share in some of this horrid ignorance, they need not be unduly chagrined. They have much company. Historians themselves, not so very long ago, were still describing the past in terms often not much less elementary than this. In its present form, historical-mindedness as a cultural tool has been largely developed during the past two centuries in response to the growth of the present, complex community.

As such, a maturation of historical-mindedness in the individual offers one approach to a more accurate comprehension of today's world. History projects an objective reality out beyond ourselves and our group, describes contours and social forces in which our emotions are less directly engaged, and thereby trains a better understanding of the present age. It broadens the vision to a recognition of numerous groups and factors bearing upon any historical episode, then or now. In practicing on materials out of the past, we forge mental tools more adapted to dealing with the world of today.

Mao to the contrary, that clean sheet of paper contains all sorts of blotches. Even the young mind grapples with various questions, and in the process comes up with answers, however rudimentary. Untutored adults adopt additional elementary concepts in order to handle the dimension of the past in their midst. Though today's world and its problems require a level of comprehension higher than that of tribes on the march, the historian is forever being rebuffed at the cutting edge of history, the ongoing processes of the present.

Street-level concepts still bear numerous similarities to those of earlier forms of history. We do not necessarily recapitulate in our personal development the growth of historical-consciousness in the human race, but the possible ways of expressing the time dimension are limited. Minds lacking the matured tool of historical-mindedness, whether two millenniums ago or now, quite naturally would adopt rather similar elementary ideas for making sense out of the past, concepts now to be further examined.

6

Many Grasses Ago:
Once upon a Time

"Once upon a time. . ." So begin many of the children's old stories. Though some of them narrate events that happened in history, no time perspective exists; they are all more or less contemporary long ago in that capacious reservoir of time, the past. They all "belonged to a misty past where heroes of all ages inhabited the same Elysian fields" (Elizabeth Eisenstein). Nor did the myths of primitive peoples reveal much sense of the sequence of happenings. Recent episodes might be remembered in a more or less correct order, but the earlier heroes, often elevated to the rank of gods, all acted on a common stage, most of the intervening period between them and the present generation disregarded.

Our own particular conception of time is by no means inborn. It is a cultural product evolved over several millenniums. Primitive peoples—if the Australian aborigines offer a typical example—held that the gods lived in a different kind of time than themselves called the "Great Time," which mortal beings could enter only temporarily through religious ceremonies or in the hunt. The Mayans believed in a "First Time," outside of and distinct from the time duration experienced by humans. Possibly we can gain a fleeting glimpse, if scarcely comprehension, of how different from our own the time conceptions of earlier peoples were from Irene Nicholson, who says that, whereas our time can be visualized as horizontal, Indian time is vertical and static. "It moves to no particular appointment in the future," and "to the American Indian the past is not gone forever but is still present somewhere."

Time perception varies greatly among different cultures. Frequent erroneous dates in the histories of India reflect a notorious lack of this sense and of historical-mindedness. History carried little meaning, being merely a record of a rather anarchic, repetitive futility in a society where only the individual person, not his or her social organization, was considered important. Quite possibly, India's climate did not inculcate an awareness of time because irrigation was not, in general, necessary for agriculture. By contrast, time as pure succession of events following one another has been much more characteristic of the Chinese.

Without memory we have no history, and without an ordered memory we have no ordered history. The earliest form of history consisted largely of a jumble of stories heaped together without patterns, sequences, or perspective. Not that organized time on a short-term basis lacked importance, for, as far as the cycle of a single year was concerned, ancient people's very survival depended upon careful and constant observation. Many a priesthood earned its keep by knowing precisely when rainy seasons, flooding rivers, drought, frost, and the ripening of certain cereals and fruits might be expected. It became necessary to know the positions of the stars, to keep count of the moon's waxing and waning, and to observe the sun's position in order to know the equinoxes. Priests also mobilized the populace for the hunt, sowing, and harvesting by appropriate ceremonials, in which, too, certain historic memories of ancient happenings were revived by reenactment.

Years were originally recollected in the most natural way, by an important occurrence, such as "year of the flood," "year of the comet," or "year of the pestilence." A remembered event had taken place "many moons" or "many grasses" ago. A year originally had no exact numerically determined length, the full sequence of the seasons constituting its completion. For peoples largely concerned, for their own preservation, with the rhythmic repetition of the successive seasons, a cyclical conception seemed natural, that is, time seemed to move in a more or less complete circle, eventually returning to its point of origin again.

Time was inextricably tied together with the gods, and, though we are rarely aware of it, our calendar still reflects this earlier practice. English-speaking people refer to the fourth day of the week as Wednesday, and thereby still unwittingly honor the name of the greatest god of the ancestral English and other Germanic peoples, the one-eyed Odin, or Wotan. Friday bears the name of his wife, Frigga. The bearer of thunder and lightning, the fearful Thor, his goat-drawn chariot rumbling across the heavens, may have been retired from his strenuous labors long ago, but he still gives his name to Thursday, Thor's Day. With Tuesday's god, Tiu, or Tyr, our memories reach back even further, for he is so ancient that Odin and Thor replaced *him* as leaders in the Nordic pantheon. His name appears in other guises in Zeus, the sky god of the Greeks, in the Latin word *"deus"* for god, and in Dyaus of the Aryans, who invaded India before 1500 B.C.; hence, he must have been worshipped well over a hundred generations ago by those who carried the ancestral Indo-European languages all over Europe and east to India and Iran. As for Saturday's Saturn, the Romans attributed to him the Greek legends of Cronus, the latter being so ancient that he seems to have been a deity of the inhabitants of Greece *before* the Indo-European Greeks arrived in the area. Cronus was the god with the sickle, Father Time himself!

So, in this procession of pagan gods, we unconsciously preserve the remote past in the present, still quite unknowingly doing our weekly obeisances to deities worshiped by the remote ancestors of many of us. Not even this is the end of the story, for a Sun's Day and a Moon's Day perpetuate the recollection of what surely must have been the earliest worship by human beings far back in the mists of human beginnings, that of the sun and the moon.

Turning to the months of the year, these were inherited from the Romans. By the time of Julius Caesar, the Roman calendar, whose year was a bit shorter than solar time, had lost three months, that is, January now occurred in the autumn. In the course of the major overhaul that resulted in the so-called Julian Calendar, including a year of 445 days (46 B.C.), Julius Caesar took the opportunity to name a month for himself. Some years later, the Emperor Augustus, not to be outdone, appropriated the next one. The seventh through the tenth months survive in the names of September through December, but Julius Caesar and Augustus replaced the names of the original preceding months, Quintilius and Sextilius, the fifth and sixth. Not that September is the seventh, needless to say; this numbering dates back to the time before 153 B.C. when the year began in March.

In 1582, Pope Gregory XIII introduced the Gregorian Calendar and in the process of doing so lopped ten days off that year (October 5–14) in order to restore the calendar to correct solar time. By the time the British changed from the Julian to the Gregorian, eleven days had to be dropped; consequently, September 3–13, 1752, never existed in Great Britain and the American colonies.

Many know that the Christmas season is a carryover, with a new name, from the Saturnalia, the Roman season of festivals. (This, in fact, commemorated the Golden Age, which supposedly prevailed in the time of Cronus, *alias* Saturn, in the remote past.) The actual birthday of Christ was put on the day of the birth of the sun god, Sol Invictus, the time of the winter solstice, and the celebrations were transferred to the new observance. The name of Easter, used in parts of northern Europe and in North America, also derived from earlier religion, from Eostre, or Ostâra, a goddess of spring, whose festival occurred at about the time of the Christian Easter.

Philosophers argue over whether time was invented or discovered, but historians scarcely need worry over these ultimate questions, their time measurements having obviously been constructed during the past few thousand years. Some of the measurements reflect the regularities of the solar system, the year precisely so and the month much less accurately, while the sexagesimal system, upon which the sixty minutes and seconds are based, goes back at least 5,000 years to the early Sumerians of Mesopotamia. Although the ordinary people needed only the cyclical time of the seasons for their activities, the demands of increased social and political organization caused the priests to work out more detailed calendars.

Advanced communities usually dated the year by the reign of the ruler, priests or scribes preparing long lists of their names as a sort of calendar in Babylonia, Egypt, and China. The Romans designated years by the names of the consuls in office and the Athenians by their archons, but the years of the Olympiad (traditionally 776 B.C.) and of the legendary founding of Rome (between 759 and 748 B.C.) also eventually came into use for certain purposes.

The Christian calendar does pose difficulties. Based on religious motives (and on the *wrong* birth date for the Founder, at that), the numbering, broken into A.D. (Anno Domino) and B.C. (Before Christ), is inconvenient, as every history student can personally testify. The year A.D. 1 occurs arbitrarily in the midst of a busy scene, of a series of historical sequences; prior to that year, we are forced to number backwards, with all of the attendant confusion. The Venerable Bede (673–735) first started the practice in his *Ecclesiastical History,* taking over the numerical system originally prepared by a Syrian monk who was trying to settle the proper date for Easter. About a hundred years later, the chancery of the Holy Roman Empire began using it, and the papal documents bear this dating beginning in the tenth century. Bede would have conferred a considerable favor on his fellow historians of the future by adopting the Jewish calendar instead. This would have had the virtue, for historical purposes, of bringing into one single straight numbering system all of the written record of even the most ancient of civilized societies.

Aside from the clergy, a preoccupation with precise time, with hours and minutes, derives from modern concerns and was made possible only by the invention of clocks, providing accurate measurement of equal intervals. Early peoples reckoned time in practical terms as being how long it took to walk to a neighboring village or to sow a certain plot of ground. Caravan routes across the Sahara were measured by days of travel, and an Arabic chronicler described the Mali Empire in West Africa as being four months long and four months wide. It is not unusual even yet in Europe to hear distances expressed in terms of hours to walk or drive. The Egyptians used sun dials and water clocks, giving an approximate time, as did the peoples of the classical age. The Greeks added the hourglass. Marked candles, burning at a steady rate, also provided reasonably useful time until quite recently. An hour was one-twelfth of daylight on a sun dial, which meant that it varied with the seasons. More exact measurements had to await the invention of machinery.

In the supposedly timeless Orient, the Chinese developed mechanical clocks, using waterpower to provide motive force, and this as early, apparently, as the eighth century. The first mechanical clock in the West, inventor unknown, seems to have appeared somewhere near the end of the thirteenth century. Dials, the face, were added in the middle of the following century. Still more precise timekeeping became possible with the advent of coiled springs, in about 1500, and the pendulum, first devised by Christian Huygens in 1657. Accurate time may be utterly indispensable for a modern, industrial society, with its factory shifts, fast communications, and transportation networks, but the need for more exact schedules in the daily routine of monasteries and churches originally stimulated the development of early Western clocks. Meantime, the machine has inculcated in us our Western sense of the "passing" of time, the incessant passage of the hours.

A "mediocre" German historian by the name of Cellarius devised the conventional division of world history into ancient, medieval, and modern at the end of the seventeenth century. A useful enough device at the time for separating his own era from the manifestly different "middle" ages and placing the ancients in still another time compartment, its woeful inadequacies have led to the insertion of additional periods or subperiods, such as the Renaissance and the Hellenistic. Looking back three centuries across industrial and technological revolutions, the present generation may feel that Cellarius's own age had more in common with the Greeks and Romans than our own. Whether, in turn, the latter belong in the same period as the Sumerians is also obviously open to question.

Furthermore, the three periods are very much Europe-oriented, reflecting the main sequence of events from the Ancient Monarchies of the Middle East through the Greeks and Romans, the European feudal age, and the early modern period on that continent. This framework is scarcely applicable, just to mention three examples, to China, India, and the Americas before the Europeans arrived. If the year 1500 is considered to be in the modern era, then the following all existed in the modern period: the Ming dynasty of the Chinese empire, the Moslem sultanate of Malacca in Malaysia, the empire of Songhai in West Africa, the Aztecs and Incas (who perhaps fit better into the age of Stonehenge), the Neolithic Indian tribes of North America, the Iron Age Bantus, the Polynesians, and the Hottentots and Bushmen of South Africa. From this spectacle of peoples running the spectrum from the Chinese, probably still more civilized than the Europeans, to the Hottentots, living on the level of most of humanity 10,000 or more years ago, some credence may be given to those who assert that "calendric time is an empty vessel."

No alternative scheme of periods in world history has ever been advocated successfully. The problem lies not only in the rich variety of cultures and the different levels of civilization in various parts of the world, it also resides in the complex nature of history itself. The historian's subject does not lend itself to such universal labeling and categorizing. As Robert Ergang wrote in the introduction to a textbook: "History cannot be sharply divided into periods as a log is cut into lengths of firewood with a saw."

Though historical periods may be artificial and subject to controversy, the historian nevertheless must use them, otherwise the past is reduced to chaos. They offer one form of meaning for individual events and developments, and, along with the places where they happened, provide what Geoffrey Bruun once called the "co-ordinates of history," the means whereby we locate events. "Once upon a time" is not enough for an understanding of history.

7

Horatius at the Bridge: The Story

School children in the Western world, from the days of the Romans on into our own century, learned about Horatius at the Bridge, the overthrow of Tarquin the Proud, the cackling of the geese that saved Rome from the Celts, and all the other stories. To these were added similar tales of the early Greeks, such as Theseus and the Labyrinth, and the Siege of Troy. To sample a long series of similarly colorful adventures of the Hebrews, one need only open the Bible to the Books of Joshua and Judges.

Roman, Greek, and Hebrew stories happened to become the common heritage of Western civilization, but these are only the best-known examples of a universal phenomenon. The Icelanders told a long series of monotonously gory tales, mostly family narratives about their ancestors and undoubtedly not so boring if it was your great grandfather who happened to have his throat cut and, especially, in the days of feuding, if the descendants of the victorious assailant still lived over on the next inlet. Highly imaginary Germanic stories, some later to be used by Richard Wagner in *The Ring,* also reflect nebulous and haunting glimpses in the folk memory of such historic men as Attila the Hun and King Theodoric of the Ostrogoths.

The legends of the overwhelming majority of human communities that have existed on this earth have long since died away with those who narrated them from one generation to the next. Few of the silent mounds, within which lie the ruins and accumulated debris of centuries of human living, will ever speak again in the actual words of their legends. Nevertheless, these towns and tribes each possessed its memories, traditions of founders, champions, and valiant deeds; explanations for the local landscape, the hills, springs, rivers, and caves, often took fantastic mythical forms. Local memories can also be tenacious. As recently as a generation ago, the inhabitants in the vicinity of Mapungubwe in southern Africa refused to climb this hill because it was sacred to the "Great Ones" of their ancestors. That is, after several centuries the villages continued to retain vague memories of the highly developed Zimbabwe culture, one of whose centers had been located near them. When archaeologists removed the mummies of the pharaohs from the Valley of the Kings' Tombs at Luxor, the villagers still remembered the ancient curse upon those who molested the dead and gathered to sing funeral chants for those who had been buried for over 3,000 years.

Early city-states and kingdoms with stronger organization usually institutionalized their oral traditions by training certain individuals to know the traditions and legends by rote, these then being recited at ceremonies and special occasions. In the days before books, some of these individuals were, to borrow the words of Jan Vansina, virtual "walking libraries" of the stories of their people. Such long-enduring African kingdoms as Benin, Dahomey, and Rwanda maintained corps of reciters, often divided into specialized branches for each kind of legend. More serious business than entertainment was involved, for they provided propaganda for the government, inculcated loyalty and pride by describing past exploits and villainous enemies, and confirmed the legitimacy of the rulers by their precise knowledge of the royal lineage. Reciters also served as a sort of human archive by their knowledge of earlier grants to favorites, of past rewards conferred for heroic deeds, and of the genealogies of the noble families.

When the Europeans arrived in the South Sea Islands, they found the Polynesians preserving genealogies orally, with accompanying legends, reaching back a millennium in some cases to these peoples' arrival in the islands. The Incas in South America maintained perhaps the most complex and organized corps of memory specialists of them all, people who combined the functions of historians, propagandists, and archivists; in the manner of modern totalitarian thought control, they carefully selected the history that might safely be narrated to the public, that which should be revealed only to the governing elite, and that which should be entirely suppressed. Many Inca stories survived because Spaniards and descendants of the Incas wrote them down. Lacking writing, the Incas recorded events, and especially their statistics, on *quipus,* an intricate device of many ropes and threads in different colors in which tied knots and their locations registered the information. In Oaxaca in southern Mexico, the Mixtecs used pictures as prompters for their historical narratives.

Though a certain amount of the Inca past has been preserved, the histories of their predecessors—the Mochica, Nazca, Tiahuanaco, and Chimu—are a total blank, deliberately destroyed by the conquering Incas while uprooting potential sources of dissidence. The Mayans suffered an equally lethal cultural blow, the only accounts of any consequence to escape destruction after the Spanish conquest being the *Popul Vuh* and the *Books of Chilam Balam,* long adventure stories from the centuries immediately prior to the conquest. Like the mounds of the world, the temples of Yucatan, of Guatemala, and of the earlier Andes lost their voices in the almost mute world of the Americas.

Other historically significant peoples have been silenced, probably forever, by enemy conquest or subsequent cultural displacement. The Carthaginians, their written records totally vanished, speak only through the writings of their Roman conquerors, while the language of the Etruscans still evades full decipherment, though evidently still a living language as late as the fall of Rome. Contemporary with the great era of the Greeks, the Etruscans must surely have rivaled them in the liveliness of their history. One wonders what the Druids of Gaul and the British Isles might have transmitted to later generations, aside from their obsession with their intricate religious beliefs. What stories were told at Stonehenge, and how long were legends afloat about the warriors buried with barbaric splendor in the earth mounds of Scythia and Central Asia?

If collected and written down, the stories of a people might survive indefinitely, hence the picturesque array in the Old Testament. Livy and others, by writing histories of Rome, immortalized the old Roman legends still extant in their time, and Bede, a couple centuries after his people had settled in Britain, did the same for the English. Sometimes the compilers themselves became mixed up; Jordanes set out to write the history of the Goths and in the process incorporated many accounts from the Getae, an entirely different people long in contact with the Goths. Saxo the Dane, trying to piece together the Viking sagas still known in his lifetime, arranged them so that no one is ever likely to disentangle them with any assurance of historical truth. The medieval troubadours perpetuated in a greatly embroidered and garbled form, in their *chansons de geste,* some heroic deeds, such as the Song of Roland and the Arthurian stories from the old Welsh folk tales.

Manifestly, the modern historians can rarely prove that any portion of the early legends, incorporated into later written narratives, actually possesses any historical validity. Nevertheless, legends might be transmitted for many generations with amazing accuracy, painstaking care being devoted to ensuring the precise preservation of the exact spoken word. Legends could be most serious matters, perpetuating the divine truth as originally handed down, and the survival of the tribe might well seem to depend upon an exact reproduction from generation to generation of what had been bestowed by the gods. A kernel of truth is frequently perceptible in a legend, some useful glimpse of an age or a people, while the specifics of the tale remain eternally unprovable or perhaps highly suspect.

Accounts meticulously preserved through the generations by word of mouth of the storytellers sometimes, when they are subject to some form of verification, turn out to have a genuine basis in fact. In the story of Theseus, Minos, and the Labyrinth, any verification of Theseus's own exploits is most unlikely, but excavations at Knossus uncovered a labyrinth-like structure, while names of some early legendary Greek heroes do, in fact, appear on excavated fragments of Greek writings, thereby at least attesting to their existence. Homer's epic of the Trojan War apparently derives from a continuous oral tradition stretching over several centuries; thus, his description of bronze armor worn by the early Greeks, long suspected to be a later insertion, was dramatically confirmed in 1962 when one such piece was unearthed.

Old Testament accounts, assumed to be largely mythical by many nineteenth-century scholars, have been broadly verified time and again in excavations and in archives elsewhere in the Middle East. Manetho's long list of Egyptian pharaohs, collected in about 300 B.C. and later quoted by other writers, proved to be substantially accurate, as has the Sumerian king list from about 3000–2000 B.C., wherever excavations divulged records and monuments bearing the names of any of these rulers. China's Shang dynasty, which ended in the eleventh century before Christ, has also been confirmed by the finding of many oracle bones inscribed with the names of kings previously considered legendary.

As would be expected, many of the legends deal with origins, plausible or fantastic, of communities. Of the numerous though usually short accounts of migrations, the forty-year wandering of the Israelites is by far the most detailed. The Aztecs of Mexico told of coming from the north (archaeology bears this out) and wandering until they saw the forecast sign, an eagle with a serpent in its beak, which in turn has become the coat of arms of Mexico. Many of the American Indians possess similar stories, nearly always providing proof of a divine origin, of a visible relationship with deities, and often offering some special role or distinction for the community. African legends of origin extol illustrious ancestors and depict tribal wanderings, usually toward the south or east from earlier homelands.

Obviously the Great Man theme plays a principal role in the elementary history of early times. Be it noted, however, that in a more simple society the role of individuals might indeed be far more decisive than in advanced communities. In the eyes of posterity, their stature grew until they were ultimately regarded as gods, and so did the number of their years in Methusaleh fashion, sometimes being reckoned in the hundreds or thousands. The classical Greeks attributed to the Great Man, in such a person as Alexander the Great, godlike qualities with drives and acts not to be circumscribed by the code of lesser men as he fulfilled his destiny.

Ancient causality, light years away from modern concepts, centers on the nature and actions of the figures themselves or on the conflict between the good hero and the wicked opponents. Gods gave assistance to the heroes or themselves determined the decisions, and otherwise nonsensical episodes could only reflect the "vagaries of the inhabitants of Olympus." The course of events might also be determined, for the fatalist, by a nebulous Something, an incomprehensible Fate, or the Norns weaving the fate of individuals.

Why did the barbarian Guti destroy the city of Akkad? Because the king of Akkad had sacked the temple of the god Enlil in Nippur, whereupon the wrathful Enlil called in the Guti. Plato said that Atlantis was destroyed because its inhabitants had become too proud. Old Testament history chronicles Jahweh's punishments when the Israelites disobeyed His commands. The absence of a sense of modern causality in the works of even the most sophisticated historical writers of the ancient world, such as Thucydides or Tacitus, is still in striking contrast to its presence in twentieth-century historiography. Thucydides, using a plurality of causes not derived from the will of the gods, still appears to the modern observer much too simple in his explanations.

Heroic Age history typically came in the form of narrative tales, spoken or sung; bards enlivened the banquets by extolling the deeds of the host, his ancestors or tribal members, to the accompaniment of a musical instrument. Organized states, however, required a knowledge of the past for confirmation of status and privileges. The Arabs have been especially diligent in maintaining the genealogy of their ancestors as a means of personal identification within the Moslem community and of sharing in the aura of prestigious ancestors. The aforementioned Sumerian king list was created by merging the lists of sovereigns of a number of cities, as though they had ruled successively, and thereby producing an impressively elongated series of monarchs. After the Burmese became a unified people in the eleventh century their priests concocted a long, largely fictitious list in imitation of the authentic Chinese compilation.

A principal purpose of history has been to teach by example, to tell tales inspiring loyalty and pride in the community and its leaders. Polybius, a Greek historian, believed that history provided the best education for politics, and, copying Polybius, much of the history written from the Renaissance well into the nineteenth century came in the guise of "philosophy teaching by example." Greek and Roman stories often contained morality lessons, the bravery of Horatius at the Bridge or the virtues of the mother of the Gracchi, all made use of by modern schoolmasters in the teaching of Greek and Latin. Livy's history of Rome illustrated the old virtues, which he believed had made the Romans great, and warned of the consequences of the declining morality, as he saw it, of his own early Augustan age. Viking sagas, full of relish for bloody violence, taught qualities necessary for survival or at least an honorable death: bravery, loyalty, endurance, and strength. We may, of course, wonder about the utility of some stories for morality purposes, such as Saxo's Viking saga about Frode the Peaceful, who ensured peace by subduing everybody else within reach.

For intensive institutionalization of the uses of history, no one has ever equaled the Chinese. A permanent register of each emperor's reign was carefully inscribed when it ended, and nothing could thereafter be altered. Though the emperor theoretically held absolute power, his acts underwent judgment by the historians in their writing of these perpetual records. He was expected to set an example of moral rectitude for his people, and should his bad conduct lose him the "mandate of heaven," he would be deposed by a more virtuous candidate whom heaven had selected as the successor. Good conduct by the ruler resulted in good fortune for the people, while evil deeds brought catastrophe, according to Taoist principles. History served as a manual for officeholders in which the past consequences of bad morality could be vividly discerned, as well as a stern guide for their own best behavior while entrusted with power. These Chinese annals, incidentally, would, translated into English, amount to about 450 volumes of about 500 pages each.

In Iran, before the Moslem conquest, the Zoroastrian concept of conflict between good and evil forms the theme for a history in which the king of kings leads all good people in the great battle against the forces of evil. El Mas'udi, an Arabic historian, reported that on the east coast of Africa in the later Middle Ages the devout people exhorted the Zanj (the blacks) to good deeds by recalling the "example of their ancestors and former kings." Zosimus, the first historian who attempted to explain the "fall of Rome," and in a sense the first to perceive it historically, chose to attribute the collapse to the "follies and crimes" of its rulers. Earlier history seldom figures as purely history; it had other purposes as well. Nor was it often a distinct area of knowledge, for religion, literature, statecraft, and history frequently blended together into a more or less indivisible whole.

Though characteristic of elementary history, the story need not necessarily be elementary. The story, gloriously told, still remains with us, written with full usage of historical methodology and painstaking attention to both accuracy and detail. With the invention of cinema and television, a whole new vista for historical storytelling has also opened up, in which the opportunities, though rarely faithfully and creatively used, are virtually limitless for a rebirth of history as a story. The promise implicit in D. W. Griffith's *Birth of a Nation* (1915) has seldom been fulfilled, but in such masterpieces as the BBC's depiction of *The Six Wives of Henry VIII* and *Elizabeth R*, the fascinating possibility arises that we may come full circle, as the storyteller returns to the audience to recreate, with all the aid of modern devices, the moods and scenes of long ago.

8

The Doomsday
Trumpet:
Catastrophism

The island of Santorini, or Thera, in the Aegean Sea is a spectacular place to visit. Located between Greece and Crete, it looms sharply out of the water as a craggy, shattered volcano, one side fallen away, with the crater serving as a deep harbor. The remaining three-fourths of the curving wall survives, a cliff up which trails a steep path to the village on top. If some archaeologists are correct, the history of Santorini, called Thera by the ancient Greeks, is equally spectacular.

According to the theory, first proposed by Spyridon Marinatos in 1939, a violent volcanic eruption, like that of Krakatoa in Indonesia in 1883, brought the sudden destruction of the Minoan civilization on Crete, about eighty miles away, through earthquake, tidal waves, and volcanic ash. Since then, an accumulation of evidence has given the theory much more credibility and respectability than such a fantastic proposal would normally receive.

Inevitably, the old will-o-the-wisp story about the catastrophic sinking of Atlantis "in a single day and night" has also been connected with the Thera cataclysm. The legend originated with Plato's famous account, which he claimed his ancestor, Solon the Lawgiver, had heard in about 590 B.C. from Egyptian priests. Though Plato located it in the Atlantic and over 9,000 years before his own time, the kernel of truth in the Egyptian tradition could plausibly be a recollection of the Aegean catastrophe, preserved in garbled form for over 800 years. With equal inevitability, certain hitherto unbelievable Greek legends are also being linked with the disaster: a war between Poseidon, god of the sea, and Zeus; possible eyewitness descriptions incorporated into other oral traditions; and even the Israelite memory of the plagues in Egypt before their Exodus.

Catastrophism does form an important part of the elementary history of the ancients, and the possibility can hardly be denied that they could have had folk memories of the occurrence of such natural cataclysms. That the ancients believed them the work of deities is scarcely surprising, considering modern descriptions of natural phenomena—strange fireballs, searchlights in the sky, volcanic ash obscuring the sunlight, tidal waves, and earthquakes with their "deep rumbling noise from the earth itself, full of menace."

A thoroughly authenticated example of catastrophe is that of the Flood, though not, of course, according to the specifics of the biblical legend of a man named Noah and his Ark landing on Mount Ararat. (The Sumerians and Babylonians, respectively, called him Utnapishtim and Ziusudra.) Deluges there were, floods of such devastating size that "the world" of the lower Tigris-Euphrates valley was "destroyed" some 5,000 years ago. In 1929, while excavating at Ur, Sir Leonard Woolley, having dug down to a soil level from a little earlier than the time of the first kings of the city, suddenly came upon water-laid silt lacking in traces of human habitation. After digging another ten feet, he once again began discovering evidences of human residence. Those ten feet had been deposited by the Deluge and its aftermath! Soon afterwards, excavators at Kish, another Sumerian city, found a similar layer, evidently the consequences of a later inundation. Whether because of "forty days" of rain (the Sumerians said seven), or the backing up of the waters of the Persian Gulf, or other possible reasons, disasters of such magnitude would be forever afterwards remembered in the legend of the Flood.

Other possible disasters have been suggested. Rhys Carpenter has argued that a climatic change, a long-enduring period of drought, destroyed the Mycenaean civilization, debilitated the Hittite Empire farther east so that it fell, and drove the Peoples of the Sea to migrate in search of new land and food, thereby explaining the return to an age of barbarism in the twelfth and eleventh centuries in the Middle East. Drought—or, conversely, flooding—has also been advanced as an explanation for the collapse of the Mohenjo Daro and Harappa civilization in the Indus Valley, a destruction formerly attributed to the invading Aryans.

Nor did the ancients lack visible proof of catastrophes caused by human beings. As early as Sumer, we encounter, on cuneiform tablets, lamentations for the fall of Ur and Nippur. Surviving written records and archaeological evidence alike are checkered with the sudden and bloody destruction of cities by barbarians looking for plunder or their chastisement by the imperial armies of Nineveh and Babylon, Carthage and Rome. No one could be certain that he or she would not be dragged into captivity to serve out his or her life as a slave of the city's enemies. In the fatal year of 146 B.C., the Romans destroyed *two* of the wealthiest cities of the Mediterranean, Carthage and Corinth.

The books of the prophets of Israel are filled with the mood of catastrophism, a virtual litany of disaster, as these moral leaders inveighed against wickedness and prophesied destruction for the unrighteous and the oppressor. Nahum, writing in the last days of Assyria and relishing its fall, foretold that "the noise of the rattling of the wheels, and of the pransing horses, and of the jumping chariots," would be stilled, and "thy nobles shall dwell in the dust; thy people is scattered upon the mountains, and no man gathereth them." Jeremiah, a virtuoso at blasting the doomsday trumpet, railed against Babylon: ". . . and they shalt not take of thee a stone for a corner, nor a stone for foundations; but thou shalt be desolate for ever, saith the Lord."

In the Book of Daniel occurs the famous biblical version of the fall of Babylon to the Persians and Medes. At a great banquet, in itself symbolizing the wicked power and luxury of the oppressive Babylonians, the fingers of a hand appeared, writing on the wall "Mene, Mene, Tekel, Upharsin." Daniel translated this to mean "God hath numbered thy kingdom, and finished it. Thou art weighed in the balances, and art found wanting. Thy kingdom is divided, and given to the Medes and Persians." And so it came to pass, though the story itself, told centuries later, is scarcely credible.

Manifestly, the ancients possessed enough evidence of catastrophe to color their history in a dramatic way. Human nature being human nature then as now, people also remembered episodes of dramatic violence, albeit their prosperous cities might continue to thrive for centuries. Peaceful decades of worthy endeavor, accomplishments in the arts, commerce, and material comforts, attracted no more public attention than in our own contemporary newspapers, with their daily and misleading chronicle of violence, accidents, and other bad news.

Not until the invention of printing did the facilities even exist for discerning enough of a recorded past for people to become fully aware of the details and of a more sophisticated pattern of change amidst persisting continuity. Remembering the fall of a great city or empire, the ancients no longer recalled the intermediate stages of decline, nor had they comprehended their nature at the time. A catastrophe may long have been incubating within the society and government itself, an enemy only pushing over a tottering facade. The ancients lacked the intellectual or technical tools to understand the contributing economic, social, and geographic factors, beyond sensing the times going out of joint or seeing initial disasters as a warning from the gods.

They saw the past in terms of a more or less set stage upon

which the actors performed their roles. Whereas, in fact, the props of the historical stage are constantly undergoing change, often with almost imperceptible slowness, they could only visualize a catastrophic event, an abrupt change, as seriously altering the background. In their narratives, modern observers miss a sense of the flow of time, the measured sequence of the years, and, above all, an awareness of the "becoming" of things, the evolutionary nature of communities and institutions. To be sure, the tempo of normal change nearly always moved far more slowly in earlier societies, while jarring events may well have comprised more of a factor in successive alterations than in later times.

In November 1970, a cyclone and tidal wave killed as many as perhaps 300,000 persons on the coast of Bangladesh, then called East Pakistan, in a cataclysm immediately recalling the biblical Flood. Soon thereafter the Bengalis rebelled against the Pakistanis and, with the help of India, became independent. An interesting sequence of nature's wrath and political acts this, precisely suited to the talents of the ancient historians!

Our century has seen world wars, numerous social upheavals, and the nuclear demolition of Hiroshima and Nagasaki in "a rain of ruin from the air, the like of which has never been seen on this earth." A generation living under the threat of nuclear weapons can hardly reject the possibility of future cataclysms. Most historians, nevertheless, must now regard a catastrophic or an apocalyptic view of history as reflecting an excessive concentration on a phenomenon whose incidence or degree of probability is infinitely less than its fascination for part of the public. It grossly oversimplifies the picture of what does take place, of the background elements leading into a dramatic episode and the subsequent developments wherein the strands of continuity reassert themselves. Later generations often caricaturize the actual scene into one of sharp violence and abrupt change by abstracting a few elements from a kaleidoscopic panorama while ignoring the remaining contours and details. Even as geologists necessarily broke with early nineteenth-century beliefs in catastrophism in order to create scientific geology, so historians usually stress the pervasive, if less spectacular, role of enduring social forces in the everyday world.

An explanation by catastrophism all too often identifies its perpetrator as an illiterate in historical processes, as lacking a knowledge of how change and continuity interact in the real world. An immature time sense particularly induces a sense of the catastrophic because of an inability to accept the reality of long-time duration and the cumulative processes operative therein. The past can then only be visualized in terms of a series of sharp breaks with continuity, to which an "end of the world" feeling may contribute, a foreboding mood and fear of the unknown future quite prevalent in recent decades. Aggravating contemporary anxieties have been the mass media, which, intrinsically for purposes of ensuring an audience, have subjected the populace to the dubious thrills of a series of doomsday crises. A pessimistic anxiety in "these dark times" about an ominous future, however, has been a constant in human thought and especially among some types of doomsday personalities throughout human history.

Those afflicted with premonitions of the apocalyptic or those disposed to taking contemporary prophets seriously should read Norman Cohn's *Pursuit of the Millennium.* He traces the strain of catastrophism from Old Testament Judaism on up through the medieval versions of catastrophe to those versions extant in the time of the Reformation. Christianity from its inception has been colored by an acute sense of living in "the last days," a belief in an impending Judgment Day and the apocalyptic vision of the Millennium. Becoming the property of dissidents and socially lower-class groups, this belief persisted as a sort of underground history, offering ready explanations based largely on biblical sources for successive crises. Articulating the aspirations of rebels, this history consisted of a past divided into successive eras that culminate in the present struggle of the last days before the coming of the Millennium. Although the devil or Antichrist rules the present wicked and hateful age, the "establishment" being made up of his representatives, the return to life of a great person or the appearance of a liberating savior will signal the onset of the final apocalyptic Armageddon.

Some elements of virtually every generation have simultaneously feared a foreboding future and desperately awaited its liberating message. "[S]tripped of . . . supernatural sanction, revolutionary millenarianism and mystical anarchism are with us still." Marxist doomsday predictions for capitalism often figure as an ingredient in popular folk history. A group of economists, meeting as the Club of Rome to discuss ecology, announced that we only had from ten to twenty years in which "to right ourselves," otherwise civilization would suddenly collapse. Today's newspaper probably contains yet another warning that unless we promptly be converted by this month's popular Jeremiah, appalling things will happen. Meantime, Jehovah's Witnesses soldier on in the ancient Christian tradition of St. John's Book of Revelation.

Individuals lacking a mature sense of time thrive on the mood of the apocalyptic, search for the "signs" that herald the coming of dramatic events, and may have a taste, temperamentally, for the Four Horsemen of the Apocalypse, the Valkyries bearing the slain to Valhalla, or the vision of the mushroom cloud on the horizon. This mood of catastrophe and the apocalyptic undoubtedly in itself serves as a causative factor in history. Political prisoners long held in detention sometimes reach a state of mind where they can visualize themselves only as being liberated in such circumstances and then returning to the midst of an adoring and grateful populace. Some revolutionaries, incurably addicted to this elementary approach, would wipe the slate clean in order to usher in a new and better world. Political extremists of both right and left chronically find part justification in an elementary version of history having little relationship to the realities of the modern society or community. Like the Plot theory, the doomsday gambit is one of the tricks of the trade.

Our modern community, hence, hears much political rhetoric and many explanations on a level as elementary as that of the ancients. Alongside the scientific methodology for the natural world, some people resolutely avoid the intellectual tools developed for comprehending our contemporary society. In an age of automobiles, airplanes, and space travel, the concepts of historical processes used by part of the public are as modern and as realistic and well adapted to our communities as Nahum's "pransing horses" and "jumping chariots" are for traveling on our throughways.

9

The Golden Age: Past or Future?

Biblical history begins with Adam and Eve in the Garden of Eden. The Sumerians recalled a time when there were no snakes, lions, or wolves, "no fear, no terror." Cronus (or Saturn) had supposedly presided over a Golden Age somewhere in the remote past when fruit grew without human tending, the flocks multiplied, and all men lived in prosperity without work or sorrow. If one of the frequent ingredients of elementary history is a feeling that we live in "the last times," another is a belief in the "good old days," or perhaps a Golden Age somewhere in the past.

Hesiod, a Greek who lived in the eighth century before Christ, talked of five successive eras, each more evil than the one before, the Golden Age of Cronus, the Silver Age of Zeus, the Age of Bronze, the Heroic Age, and his own, the worst, the Age of Iron. That Hesiod should believe himself living in the Iron Age is typical; most generations, all too well aware of their own troubles, would probably echo fourteenth-century Petrarch's opinion that he would have preferred to have been born in any era other than his own. Many people tend to look back nostalgically to the good old days long enough ago to have forgotten the sufferings and strife of those years. A more simple rural society may now seem to have been a veritable Golden Age when shorn of its quota of distress by posterity's forgetfulness. Some citizens exaggerate the sterling qualities of the Founding Fathers, not realizing that they were as human as ourselves.

Oftentimes, the ancients combined the notion of a gradual deterioration from a Golden Age with the concept of a cyclical pattern of time. The Hindus visualized a cycle as made up of four eras: a Golden Age of perfection; a second period in which virtue declined; a third period of increasing sinfulness; and a final era of much wickedness. Needless to say, humanity now languishes in the latter. Though Chinese historical scholars generally used linear time, some Chinese cyclical theories also appeared, especially in Taoism and neo-Confucianism. The Mayans employed a fifty-two–year cycle, but they also had other cycles, the longest being the *kincultun,* lasting about three million years.

Usually a cycle was visualized as being terminated by a gigantic catastrophe, the end of the world, with possibly a new sequence then beginning. Appropriately enough in view of their climate in the Far North, the Vikings believed the world would first grow cold and dark, then the gods themselves would perish in battle with the forces of destruction at Ragnarok. In some versions, however, they made provision for a new world to arise and humanity to reappear from one surviving couple. Graeco-Roman tradition vaguely recalled the shift from one era to another in the unseating of the earlier gods by Zeus-Jupiter and his family. In the cyclical pattern, be it noted, history consists not only of the past; it also includes the future, a future broadly predictable because history repeats itself in the ultimate return of the various ages of the cycle.

Some Greek philosophers believed in cycles, Parmenides, Empedocles, Anaximander, the Stoics, and, possibly, also Plato and Aristotle. The latter detected a political cycle in Greek cities from aristocracy to democracy to rule by tyrants. Polybius elaborated a pattern running from monarchy to tyranny, to aristocracy, and thence to oligarchy, moderate democracy, and mob rule, a point of view defensible due to what happened in many Greek cities. Nevertheless, in writing about the past, Polybius used linear history, and so did nearly all of the Greek historians.

Jewish history follows a linear form. It has a beginning and an ultimate goal, the Jews, as God's chosen people, working out a destiny to be realized in the future with the coming of the promised Messiah. The Christians developed this kind of linear history, though some early Christian writers also thought in terms of the cyclical.

St. Augustine, in an age of barbarian violence and manifest erosion of Roman power, molded the shapes of Western history for many centuries to come by adverting to an apocalypse of the coming of the City of God. He drew from the classical and Jewish past—his history still deals with famous individuals and their deeds—but the stories are oriented around a greater theme. Well grounded in Rome's secular history, he treats it as material evidence of God's plan being unveiled upon earth, that in the divinely ordained scheme of things the Roman Empire had been created in order to make possible the emergence of Christianity. For the Romans, their long-enduring power disintegrating before their eyes, this explanation also served as a great consolation.

History now had a goal, and historical events, however inscrutable to humanity, occurred according to a definite design or pattern. Events derived their meanings from the overriding cosmic drama; heroes and villains still flourished in this history, but they did battle on behalf of something greater than themselves. The culmination of earlier historical development, the rise of Christianity, figures as a *unique* drama, hence not cyclical, and the past "acquired a dynamic, almost a propulsion" (Plumb).

Another concept, too, lay implicit in St. Augustine's view of history; the complete triumph of the City of God lay in the *future*. Albeit originally conceived in a religious sense, the notion of a Golden Age in the future was eventually appropriated by those of a more secular mind. For the ancients, the return of a Golden Age formed part of the cycle, hence in a remote future beyond the capacities of the people to hasten it. Graeco-Roman history may have been largely linear, but that line did not ascend upward, and what modern generations call progress was considered by the Romans to be a "corruption" of the natural order of things. Throughout the medieval period, people continued to look to Rome and the church fathers for authority, and Renaissance scholars, attempting to recreate the age of the classical thinkers of the past, were still looking backward to the ancients.

Meantime, the Christian millennial version of a future Golden Age, of a "New Jerusalem," continued to be propagated throughout the medieval period. The persistently popular Sibylline Oracles added the prediction of a coming messianic suzerain, an Emperor of the Last Days, and the expectations of underground rebels focused successively on the return of Constantine, Henry IV, Frederick Barbarossa, and others to set the world aright. Each century's crises were interpreted with the help of the Oracles, the prophetic Scriptures, and the utterances of a series of would-be deliverers, a procedure regularly denounced by an inconvenienced church and as regularly flouted. Joachim of Fiore (1145–1212) dreamed of a future Age of the Spirit in which the whole world would become "one vast monastery" inhabited by "contemplative monks" (Cohn), not necessarily a Golden Age for ordinary flesh and blood people! Later, in the period of the Reformation, Thomas Müntzer predicted that the Turks would conquer Europe as a preliminary to the Second Coming and the Millennium. Soon thereafter, John of Leyden reigned briefly in Munster as the "Messiah of the Last Days."

By the eighteenth century, some versions of a Golden Age had become increasingly secularized, and a growing conviction that linear history led upward brings the fateful word "progress" into play. Thinkers could now believe that they had outstripped the level of the ancients by revolting against their intellectual authority. In mathematics especially, obvious advances had been achieved, while the Newtonian viewpoint summarized an equally dramatic change in outlook toward the physical world. Scientific experimentation and new models of machinery opened up a wide new world of possibilities, one quite different from that of the ancients. The witchcraft mania, rampant until the middle of the seventeenth century, had ceased to torment the Europeans. A definite population growth in France and some other countries reinforced the mood; no longer did bad crops, to quite the same extent, bring hunger, disease, and death to the most vulnerable. An increasingly cultured cosmopolitan aristocracy, nourishing the arts and letters, knew how to live more gracefully than anyone in the West since the Greeks, and so a man like Condorcet could now sense and express the growing feeling of general improvement by elaborating his famous concept of human progress.

In the nineteenth century, the West embraced progress as an article of faith. Political philosophers, some still influential, envisioned a Golden Age in a secular future, seemingly attainable by humanity on this earth through its own planning and labors. Faith in progress, and the desirability of harnessing our efforts to its exhortations, became a major theme, perhaps the predominant, in historical writing.

Much less so in the present century. Oswald Spengler, during World War I and the defeat of his Germans, turned to a cyclical theory to express forebodings about the future of Western civilization. Arnold Toynbee, a little later, would devote many years to writing a pessimistic version of cyclical history. The pollution brought by industrial revolution, the threat of overpopulation, bloody revolutions, and world wars, these and others have introduced their ugly presence into the Golden Age future envisioned for us by our immediate ancestors.

In our secularized culture, another variant of the Golden Age has also become exceedingly common, a belief that somewhere on earth a group of people actually has found the road to a Golden Age or possibly even achieved it. Chinese civilization and the newly discovered South Sea Polynesians enjoyed periods of popularity. Many Europeans once looked to the United States as the land of promise. More recently, the Communist societies of the Soviet Union, Castro's Cuba, and the People's Republic of China have attracted numerous devotees. Scores of other versions of future utopias and how to reach them have appeared, as humanity's hopes and despairs drive it to disregard the customary historical processes in favor of repeated attempts at a great leap forward.

10

The Unholy
Railroad Train:
Progress or Decline?

Humanity has never quite shaken off the traumatic memory of the fall of Rome and the relapse of western Europe into the so-called Dark Ages, "the worst setback in the history of civilization" (Herbert Muller). The Greeks themselves dimly remembered the earlier Minoan-Mycenaean culture and the subsequent barbaric Dorian invasion. Islam, after the splendors of the early caliphate, slowly subsided into the Moslem equivalent of the Dark Ages.

Some would have us believe that Western civilization has passed its zenith or even insist, like Toynbee, that it is far along the road of decline. Spengler's monumental *Decline of the West* (like Toynbee's work, thoroughly disliked by professional historians) spelled out the stages in the cycle of history and purported to prove that the West was retrograding. Meantime, the residents of our blemished Golden Age of technological wonders grow ambivalent, having their belief in progress now intermingled with doubts. For some, the rack of progress becomes intolerable, especially in its guise of ever more material acquisitions and incessant promises of better deodorants and the car of tomorrow. If progress is real, then the latest must be the best, so runs the faulty logic of those trapped in the compulsive procession of ephemeral fads. Some ostantatiously drop out of the rat race, only to adopt the ultimate Golden Age version of progress, the "cult of the future."

Paradoxically, those who consider the past as worse than worthless because it has bequeathed burdens that retard rapid advances may be thereby endowing the past with more significance, in a negative way, than those believing in less drastic patterns of change and continuity. Worshipers of the idol of progress, fervently convinced that the future comes too slowly, may be prepared to inflict suffering upon their own generation in the hope of accelerating advances and attaining the good society sooner.

To be sure, this devotion to progress has become deeply engrained. Elderly people can still remember the competition in the setting of new speed records by trains. Steamship companies vied for records in crossing the Atlantic and in the size of the ships. The first transoceanic voyage by a steamship, the invention of the screw propeller, the driving of the final nail in the first transcontinental railroad track, the stretching of the first telegraph line from Washington to Baltimore, the invention of the telephone, the coming of the wireless telegraph, all of these were celebrated conquests at the time, each confirming continued progress. In the 1920s, the nations competed in the building and flying of dirigibles, and Charles Lindbergh was the first to fly nonstop across the Atlantic. Newspapers reported the opening of each major link in continental and overseas airlines.

And now? Where eight passenger trains passed through our town each day, now there are none; driving to Washington takes less than eight hours, but the last lone train took twelve. (It stopped for dinner somewhere in Appalachia, the crew and we six passengers went into a trackside restaurant, and this writer suddenly found himself expecting to hear the clopping hoof-beats of an approaching stage coach.) Where the residents of American cities once bragged about their rising census figures, they now worry about overpopulation. Town boosters formerly cheered smoke pouring from factory smokestacks as a sign of growth and modernization, not of pollution. Automobile traffic on big city streets moves at an average rate of twelve miles an hour, about the same speed as a horse.

Those who still need or happen to like to ride on railroad trains obviously see a decline, though now the great through-ways and swift airplanes have replaced them. Railroads themselves outmoded the canals, whose rapid digging and abandonment in the United States constituted one of the swiftest examples of rise and fall on record. Railroads also created unemployment among the drivers of Conestoga wagons and stage coaches; there had been 106 stage lines running out of Boston alone. Mark Twain described the races by Mississippi river boats with exuberant gusto, happily listed the progressively faster times achieved between New Orleans and such cities as St. Louis, and begrudged the triumph of the "unholy train," "ripping the sacred solitude to rags and tatters with its devil's war-whoop and the roar and thunder of its rushing wheels."

Handicraft arts deteriorated as the Industrial Revolution progressed, along with some of the skill and beauty in everyday life for both the viewer and the creative peasant artists. The coal industry dwindled as newer forms of fuel gained ascendancy; ignoring American industry's increasing reliance on other forms of energy, the Soviet press in the 1950s pointed to the lowered production of American coal in contrast to Soviet increases as one indication of the decline of American capitalism. Italy is said to have declined in the sixteenth and seventeenth centuries parallel to the rapid advance of oceanic travel on the Atlantic. However Mediterranean trading in this period may have been quantitatively larger than earlier, it was simply cast into the shadows by the conspicuous growth in the Atlantic area. In each case, the initial impression of decline more broadly examined is seen to be only one facet of a larger process. In these instances, progress can be visualized as being somewhat like a relay race, with the baton passing repeatedly to new runners and the bearers, once successfully attaining their goal, creating the conditions for their own replacement. The Marxists have one version of this: out of decline emerges progress, that is, according to them the fulfillment of the goals of capitalism and its subsequent crisis prepares the way for a so-called progressive step forward, the emergence of socialism.

Perhaps the victims of progress, those who lose out in each stage, talk about decline. Spengler's Germans had lost a war, and the British, firm believers in progress in the nineteenth century, became much less convinced when their national fortunes turned. Members of a growing and vital nation, occupational group, or other association will think in terms of progress, while those suffering defeats and setbacks search for a different rationale.

The British Empire, still existing in 1945, had vanished by 1965. Close to thirty independent countries, most of them members of the Commonwealth of Nations, stood in its place. Had the British Empire "declined" or "fallen," or are these words inadequate to describe what really happened, merely words used in elementary history? An empire, outmoded as a political form, underwent a transformation, a rapid metamorphosis in response to the necessity of intelligently adjusting to changing circumstances.

At the opposite extreme in duration, Edward Gibbon carried his account of the decline and fall of the Roman Empire clear down to the end of the Middle Ages. Constantinople, of course, remained a "Roman" capital until 1453, though Rome itself, as we popularly think of it, falls in 476. Territorially, the empire did contract for over a thousand years, though by no means constantly or evenly, until it embraced little more than the capital city. Is "decline" quite the proper word to employ for something continuing this long? Contemporaries of the end of the Western Roman Empire, living as close to it as we do to the vanishing British Empire, did not generally realize that it had fallen at all. Invading tribes, the Franks, Ostrogoths, Visigoths, Vandals, and others, occupied various areas but usually continued to use much of the old surviving governmental apparatus and practices in what, at the time, seemed a continuation of the empire.

Early modern Europeans arriving in Africa considered the blacks backward. Unknown to the Europeans, the Africans were at that time in the later stages of a major historical achievement, the repopulating of the southern half of the continent. Concurrently, they were developing an iron industry, absorbing useful skills and techniques from the Nile valley and the Mediterranean area, adapting farming methods to a sizeable portion of Africa, and creating their own type of society. The blacks were successfully responding to the challenge of the African environment and within the context of their history achieving necessary goals, though this very effort may have precluded advances along some lines then considered important by Europeans.

Are the Dark Ages just possibly an optical illusion foisted on us by earlier writers? The fifth century, the dismal years of increasing disintegration in the West, seems to have been one of "growing prosperity" in the eastern Mediterranean. Arabic historians would scarcely regard this period as a Dark Age, inasmuch as the Moslem world passes through its great period in commerce, architecture, and medicine between 700 and 1100. Our periodization reflects conditions, especially, in France, England, and Italy, that is, the conventional concept of world history still carries the imprint of what, in world perspective, was a local decline in part of Europe.

Other questions emerge, whether the Colosseum crowds, slaves, and praetorian guard really represented a higher civilization than medieval society and government, or whether medieval men were more warlike or cruel or generally backward than the Romans. Granted that Italy went through a positive decline, evidence exists for an advance in northern Europe, a leveling off of different parts of the continent. Moslem Spain, at its pinnacle in these centuries, was surely the equal, culturally and materially, of imperial Rome, the early eastern caliphate, and the Byzantine Empire. In technical matters, the Roman Empire definitely was less advanced than many areas during the Middle Ages; a well-equipped feudal army, possessing more advanced weapons, would have defeated the Romans.

Obviously a Dark Age existed for intellectuals of a secular cast of mind, including the sort who now write history. The intellectuals, however, retreated to the Church and entrenched themselves there as clergy, in the process asserting a very great power over the community. It is equally obvious that the earlier Middle Ages were a poor time in western Europe for those whose talents ran in the direction of trade and commerce; because they were important members in the subsequent middle class, their attitudes would be influential in the nineteenth century when historians devised our conventional views of history.

The Renaissance was long regarded as a period of impressive advances. Some recent historians, however, have contended that a period of decline lasted through the fourteenth until the middle of the fifteenth centuries, while the sixteenth also witnessed a hardening of religious orthodoxies, plus a rapidly growing belief in witchcraft and astrology. A consensus places the beginnings of modern times in the Renaissance, but in terms of an age of science and technology the real dividing line of development comes in the seventeenth and early eighteenth with the breakthrough of modern science.

If comparable at all, how does the quality of contemporary art compare with that of the Renaissance? Do the arts command as much proportionate interest as they did 450 years ago, and is this relevant to the measurement of progress? The point is that we regard science as the touchstone of progress, whereas the society of the Renaissance considered the arts, painting especially, as the highest form of achievement.

Any judgment of progress or decline seems to depend largely upon the criteria used, whether based upon materialistic growth, power, the refining of scientific methodology, the appreciation of beauty, the prevalence of democratic government, or the happiness of the average human being. Toynbee virtually ignored science and technology and, having thus effectively stripped the modern world of its most vaunted forms of achievement, could easily find decline from the sixteenth century onward. Spengler's particular interest lay in art, by no means the strongest suit of the twentieth century. Undoubtedly parts of western Europe passed through Dark Ages if measured in terms of the collapse of Rome's central authority or the decline of urban civilization, both cherished now because we live in an urban civilization with strong central authority. Genghiz Khan's warriors in Central Asia probably thought that they were improving the world when they wiped out the cities and slaughtered the farmers, thereby making room for pastoral activities! The world obviously did not grow dark, as at Ragnarok, during the Dark Ages. People lived, had their pleasures and sorrows as always, amidst the changing seasons and the annual routine of sowing, cultivating, and harvesting.

For building with stone the world may have been declining since the end of Gothic architecture; in terms of gracious living, civilization climaxed with the eighteenth-century aristocracy; the summit for civilized politics came in the nineteenth-century British parliament; and if control of nature's energies be the criterion, then we are now at the peak. A future age may regard the obsession with controlling the forces of the physical world and the concomitant faith in material things as a form of barbarism characteristic of this lap in the relay race of mankind.

Having surmised that progress is relative, we can scarcely leave the discussion at this point. At the pots and pans level, which is approximately where historians start their story, we do eat better and have made remarkable advances in health and medicine as our span of years upon the earth continues to lengthen. To doubt a fundamental sort of progress is to be in the position of a driver in the mountains who believes that the highway is going downgrade until, hearing the motor laboring, looks back and sees that the car is climbing; the driver has been fooled by the slow upward direction of the road relative to the rising contours of the mountain terrain itself. Perhaps the mountain of our rising expectancies deceives us as to the genuine progress achieved.

The words "progress" and "decline" do have their uses, but, like so many terms in history, they carry valid meanings only within the realities of specific situations. When someone advocates a course of action in the name of progress, the criteria being used and those being omitted should immediately be brought to mind and the proposed victors and victims specifically identified. Like the "last days" and the Golden Age, the concepts of progress and decline, reduced to a simplistic level, are characteristic of elementary historical-mindedness. As such, they are common coinage for historical processes far more complex than their frequently glib usage would indicate.

11

From Elementary to Basic: The Shaping of History

Two more elementary devices for the shaping of history remain to be mentioned, the trick of the Outer Darkness and the short cut of the Philosopher's Stone.

Sir Herbert Butterfield once referred to the habit of relegating to "the outer darkness" whatever we do not like or understand, a mental sleight of hand practised by most of us. Human nature whispers that we are the children of light in contrast to the children of darkness. Marxists regard as "backward" all those not holding their "advanced" or "progressive" views. Intellectuals tend to disdain people in business for operating according to economic interests, while many of these people deride intellectuals for judging by abstract ideas. Various American groups tend to enhance their own self-esteem by consigning to the Outer Darkness certain other groups within the national community.

Writ large, the playing of this trick on the dead often helps to shape the contours of the human past. Members of our generation regularly boost their own egos by using the enlightened present versus the benighted past dichotomy. People of the Enlightenment prided themselves on being more civilized than their predecessors, and so the concept of the medieval as being the Dark Ages became one of the enduring shapes of history. The Arabs long ignored their past before the coming of Mohammed; they considered this to be the Jahiliyya ("the Ignorance"), consequently unworthy of being remembered. By so doing, they dropped into oblivion the achievements of the South Arabs, especially the high culture of the Yemenite Sabaeans, as well as the wide commercial enterprises of the earlier period. Orthodox Russian Communists have imposed an Outer Darkness on the decades before the Bolshevik Revolution of 1917 and on the details of this momentous development. Seen in Russian museums and books, Lenin appears lonely—he does it all. Smolny Institute has thousands of photographs of the revolution which cannot be shown because they do not fit the official shapes of history and because most of the leading participants, as a result of political feuding, were subsequently cast into the Outer Darkness.

As for the second device, alchemists formerly attempted to transmute base metals into gold by means of the so-called philosopher's stone, and now political alchemists endeavor to transmute the normal community into a Golden Age society by means of an ideological philosopher's stone. A magic formula is sought, a single standard or some obsessive insight, against which society, its leaders, parties, and institutions, all must be measured. An engineer, trusting his philosopher's stone, may plunge into political crusades with mental tools and skills that if applied to building bridges would swiftly cause girders to collapse because the pertinent laws of physics and the nature of metals would have not been taken into account.

These complete a list of elementary concepts, the imagery that naturally occurs to the human mind in the absence of more sophisticated shapes and explanations of historical processes. To recapitulate, the street-level devices include the good-evil dichotomy, the Great Man theme, the Plot theory, monocausal explanations, and the Gordian sword of action. Catastrophism often appears in lieu of more mature concepts of change and continuity, while for the broader shapes of history, the Golden Age, progress, and decline frequently provide the contours. Used in innocent unawareness of a higher level, these devices have been rendered obsolete by the development of a more thorough knowledge of historical processes. When flagrantly employed by street-level peddlers, they indicate the quake, signal the presence of intellectual charlatanry.

However, the appearance of one of these concepts in a narrative otherwise constructed with the aid of historical processes can be entirely legitimate. Using progress or decline as a unifying thread for a narrative, focusing on a catastrophic event, or even employing the Outer Darkness as background to highlight a certain development can be respectable enough practices. It is a matter of how they are used and of gradations of acceptability. The careful handling of these themes by scholars contrasts sharply to their *exclusive* use on the street level, where they serve as simplistic substitutes for concepts more faithfully depicting reality.

An imprecise usage of terms also characterizes the elementary level of historical-mindedness. The historian's language appears deceptively easy, only "a prolongation and a refinement of ordinary language" (Raphael Demos). Unlike the scientists, historians do not operate with specific technical terms, and, couched in the common vernacular and using familiar terms, the discourse of the professional tempts the untrained amateur to assume the prerogatives of an historian. Beneath the superficially plain surface, however, lie a wealth of associated meanings, unspoken assumptions, and a skillfully balanced juxtaposition of interwoven historical factors.

Analogies and terms or labels require careful handling. An empire is said to "fall," like a house or tree, but the expression actually symbolizes a much more complex process. Analogies are useful for a quick transmission of mutually understood ideas and for communicating an approximate comprehension of something hitherto unknown by means of the already familiar. The essentials of a larger picture can be conveyed in capsule form by analogy, as in the usage of the image of the Mansion of History in this book. They also frequently suggest additional, though sometimes deceptive, insights. Analogical explanations, however, remain only approximations; pushing the analogy too far tempts the unwary and arguing proof from them is an utterly treacherous business. As a probably necessary, or at least convenient, form of mental shorthand, they can easily trap their users, perhaps resulting in an unwitting shaping of history by reducing it to the contours of extraneous images.

Quite possibly the most commonly used image of them all is the conception of politics as being based upon a left-right prism of politics, in which the left consists successively of liberals, socialists, and Communists while the right extends through conservatives, reactionaries, and fascists. Originating with the seating in the early nineteenth-century French assemblies, where liberals sat on the left and conservatives on the right of the presiding officer, the imagery was later projected upon the whole range of politics. Though having the obvious advantages of simplicity and clear classification, this device can also be deceptive; thus, the extremes of right and left may have more in common with each other than with those in the center of the prism in their attitudes towards human liberties, violence, and desire for change. (Bending the straight line into a circle, wherein the extremes impinge upon each other, might, in fact, provide a more accurate image of reality.) The significance is that the device has served as more than a passive mirror of reality, it has greatly influenced our political attitudes.

Historical terms, inescapable as a simplification of complex reality, must be resorted to constantly, and familiarity with their usage, knowing the range of associations that go with them, forms an integral part of historical-mindedness. Time periods, broad names for social groups, and terms for specific phenomena in historical processes depict, when properly handled, realities in the past. At the street level, the terms usually lack precision, tend to appear as stereotyped labeling of groups or to carry value judgments as in "revolution," "feudal," or "fascist." Because many of these terms were minted in the Forum—and sometimes by other disciplines—they reflect their own histories; the vocabulary has grown rather than being invented, hence a short definition rarely conveys the full accouterment of meaning acquired in past circumstances. Part of the skill of the historically minded person resides in an ability to define a term within the specific contexts in which it successively appears. Once mastered, this occurs as an automatic response so that not much in the way of effort is required to decipher each usage. Actually, children learn most of their vocabulary similarly, much of it picked up through usage rather than in the dictionary. Exaggerating a bit, the historian is somewhat in the position of the Chinese, who use the same symbol for a number of words and must learn rapid comprehension of which word applies in each case.

Only repeated experience with a term in various contexts can instill a sensitivity to its particular nuances. A knowledge of word origins in itself helps to provide a useful perspective on their usage. Thus, "capitalism," derived from "capital" through the German *"Kapitalismus,"* has been broadened, due to ideological reasons, from a financial term to one denoting a form of society; for that matter, in the original sense "capitalism" varied greatly in the Renaissance or even in the nineteenth century from its present form. Babeuf and Karl Marx took "proletariat" out of its Roman context and applied it to factory workers. "Industrial revolution," first coined in France early in the nineteenth century in imitation of "political revolution," was first popularized late in the century by an uncle of Arnold Toynbee of the same name. "Progress" apparently was first given its modern meaning by Sir Francis Bacon. "Democrat" came into use, evidently, in the Low Countries in the 1780s, became popular usage to a certain extent during the French Revolution, and was current all over Europe by the end of the 1790s. Its present meaning in Communist countries is rather different from that in the West. A "tyrant" was the title for a dictator in the Greek city-states, without the later pejorative associations. As for "liberals," an early nineteenth-century word for those opposing state controls essentially, it has been appropriated for so many different and sometimes opposing meanings that any honest identification has become virtually hopeless except as a vague synonym in wide circles for the "Good Guys."

Shaping the contours and ascertaining the basic processes are not usually considered to be the ultimate goals of historians; they are only tools necessary for the commonly accepted mission, the accurate narration of what historians discover during visits to the past. Unlike social scientists, they do not search for universal laws, exact formulas of relationships, or slide rule exactitude; events of the past being essentially unique, never quite the same twice, their generalizations of relationships necessarily lack the precision of the sciences. Secure analogies between past and present, patterns in history that confirm our struggle and prophesy victory, the guidance of a dominant idea, or the comfort of scientific terminology and measurable units that give the twentieth-century mind its assurance—most historians do not offer these street-level attractions. As "guardians of mankind's collective memory" (Pieter Geyl), they cannot do so because the evidences out of the past do not permit it.

What the historian does discern are tentative uniformities that seem to recur repeatedly in various locations in time and place. Though every event is unique, it is not totally unique, it shares similarities with other events. Perceived within the range of the probable, the basic historical processes—the commonly accepted judgment of how things tend to happen in history—are used by the historians in the way the evidence seems to indicate. These generalized relationships are deemed to fit the bulk of the evidence and, unlike the elementary concepts, necessitate at least a basic knowledge of the past for them to become persuasive. The gist of each of the processes, whose essence is less of science than of shrewd wisdom derived from a many-faceted experience with the past, can best be set forth by a number of suggestive examples rather than in one explanatory model.

In the basic historical processes, something more credible than catastrophism and more specific than progress and decline emerges out of the interacting forces of change and continuity.

Certain major social forces, energies in the community, help to create cohesion and movement in history: geographic, economic, religious, technological, institutional, and ideational. A multiplicity of these forces bear in varying degrees upon any given historical episode, as do the unpredictability of the human personality, the happenstance of timing, and the element of pure chance. These constitute some of the chief components of the basic historical processes, now to be examined in detail.

III

BASIC HISTORICAL PROCESSES

12

With Glacial Slowness: Change and Continuity

One day a great man called Oog ambled out of his cave and in an hour of inspired illumination proceeded to invent the wheel. By the time of the Flintstones, a tribal legend asserted that the wheel had been bestowed upon the people by a god named Oog.

Somehow, this account does not have the ring of total veracity. An invaluable attribute of historical-mindedness consists in knowing how things do not happen.

Matters, as usual, are distinctly more complicated. To the best of present knowledge, the first wheel appeared in the Sumerian town of Erech sometime after 3500 B.C., but more than another millennium passed before a fully satisfactory model had been developed. Apparently the first wheeled vehicles consisted of sledges to which wheels were attached. Toboggans go back at least 15,000 years, and sledges, dragged along on the bare ground, had long been in use. Probably the innovators fashioned the first wheels by joining three short planks at the edges and rounding them off; these were then attached to revolving axles and a sledge mounted thereon. One of the most significant inventions in all human history had occurred, and yet it happened in a most natural way as only a practical change within what had been long and continuous practice. Sledges became wagons by a halfway alteration much like the automobile originating as a horseless buggy.

Eventually, to prevent rapid wearing, the Sumerians began to stud the wheel with copper nails, then a rim was added, and finally, a thousand years or so after the original invention, came copper or leather tires. Solid wooden wheels were heavy and awkward, quite suitable for hauling goods in from the fields or manure out to them but scarcely adequate for other transportation. Though they used clumsy chariots in their armies by about 2500 B.C., the Sumerians needed something on the order of 500 years more to produce light, spoked wheels that afforded greater speed and maneuverability.

Developing with glacial slowness, this artifact evolved in a natural, piecemeal fashion, dictated by successive needs. Solid wooden wheels long persisted (and have not entirely vanished yet) in rural and pastoral surroundings. Across the centuries echoes the agonizing screech of ungreased rotating wood, the dusty wagon trains of invading Celtic, Germanic, and Turkic barbarian hordes. Wheels did not move, however, in the Indian Americas; though toys with wheels existed, the invention remained stillborn.

Oxen, already pulling sledges and primitive plows, naturally were the first to enjoy the dubious privilege of being hitched to carts and wagons; 5,000 years later they can still be seen, in an example of prolonged continuity, serving as draught animals in some parts of the world. However, oxen are slow beasts, scarcely suitable for a brigade of charging chariots, and the onager, a Middle Eastern relative of the horse, was recruited for military service instead.

The horse presently replaced the onager; only the size of a pony, however, the horse still lacked the sturdiness for riders. This combination of horses and better wheels with spokes, facilitating greater speed and mobility, revolutionized warfare and, with the addition of the compound bow, gave decisive military advantage to the Hyksos invading Egypt, the Hittites creating an empire in Asia Minor, the Aryans invading India, and the Shang dynasty (c. 1520–1030) building a larger Chinese state. Faster communications also permitted the maintenance of larger empires, once conquered. Later, the Persians, bordering on the nomadic horsemen of the steppes, would ride horses to conquer most of their known world. The cavalry replaced chariots as the most important military arm in the Middle East, though not yet in the Graeco-Roman world.

Long after their military function had in fact ceased, chariots continued to be used on ceremonial occasions in Rome, a typical example of how continuity often persists in traditional vestments long beyond practical utility. Chariot races in early medieval Constantinople offered the Greeks the excitement and emotional outlet Americans get from major football and basketball games. In the United States, the Kentucky Derby has survived the virtual disappearance of the workhorse.

Another lengthy evolution separates the Persian horsemen, fighting with bow and arrow or javelin, from medieval knights charging with tilted lance and swinging their swords in the mêlée. Staying on a mount by knee pressure, before the invention of stirrups and saddle, required a bit of dexterity. Bridle bits made of bone or metal were evidently invented by necessity as soon as horses were attached to chariots, but the other seemingly obvious changes were long delayed. Not until near the end of the Roman Empire did the padded saddle appear in Europe, though the Chinese had it a little earlier. Later, the stirrup arrived and, finally, expensive big horses who were voracious eaters of costly grain. All three very likely trace their origins to the steppes of Central Asia, where the horse had almost certainly been domesticated in the first place. Though the late Romans and Byzantine Greeks perforce developed armored cavalry units—somewhat resembling the later knights in appearance—in order to cope with incursions by these Asiatic horsemen, mounted men obviously remained handicapped until the combination of saddles, stirrups, and larger horses made possible the creation of the formidable medieval knight.

Here, in excruciatingly slow motion stretching over several thousand years, a basic pattern of change and continuity emerges. Over long stretches of the past, the compulsions of habit and tradition create a continuity so strong in some areas as to seem entirely static. Nevertheless, in the long term perspective, sequential movement and causal molding are perceptible even in these ages when seemingly self-evident alterations took centuries to consummate.

Occasionally the pieces fall together into a new creation with comparative swiftness, as in the relatively sudden development in the eleventh and twelfth centuries in central Europe of horseshoes, padded collars, harnesses, and shafts, which made possible, finally, the employment of the workhorse. Sometimes a seeming breakthrough is not followed up. Water power, by use of some form of paddle wheel, appears not long before the beginning of the Christian era, seems to be quickly adopted in a number of places, then fails to make further headway. (An ample and cheap labor supply, a positive need to find employment for idle hands, and religious scruples apparently prevented its greater adoption.) A Greek named Hero actually devised a steam engine (c. 130 B.C.), but like the Mexican toy with wheels, nothing more happened. Nobody in Europe thought to invent something as simple as the wheelbarrow until the later Middle Ages.

Change may also occur in the form of retrogression. With the decline of cities and their larger market, late Roman and early medieval production, such as in textiles, moved to the villages and households, and a positive loss in skills and techniques resulted. In iron, however, the typically medieval demand for swords and church bells, as well as for axes, spades, and plowshares, kept standards up. The spread of the church stimulated the making of iron church bells, first developed from the small Roman table bells in the fifth century; bronze bells became widespread in the days of the Carolingians.

Contrast this infinitely slow pattern with the tempo of

technological change in the twentieth century. Patents on a movie camera and a projector were applied for in 1891 as a result of the work, particularly, by Thomas Edison, William Dickson, and George Eastman. The first picture arcade opened in New York City (where else!) in April 1894, and the first regular theater showed moving pictures two years later. In 1911, the United States already had perhaps 13,000 movie theaters, talkies began near the end of the Roaring Twenties, and in 1946 admissions amounted to 82 million persons a year.

The invention of the audion tube in 1906 by Lee De Forest made the radio possible, the first scheduled broadcast, by KDKA in Pittsburgh, occurring on November 2, 1920. Within three years, the country had 500 radio stations, and in the thirties and forties most people listened regularly to this medium. Then came television at the end of the 1940s, though it had undergone experimentation for over twenty years before that. In the following two decades, after its real commercial breakthrough in 1948, the number of television sets in the United States grew to 79 million, thereby greatly reducing attendance at movie houses and forcing radio to retreat from its wide and ambitious programming to a routine of what it could do best, news, weather reports, and music.

For modern generations, the changes involving the wheel, the cavalry, and the others appear to move with glacial slowness. In long-term perspective, however, they *do* move. The comparison should not be made with the present velocity but with the preceding millennium-long sameness of Paleolithic life. Seen against this background, change had started to filter into the rigid contours of continuity, a genuine interaction of change and continuity, as the historian knows it, materializing. Now, in our own century, changes flow so swiftly that one form scarcely has time to reach fruition before alterations appear. So rapidly do changes come in many fields of human effort that the pattern of change and continuity has become one of incessant transition from one form to another.

Behind the surface facade of prevailing continuity in history, the forces of change never quite cease working, and in periods of conspicuous change the tenacious ties of continuity reassert themselves. Usually, the safest initial assumption, pending specific evidence, is that of prevailing gradual change.

Nominally, in the textbooks, the Holy Roman Empire is founded on Christmas Day, A.D. 800, with the coronation of Charlemagne and survives until 1806 when Francis I, by agreement with Napoleon, gave up the title. Though this seems an example of long-term continuity, Geoffrey Barraclough has called it "a story of discontinuity." After Charlemagne had been crowned Roman Emperor by the Pope, the title continued to be borne by a long succession of rulers. Charles, however, became a second emperor in what was still generally considered to be one Roman Empire, a state of affairs like that of the fifth century. In 962, Otto I revived the title, not representing any particular area of land, but by the following century the domain itself was beginning to be considered a separate territory, as indicating a political entity. The actual name of Holy Roman Empire does not come into use until the twelfth century, and whether the "Holy" actually constituted part of the name then or was merely a prefatory adjective seems to be a matter of opinion. Eventually the emperor only nominally ruled Germany and was suzerain of a state, to quote Voltaire, neither holy, nor Roman, nor an empire. The assumption of the title of Emperor of Austria in 1806 only officially confirmed a long existing situation. Continuity, yes, but also the discontinuity of repeated changes over a millennium.

One of the most rapid changes to occur in the Middle Ages, seemingly of catastrophic dimensions, was the Arabic explosion of the seventh and eighth centuries, which, starting in the late 630s, reached within a century the Pyrenees in the West and the borders of India in the east. And the strands of continuity? Mohammed claimed as a Prophet to be the successor of Moses and Jesus. Judaism and Christianity both contributed to the beliefs of Islam; in fact, Mohammed begins by transplanting these two religions into Arabic idiom and experience. No immediate mass conversion followed the conquest. Christian communities continued to exist and, as minorities, still survive in several Moslem countries. The brilliant philosophy and science of the early caliphate stemmed directly from the Greeks, as did much of the early architecture. Change, yes, but also much continuity. For that matter, the Christian conversion of northern Europe and Latin America was made easier by the identification of Christian saints with local gods or spirits and the use of the old holy places and festivals for Christian worship and Holy Days.

Medieval and early modern history offers a long series of examples of that gradual change that constitutes the norm in much of history. Long-distance trade gradually increased over a number of centuries, first of all in southern Italy and the Adriatic where it had never ceased because of continuing Byzantine sea power in these waters. Commerce and cities grew in importance over the centuries, spreading from northern Italy into the Rhineland, France, and the Low Countries. In the sphere of government, feudalism gradually diminished in importance, the trend varying greatly from country to country and occasionally punctuated by a great victory of a centralizing monarch until the long-term development led into the Age of Despots. The power of Christian Constantinople slowly ebbed, while at the other end of the continent the Christian victory in Spain was centuries in the making. The Christians advanced very gradually, no visible expansion occurring for a century or more. Occasionally they lost ground and at times made great breakthroughs, but not until 1492 did the fall of Granada mark the end of the long process in Spain.

These are all seen in the long perspective, overriding the flux of immediate events. Manifest drastic changes, examined more closely, usually prove to have a long background of preparation, sudden alterations being only the culminating episode in which change breaks surface dramatically or confirms the slower earlier developments. Even where it comes with dramatic swiftness, history often eventually balances things out. Continuity seemed drastically violated in England in 1066. The Normans abruptly seized control, and yet two centuries later an observer might have thought, firstly, that the English had absorbed the conquerors and, secondly, that if the Normans had never arrived the English might well have long since adopted many of the Norman ways. Much earlier, the Angles and Saxons had conquered England and made enough of a clean sweep to change the language and nearly obliterate Christianity, and yet the evidence indicates that by no means all of the earlier inhabitants fled or were killed. Over on the other side of Europe, the Mongols swiftly conquered Russia in about 1240, a Russia that had already disintegrated politically. During the next one to two centuries, the balance was redressed as the Russians gradually regained their freedom and resumed the direction of their own affairs.

Creation and transition both characterize the fundamental flow of historical events and developments, however greatly they vary in tempo in different ages, societies, or areas of human endeavor. Taken too literally, some of the historian's working concepts may seem to violate the reality of these continual transformations. Historical eras slice asunder the unity of the successive sequences. So does the focusing on a series of "firsts," the first telephone or the first parliament, by distracting attention from the actual processes of preparation and subsequent unfolding of possibilities; a long evolution is telescoped into a short episode, which thereby is made to seem as if it were the development itself.

Basic to any understanding of history is the comprehension of change and continuity as two interacting parts of a permenent and incessant process, whatever may be the tempo and balance of social forces in any specific historical sequence of developments. In the words of G. M. Young, quoted by Wedgwood, "Movement and continuity are the conceptions with which he works, and what aesthetic writers claim a passionate apprehension of form to be to the painter, a passionate apprehension of process is to the historian."

13

Beyond King Cuthred: Uniformities

746   *In this year king Selred was slain.*
748   *In this year Cynric, prince of Wessex, was slain, and Eadberht, king of Kent, passed away, and Aethelberht, son of king Wihtred, succeeded to the kingdom.*
750   *In this king Cuthred fought against Aethelhun, the presumptuous ealdorman.*
752   *In this year, in the twelfth year of his reign, Cuthred fought against Aethelbald at Beorgfeord.*
753   *In this year Cuthred fought against the Welsh.**

This is history? Yes, they are typical annals or chronicles and are certainly much more accurate than certain stories from the

*From *The Anglo-Saxon Chronicle,* translated and edited by G. M. Garmonsway. An Everyman's Library Edition. Published in the United States by E. P. Dutton & Co., Inc., and reprinted with their permission.

general era such as *Beowulf* and *The Song of Roland* or the tales of King Arthur's Round Table. Chroniclers have also served the historians well in providing details and a measure of certitude. Manifestly, however, there is more to history than annals, what Arnold Toynbee once called, if memory serves, the "one damn thing after another" kind of history.

Novices have been known to perpetuate this sort of thing by submitting examination answers consisting of little more than a collection of events dumped on a piece of paper without order or relationships. History is likely to be tedious for those who cannot see beyond King Cuthred. Aware that something more seems called for, the novice may tie the facts together by one or more of the usual elementary concepts, including the mighty deeds of King Cuthred and his smiting of presumptuous ealdormen in the continuing battle between good and evil. These are the usual expedients resorted to when groping for interrelationships before knowing the commonly accepted regularities or uniformities.

Historians, dealing constantly with multitudinous facts and events, have discerned a considerable number of these tentative uniformities. Perhaps, in view of the uniqueness of each historical event, scholars tend to make them too sharp and tidy to fit the rough edges of reality, but the regularities do provide an utterly necessary intellectual tool for making history make sense. Although no event has ever occurred before in precisely the same way or form, striking resemblances can scarcely be denied. History shares this characteristic with some other areas, such as geology or zoology. That no two rocks are ever physically identical does not prevent the geologist from classifying them as granite, quartz, or whatever. No two English Setters are quite the same, but they undeniably belong to a specific breed of dogs. And so, in greater complexity, with historical events. For the devotee of history the fascination may begin here, the excitement and challenge as well as the problems and frustrations.

Most common of all, and least exciting today in the Western world, has been the grouping of factual information about such manifest continuities as the long enduring authorities of church and state. The Papacy in Rome, the Holy Roman Emperors, and the succession of national kings, once their respective offices came into being, have served as convenient compartments for narrating history and have provided pivotal figures for the inculcation of loyalties. To some extent reflecting true realities of the past, this traditional practice has often been overdone to a point where the omissions become nearly as stultifying as those in the annals. Then, too, a modern observer, with preconceptions of a strong national state, customarily sees more than actually existed at the time. A series of other regularities offers a deeper understanding of what happened in the past.

One cluster of uniformities encountered in medieval history is customarily expressed by the word "feudalism." Not used in the Middle Ages, the term was invented in the seventeenth century and subsequently popularized by scholars and lawyers interested in describing a regularity seemingly present in that earlier era. Originally denoting a localized phenomenon in western Europe, the word has later also been applied, with varying degrees of justification, to societies and governments at various times in other parts of the world, among them Egypt, Iran, Russia, India, and China. The word "feudal" now sometimes occurs erroneously as an epithet in describing some contemporary societies or governments.

Probably the most usual undergraduate conception of feudalism is still summed up by a map of eleventh-century France hanging in a classroom, the country chopped up into duchies and counties in variegated hues. Associated with this are ideas of a very weak central government, strong local lords, knights in armor, and an overabundance of turbulence; it may also be falsely identified with manorialism only, the prevalence of large landed estates. Unfortunately for definitions, the Franks originally involved in the emergence of so-called feudalism in the eighth to tenth centuries had no broad viewpoint of what they were doing. "It was not a system; it was based on no theory; it was an improvisation to meet a desperate emergency" (Joseph R. Strayer). The authorities pieced together a governmental apparatus out of that which existed and out of what was possible at the time. It never could be "uniform, consistent, or logical," except when scholars and lawyers later tried to make it so. Some historians now would prefer to drop the concept entirely.

Shortly after 730, Charles Martel of the Franks created a force of armored horsemen equipped with the larger horses and using stirrups. Grain-fed horses and armor imposed a heavy financial burden, which the government met by confiscating the lands of the church for distribution among the horsemen. Presently the king allocated additional villages and stretches of land, each community being obliged, as a contribution to its defence, to help maintain one or more knights and their mounts. The land was held as a temporary fief from the king in return for military service, and the resultant potent body of knights accounted for much of the success of the early Carolingians.

This military revolution took place in a largely rural economy without much circulation of money and in which each community often had to depend upon local resources for defending itself against both external attacks and internal violence. Bereft of a strong power base himself, handicapped by poor communications, and lacking effective means for mustering countrywide support by the devices of more advanced states, the king had recourse to a traditional custom, that of homage or vassalage. Its ancient origins stemmed back to the Roman patron-client relationship and to the Germanic war band, in which the warriors were pledged to follow their leader through every extremity on the battlefield. Briefly put, the king used his personal relationship with his principal followers to hold the state together. In terms of the concepts described in the last chapter, the continuity of the leader-warrior bond was maintained, while the change of bestowing a fief upon the warrior, now mounted, produced a new arrangement called feudalism by modern historians.

Feudalism attained its most complete form—though it was never entirely completed—in northern France, apparently in consequence of a need for defense against Viking raids at a time of disintegrating Carolingian rule. Increasingly, the holding of a fief carried with it certain other attributes of government, actual administration of the area and the maintenance of law courts, functions which the monarchy lacked the means to sustain. What else could a king do, "too poor to maintain a professional bureaucracy" in a rural economy, than fall back upon such a device? Without it, France might have disintegrated completely into local states the size of the Celtic tribal areas before their conquest by Julius Caesar. Perhaps the memory of earlier centralized government provided the continuity that prevented complete collapse. In other places than western Europe, too, feudalism has occasionally materialized in the aftermath of a strong central government, a feudal arrangement presided over by the "ghost" of the vanished regime.

A group of practices intended to strengthen the Crown in France had the opposite effect when the later Carolingians proved unable to enforce their mastery. Supposedly temporary fiefs became hereditary, the vassals building up their own local power to such a level that they could virtually ignore the wishes of the king. In England, where the Normans imposed feudalism after the Conquest, the kings, well aware of the collapse of royal power in France, took good care to limit their vassals' power from the beginning, and the arrangement worked more in accord with original expectations. Feudalism came more slowly and less completely to Germany. Feudal practices, ideals, and forms continued to be used in Europe in the later Middle Ages long after the disappearance of the conditions that had brought them into existence had vanished.

Here, then, is a long-term uniformity (or, more accurately, a cluster of them), originally involving a breakthrough in military technology entailing big horses, stirrups, and armor. Once this powerful war machine developed in the West, the Byzantine Greeks, the Spanish Moslems, and those in the states in the Middle East necessarily copied the Franks. A knighthood in armor eventually appeared in West Africa and the Sudan, to survive in some places until the eighteenth century.

The Franks had not been the first to face similar circumstances nor the first to make a response somewhat of this nature. Fighting horsemen had characterized Iran ever since the days of the Achaemenids. Still confronting the problem of the raiding nomads on the northern frontier, the Parthians set up a force of mounted archers, wearing armor for protection against nomad arrows and riding big horses strong enough to bear them. At this point, the large horses apparently first appeared on the scene, the result of selective breeding on the steppes or possibly in Iran. As heavy a financial burden for the Parthians as they were for the Franks later, the warriors here too were dependent upon the villages for their livelihood. Iranian society under the Parthians and the successor Sassanid Empire was dominated by a group of landed families, who served as the mainstay of the military officer class.

Theoretically, for a wealthy state able to equip and pay armored horsemen as a professional army, the maintenance of such a force need not necessarily have entailed the establishment of manorialism, much less feudalism. Nevertheless, even in the rich Byzantine Empire in the tenth century, the transformation of the mounted horsemen, the cataphracts, into a military force like that of the Franks stimulated the emergence of a special landowning gentry doing military service. Wherever they appeared, the armored horsemen put their imprint upon society in the form of a landed aristocracy and at least some of the characteristics of feudalism. The Chinese, in their perennial conflict with the northern nomads, went through a "feudal" phase in this period. Much earlier, the emergence of the charioteers as a costly military weapon in the Middle East seems to have created kindred results throughout the known world in 1700–1300 B.C. The phenomenon very loosely called feudalism has recurred in the past in various parts of the world, called forth by somewhat similar circumstances, and each time manifesting sufficient traits in common with other such occurrences for all of them to be considered uniformities in history.

Amidst the stories out of the medieval, the historian detects certain general uniformities associated with the prevalence of feudalism. Closely inspected, the regularities are by no means as regular as they may seem to the casual observer, but they do serve to depict, in general terms, the age. Something much broader and pervasive than the deeds of individual knights is operative, and understanding its nature gives a far greater comprehension of the whole era.

Another equally useful uniformity (or group of them) involves the city-states, which, wherever they appear, tend to have certain characteristics in common in terms of social groups, occupations and preoccupations of the inhabitants, town governance, and relations with other city-states. To read about Florence or Lübeck is to learn much, also, about Milan, Ghent, or Novgorod in that period. European towns, dotting the continent in the middle and later medieval, display rather similar polity and spirit, of which more later. As with feudalism, the phenomenon has been recurrent, and this particular set of uniformities can also be applied usefully to other eras of city-states, to classical Greece and its colonies all over the Mediterranean, to the Phoenician towns, and to the very ancient city-states of the Tigris-Euphrates valley. No two are ever alike, each one is unique, and yet the parallels clamor for attention.

Nomadic societies, living in a virtual symbiosis with horses or camels, tend to have certain traits in common. The peoples of Arabia, Mongolia, and the Sahara were molded by the "harsh realities" of their environment into "highly cohesive" groups in which the individual counted for little, and blood kinship provided the principal ties in the community. A number of other uniformities help provide the warp and woof of history, some of which will become apparent in the discussion of social forces.

These regularities are short cuts to more rapid knowledge and understanding of the past. Learning them by short definitions limits their meanings too much in a history made up of infinite variety and nuances. A few appropriate images of the basic structural pattern serve better, model pictures which with later experience acquire a cluster of associations flexible in usage. Having learned the basic patterns, a student then knows the expectancies and, especially, takes note of the exceptions, the variations, in each individual case. The jigsaw puzzle of history, each piece unique in shape, cannot be assembled without them.

As long as terms like "feudalism" and "city-state" remain nonsense syllables, the reader is deprived of much of the complete story and is likely to remain intellectually mired at the King Cuthred level of annals. Once they are mastered, the broader contours and the shapes of social forces emerge as the tools enabling the aspirant to develop a personal style of historical-mindedness.

14

Forces in History: Geographical

Black was beautiful in the rain forests of Africa, and blond was the fairest in the pale sunlight of the Baltic coastlands; so run current theories on the origin of races. Mother Earth molded her diverse children with characteristics that have the highest survival value in different climates and regions in ways not fully understood but in which the survival of the fittest played an important role.

According to one plausible theory, the color of the blacks evolved because a very dark skin offered the most effective protection against excessive ultraviolet radiation in the rain forests. Blond skin prevailed in northern Europe where the oblique sun rays, short summers, and heavy cloud cover deprived the inhabitants of sufficient ultraviolet radiation, hence those with the lightest skin, capable of absorbing the most radiation, had the advantage. Severe climatic conditions in northern Asia during the Glacial Ages, in one theory, nurtured the Mongolian physical type, the flat cheeks, small noses, and short arms and

legs, which exposed the least body surface to the cold and resulted in the least loss of body heat. A relatively warm climate
and the need for an organism capable of staying cool resulted in
the short, wiry Mediterranean physique, while the taller, fatter
northerners generated more body heat in the cold weather. Not
to forget the short, barrel-chested Indians on the Andean Alti-
plano in South America, who adapted to the high altitude in their
physique and by producing an unusually high number of red
corpuscles in the blood stream.

From humanity's beginnings, geographical circumstances
determined the odds in the perpetual lottery of life, with its
often narrow margin of survival. Those not accepting nature's
tutelage perished, while groups responding to the environment
the most successfully perpetuated their pattern of conduct, a
pattern sanctified and assured continuance by rigid religious
sanctions. Different geographical conditions, opportunities, and
dangers led to a rich variety of human societies.

The earliest known states emerged in the Nile and Tigris-
Euphrates valleys because control of the river water, especially
for irrigation, required strong government. Egypt's nearly three
millenniums of a continuity so rigid as to seem virtually static
reflect its geography: security behind deserts and seas, while
the Nile provided a reliable cycle for food production, a base
upon which the Egyptians could maintain a civilization perfectly
adjusted to its circumstances. In the Tigris-Euphrates area, on
the contrary, a more spectacular history took place, caused by a
much less dependable river system and the proximity, repeatedly, of dangerous enemies. Successive Akkadian, Babylonian, and Assyrian empires did not arise only out of the ambitious plans of conquerors like the first or second Sargon, Ham-
murabi, or the Tiglath-pilesers; these empires were responding
to the circumstances under which the valley required unity in
order to fend off invaders eager for plunder and to protect its
wide commerce in the Fertile Crescent and beyond.

Maritime influences may be largely invisible to people accustomed to continental circumstances, and former travel difficulties
may not seem impressive in an age of rapid transportation. Politi-

cal states, for those accustomed to modern maps, consist of solid, territorial blocks of contiguous land. Lacking a knowledge of certain historical regularities important at that time, we may look at a map of medieval Europe without seeing what is there.

On maps of the later medieval and early modern periods, one may note that the Venetians, possessing only a small home base, had unfurled their winged lion banner over islands and stretches of the coastline on the eastern Adriatic, numerous islands in the Aegean, and even, at times, in Crete, Cyprus, and the Peloponnesus. On a somewhat smaller scale, the Genoese followed the same pattern, including among their possessions Corsica (earlier held by little Pisa), the Aegean, and important trading posts on the Black Sea. The seas, far from separating the political units, here unite them. Superimposing a map of trade routes, the Venetian and Genoese possessions fit neatly along the arteries of trade to the Levant, where they hook up with caravan routes from parts of the Middle East, Central Asia, India, and China.

Anyone traveling in Greece and seeing the barren hills and small farming areas in the valleys will understand why the Greeks, from the beginning, found it necessary to farm the sea; they had little choice. The sea also lured them on, the islands usually lying within sight of one another across much of the Aegean and easily accessible by even the most primitive boats. Water highways account for the innumerable city-state colonies planted by the Greeks and by the Phoenicians, huddled on a narrow strip of Lebanese land. The Byzantine Empire, its territories fringing parts of the Mediterranean, depended greatly upon sea power, though its base was the metropolis at Constantinople and a prosperous Asia Minor. Judged only as land area, its earlier domain looks rather grotesque, but the sea united rather than separated the scattered possessions.

Even at the beginning of the twentieth century, a large Greek population continued to live on the shores of present-day Turkey, a violation of the contemporary scheme of national state territorial blocks. Attempting to annex this strip of land after World War I, the Greeks, after three millenniums of continuous habitation, were themselves expelled. The ancient and long-enduring Greek population in Sicily and southern Italy had long since been Italianized, but even in the 1960s and 1970s the overseas Greeks on Cyprus, four-fifths of its population, created international crises by the desire of their militant elements for *enosis*, or union, with their compatriots.

In northern Europe, too, the water routes united and the land separated peoples. Norway's narrow, elongated shape reflects the easy access to the sea by a country hemmed in by mountains, and water unites the peninsula and several islands of the Danish realm. The Swedish nation originated on its central Baltic coast and around the great lakes, which nearly bisect the country. When the Swedes began to expand, they left the northern interior to the Lapps and Finns, the latter having adapted expertly by long experience to the hunting and fishing of the forestland. Then the Swedes themselves crossed to the shores of Finland, helped along by the existence of archipelagoes like those of the Aegean. To take to the water as Vikings came naturally to the Scandinavian peoples.

Changing the sea from a barrier into a highway required knowledge of currents, storms, and winds. The discovery of the timing of the monsoons, with the wind blowing consistently from the northeast for about six months and then from the southwest during the following half-year, made traffic between Arabia and both India and East Africa much easier. Greek pilots were taking ships across the Indian Ocean from the Red Sea to India in the first century A.D. Many centuries later, a string of Arabic towns sprang up along the East African coast, and it was no accident that the Arabs halted at Cape Delgado, across from Madagascar, this being the southernmost point reached by the monsoon winds.

Deserts may serve as barriers, but not necessarily. In West Africa, south of the Sahara, the blacks originally developed their own communities, undisturbed by invaders. Meanwhile, the North Africans, protected by the same desert to their south and by Mediterranean navies to the north, grew prosperous. Then the Romans brought the camel from the Middle East in the third century A.D., and this "ship of the desert" enabled the barrier of wilderness and sand to be breached. Eventually the nomads adopted the camel, thereby gaining mobility and destroying the security of the wealthy North African coastal towns. Caravan routes spread south, based on the exchange of gold from the African forest belt for products from the Mediterranean; out of gold sprang power and empire, first Ghana, then, successively Mali and Songhai.

Across the vastness of Eurasia from Manchuria to Hungary ran a frontier, historically the border between the civilization to the south and the barbarians to the north. Hungary's own plain made it the spearhead for Europe of the elongated domain of the nomads, and here, in turn, came Huns, Avars, and the Magyars, or Hungarians themselves. The further east on these steppes, the so-called Earth Girdle, the less the rainfall, and consequently the repeated movement westward toward better grasslands. For over half a millennium, these successive invaders, accustomed to the milieu of the steppes, created a troublesome anomaly, a dissonance, in the heart of Europe. Whether in the middle of Europe, in Central Asia, or in northern China, two different kinds of societies clashed, the edges of separate worlds in collision.

Varying geographical conditions, opportunities, and dangers in various parts of the world molded, broadly speaking, four intrinsically different kinds of communities: the hunter's deep forests; the nomad's wide pasture lands; the tamed ground of grains, vines, and orchards; and the seafarer's maritime milieu. To which, overlapping the third and fourth, should be added a fifth, the society of the townspeople.

Returning to the subject of maps, innumerable insights into the past await those who know how to read their meanings. Why should London, located in the southeastern corner of the country, be the capital of England? Primarily because of the gravitational influences of the continent; a trading base for the collection of exports and distribution of imports would naturally be found in southeastern England. The Thames provided the best and most secure harbor from weather or raids in the region, and the point at which the river could be fairly easily bridged for north-south traffic determined the specific location. No major hindrances barred movement into the interior of the island from London.

At first glance, the selection of Kiev as the medieval capital of the Russians seems downright stupid, situated as it was at the southern extremity of settlement within close proximity to the dangerous steppe dwellers. However, the slow-moving Dnieper offered the main artery of communications, and Kiev was located conveniently below its main tributaries, thereby giving access to most of the country. Again, as with London, the gravitation of centers of civilization also helped determine the choice, in this case the southern metropolis and great emporium of medieval Christianity, of the city of Constantinople.

Why Paris? Why did the Capetian kings, who restored the power of the Crown by subduing the great feudal lords, choose Paris as their headquarters? It was not in the center of the country or in the most civilized southern portion. At one time the capital of King Clovis, Paris, whose original nucleus on the largest island in the Seine made it particularly defensible, became the base for the Capetians as a forward position from which to fight the marauding Norsemen. With easily defended bridges over the river, it also happened to provide a good junction for major trade routes. Commerce coming up the Rhone from the Mediterranean could readily be portaged to the upper tributaries of the Seine, thence transported to the Channel. Other trade routes from present-day Belgium and the Rhineland converged at Paris, and from here a 70-mile portage southward carried to the Loire and another network of routes. Though by no means the only possible or convenient site for a capital—it could have been Rheims, Orleans, or Tours—Paris had excellent credentials.

Vienna started as a forward position for the Germans against the Magyars and Slavs but became a natural capital for the Middle Danubian basin because of a series of tributaries offering easy contact with the whole region; a network of land routes eventually also made Vienna a focal point between the Adriatic and the headwaters of the Vistula and Oder. In Spain, Cordoba, long the capital of the Moslems, probably owed its position to the survival of a Roman-built bridge over the Guadalquivir.

Locations of cities usually have cogent geographical explanations. Travelers in Italy, Spain, and Germany catch poignant glimpses of medieval life in the regularity with which old towns sought security by perching on the top of the hills. A bend in a river, giving added protection, often determined the site of a town, as did the terminal point of a mountain pass, a junction of trading routes, and the places where water and land transportation met. A list of the probable locations of fifty towns could easily be compiled simply by noting the junctions of trading routes in the medieval period: Vienna, Novgorod, Bologna, London, Wroclaw (Breslau), and many others. Towns were strung out like fruit on a vine, growing in size and vigor if commerce increased, then withering if trade dwindled.

Sometimes nature intervened, as with Ravenna and Bruges, once busy ports whose harbors silted up. At Ephesus, one of the most splendid of ancient cities, the harbor was ruined, perhaps by mud deposits but more likely by the uptilting of the ground in an earthquake; malaria in the ensuing marshes completed its downfall, and now Ephesus lies nearly deserted, the distant blue Aegean shimmering beyond a grassy swampland where ships once anchored.

These are only the merest samplings of geographical factors. Many others could be illustrated, for instance that mountains separate peoples, thereby helping to create local dialects and nationalities, but rivers do not make good boundaries for countries because streams unite the people on the two sides. Ibn-Khaldun (1332-1406), Arabic medieval historian, discovered his historical regularities in the interaction between the desert and the sown, between the bedouin and the farmer.

A number of sweeping and influential theories based on geographical factors have been propounded. Ernest Renan suggested that monotheism was the product of the desert, a view now abandoned. Admiral Alfred Mahan elaborated his theory of sea power as a major determinant of the fate of nations. Henri Pirenne argued that the collapse of Roman civilization came later than the Germanic invasions, that it actually occurred as a result of the Moslems assuming control of the Mediterranean waters and virtually cutting off western Europe from trade with the East. Ellsworth Huntington tried to prove that periods of long drought helped to cause the repeated barbarian invasions out of Central Asia, a phenomenon he called the "pulse of Asia." Inevitably, these broad generalizations drew heavy criticism, resulting in modification or rejection.

Long-term factors of a geographic nature strongly influence human behavior and oftentimes exercise compulsive pressures forcing people to act in certain ways. Enduring uniformities emerge out of successful responses to geographical circumstances, the resultant social forces contributing to the broad, sweeping patterns in the shaping of history. Learning to discern and use them in order to see below the surface of ephemeral happenings is one of the pleasures of historical-mindedness. Geographical regularities may also become so seductive that other categories of social forces are brushed aside and the role of chance and of the individual forgotten. One of the nineteenth-century founders of historical geography, Henry Thomas Buckle (1821–1862), made a most valuable contribution to knowledge but fell into this determinist trap by elevating geographical causality to the same sweeping level and compulsion that his century attributed to scientific causality. Carefully used, and with proper respect for other forms of causality, geographic factors provide a series of uniformities that enable us to see much more of the past than stories and chronicles.

15

Forces in History: Economic

Other social forces than those emerging from the geographic obviously helped determine the location of towns and the Venetian and Genoese overseas possessions. Humanity's activities in search of food, shelter, clothing, and adornments, the sheer necessities of making a living, put a strong imprint on the contours of history, and a variety of uniformities helpful for understanding the past derive wholly or partly out of economic circumstances. A brief look at the medieval and early modern city-state reveals a number of illustrations of these regularities.

Merchants, the long-distance traders who moved goods from one area to another, made up one major element in the history of many towns in the Middle Ages, some of the medieval uniformities arising out of the type of interests they held in common. A single peddler had these interests, but as an individual such a peddler would be virtually helpless in an essentially alien, rural world dominated by the church and the feudal holders of land. Banded together in an organized form, however, the merchants generated a social force sufficiently potent to enforce their wishes successfully over the passage of years.

They needed, first of all, protection for their kind of property—trading goods—from brigands along the road or greedy lords disposed to seize whatever took their fancy. The organized mutual help of traveling in convoy offered the safest recourse, whether in Europe, the Middle East, on the caravan routes to China, or across the Sahara, and a protected market or fair benefited local lords or bishops by enhancing their revenues. Since serfs were bound to the soil, the traders required group recognition and freedom to come and go; their activities also necessitated escape from oppressive obligations of a feudal nature and liberty to set up their own laws and courts for matters scarcely adjudicable by feudal methods.

Wherever a group of merchants became a vital force in a town, the governing authority, usually a feudal lord or bishop, came under increasing pressure to grant these privileges. Guilds, originally organized for social purposes and to help members in distress, soon also became voices for the economic interests of the traders. Guilds had various weapons at their disposal, the principal one being money and, thereby, the capacity to guarantee a lord a certain amount of regular revenue in return for recognition and privileges. If, however, the appeal to the lord's self-interest failed, force might be used in cooperation with other elements in the town in order to gain greater freedom for those involved. Regardless of other circumstances, the medieval towns of any size almost without exception achieved some form of internal autonomy, the right to govern themselves by their own elected officials and laws.

At first, this often meant a government dominated by the traders, an arrangement not to the advantage of the craftsmen who originally often belonged to the same guilds as the merchants. As time went on, they naturally began to bargain for their own interests, which were not necessarily parallel to those of the merchants. Resenting the meddling of merchant patricians who controlled the town offices, the craftsmen sought group differentiation, the right to regulate their own shops, protection for their products, control over their prices, and some way of escaping a disproportionately high amount of taxes. The history of most towns is enlivened by the efforts of the craft guilds to secure representation in the town government.

Below the level of the masters in the guilds, the apprentices, journeymen, and others nourished their own grievances. Guild masters, having attained political power, refused to pass these gains on to the workers, who found it increasingly difficult to advance to master status themselves. Complaining of low wages, high prices, and oppressive working conditions, the artisans' rioting punctuated the history of these towns, though rarely did they obtain any long-term gains. Hardly ever does the broadening out of power culminate in any genuine democracy for the masses. The final stage of the city-state in Italy more than likely brought a personal dictatorship, evolving into some form of hereditary government like a duchy, while north of the Alps the power usually became firmly entrenched in the hands of a narrow class oligarchy.

Based on the foregoing pattern, a prototype or model could be set up of the history of several hundred sizeable towns in Europe during this period, a broad uniformity useful as a learning device and subject to later elaboration and modification as specific examples are encountered. History being the story of the unique, the variations in the pattern take many different forms. Factors outside of the town itself often imposed deviations from the above model. A city like London will obtain a charter, the right to elect a mayor and council (this by 1200) and to levy its own taxes, but the presence of strong kings or queens, usually sufficiently appreciating the financial advantages conferred by the town for their conducting of policies useful to the burghers, make greater autonomy unnecessary. French towns evince an early drive for autonomy, including revolutions in several municipalities in about 1100, only to collide with the Capetian centralization at an early stage. Cities like Bruges and Ghent in the Low Countries reach compromises with the counts of Flanders. In all of these, the mercantile and craft interests are absorbed, to a greater or lesser extent, in the policies of the central government. In Germany, the cities achieve a great degree of independence in the so-called Free Cities, but occasionally the Emperor intervenes, or is called upon for help in cases of civic discord or revolt. The cities of northern and central Italy become totally independent.

The merchants did not necessarily share some of their power with the craftsmen. Some of the Hanseatic cities of northern Germany, with a strong merchant class and relatively weak local industries, remained under merchant patrician oligarchies. Venice, however, offers the classic example. Here the merchant families, at the end of the 1200s, excluded commoners from the Great Council, and approximately 200 families henceforth limited governmental offices to themselves until the end of the republic in 1797. They also reduced the doge, the official head of state, to a mere figurehead, and Venice consequently never fell under the dictatorship of one person.

The model more nearly approximates reality in some other towns. In southwestern Germany and the Low Countries the weavers and other craftsmen—half of the inhabitants in Flanders were involved in textile manufacturing by 1400—aggrandized considerable power for themselves. Cologne, the largest city in Germany, probably came the closest to an equitable distribution by sharing the government among twenty-two guilds, and Siena, where the merchants lacked strength, may have been its closest counterpart in Italy. Florence, with numerous economic interests, also underwent a series of upheavals and ensuing constitutional experiments before gradually falling under an oligarchy and, finally, the direct rule of the Medici.

This rough model, it must be hastily added, has the fault of all such models, the exclusion of other elements in order to highlight some specific aspects. The most potent factor in the early growth of some of these towns may have been their defensibility; in others the presence of state or church administrative personnel (or monasteries) may have attracted artisans and traders. In addition to these, a very large number of thriving towns came into existence out of a somewhat different set of economic motives, the interaction between the market town and the growing population of the countryside.

Where most facets of an autonomous city's foreign policy, and part of the propelling energy of the history of the times, derived directly out of the needs of the merchants and the craft guilds, the circumstances and the power to enforce their wishes would naturally vary from town to town. In general, however, the motives would include controlling trade routes by land and sea; trying to secure and maintain a monopoly in the trade or manufacture of certain articles; obtaining special privileges in other markets for purchase and sale of goods; and refusing foreign merchants permission to exchange goods with one another in the home market. Venice prevented Dubrovnik (Ragusa) from trading in the North Adriatic region and forced Ravenna to sell its grain and salt only to Venice itself, Bruges destroyed the rival town of Sluys, and Genoa built up a mole at the mouth of the Arno to cause the silting up of Pisa's harbor. Like plants in a forest competing for soil and sunshine, the commercial agencies fought a life and death struggle for economic sustenance.

Starting from Lübeck, German merchants moved eastward along the shores of the Baltic, setting up a chain of Hanseatic cities: Stralsund, Wismar, Gdansk (Danzig), Tallinn (Reval), Riga, and others. Originally drawn largely by the profits available from acquiring furs at Novgorod and selling them in such cities as Cologne, Bruges, and London, the Hanseatic merchants established a Baltic monopoly lasting until nearly the time of the Reformation. Inland, German traders also pushed routes eastward to Leipzig, Dresden, Wroclaw, and Vienna, the latter accomplished by Regensburg merchants seeking a base on the way to Kiev.

Emerging out of the debris of the Byzantine Empire, the Venetians inherited much of the trade between the East and the emporium of Christendom, where they held special privileges. When anti-Venetian hostility in Constantinople near the end of the twelfth century caused their revocation, the Venetians retaliated by persuading the leaders of the Fourth Crusade to storm the city. In 1261, the rival Genoese assisted the Greeks in regaining the imperial city, and henceforth the Genoese, now holding the special privileges, monopolized all trade coming out of the Black Sea. Having fought a series of wars earlier with the Pisans to gain control of western routes, the Genoese centered their activities on the Black Sea and in North Africa, while the Venetians concentrated on Syria and Alexandria.

Though not responsible for starting the Crusades and in fact originally fearing that they would disrupt their trade with the Moslems, the Italian cities, by their later support of these wars, greatly lengthened the stay of the Crusaders in the Holy Land. Venice, Genoa, Pisa, and others all appropriated quarters in the coastal towns for themselves, and after the fall of Jerusalem (1187) it was the commercial interests of these cities, plus the military crusading orders like the Templars, which kept the Europeans in these cities for another century. Even after the fall of Acre in 1291 and the end of the European Christian domain in Palestine and Lebanon, the Italians long used Cyprus as their base in the area; the Genoese held Famagusta from 1376 until 1464, then the Venetians ruled the island until the Turkish conquest in 1571. Meantime, the latter also held islands in the Aegean as the result of the debacle of the Byzantine Empire, and the island of Crete remained in Venetian hands until 1669 (and a few places were held by Venice until 1715). This widespread enterprise over several centuries clearly foreshadows similar developments, dictated partly by economic motives, in the Age of Discoveries and again in the period of European imperialism.

The Venetians had originally brought from Constantinople the products of numerous Greek workshops: silk, cloth, wrought ivory carvings, gold and silver plate, and precious stones. Goods from the Middle East itself in the period of the Crusades included, among others, sugar cane, textiles, Persian rugs, glassware, and steel. Merchants purchased in Moslem ports, and especially in Alexandria, products carried there by caravan or Indian Ocean vessels from further east, such as pepper, cloves, nutmeg, silk, indigo, perfumes, and porcelain. (In about 1420, the Venetians owned about 3,000 ships, commercial and military, of various sizes). When the Mongols created their great empire in the first half of the thirteenth century, which stretched from China to the borders of Poland, the caravan routes across central Asia to the Crimea became safer for traveling, hence the great attraction of Black Sea trade.

Out of the need for spices for food, a desire for luxurious dress, and other economic considerations, the Italian city-states, seeking a profit, created large empires. Venice and Milan in the fourteenth century had populations close to 200,000, and Florence and Genoa were each over 100,000. Outside of Italy, only Paris possessed over 100,000 inhabitants. Cologne, as the largest German town, was over 30,000, Lübeck the second, around 25,000, and eight other towns exceeded 10,000 in about 1400. Considering their comparatively low total population, the towns were responsible, largely due to economic motives, for a remarkable amount of history in this period.

Manifestly, the feudal nobility, with its territorial baronies, did not lack economic motivations either in trying to enlarge revenues by various taxes, imposts, tolls, or market dues. Land hunger accounted for large numbers of volunteers for the First Crusade, poor nobles or younger sons of nobles without prospect of inheritance. Many peasants who came along hoped to better their material lot in a land rumored to be wealthy.

All over western Europe the great forests, hitherto practically intact, were being cut down to create more tillable ground. A better kind of axe became available, while the old scratch plow was replaced by a heavy one capable of making deep furrows. The new plow originally required eight oxen to pull it, which in turn forced village cooperation and, according to Marc Bloch, was instrumental in the beginnings of a manorial economy. Starting in the late eighth century, the coming of the three-fold system enabled a 50 percent increase in productivity and more cultivation of oats, necessary for the horses who began to replace oxen as draught animals by the eleventh century. The backward European peninsula of Eurasia was coming alive in an economic sense, beginning to forge the destiny that eventually made it the world leader.

These are some of the uniformities emerging out of economical social forces, though they are intermingled with geographic and technological stimuli. Economic regularities can, like the geographic, be vastly tempting in their sweep and in their obviously effective suasion on human behavior. Here, some may think, lies *the* key to the shapes and meaning of history. Karl Marx, while making an epochal contribution to the understanding of economic regularities, walked into the same trap as Buckle. Convinced by the class conflicts of his own century, and finding the key to historical evolution in the means of production, he elevated certain uniformities, while minimizing others, to the determinist level of nineteenth-century scientific laws. Of which more in a later chapter.

16

Forces in History: Religious

Pope Urban II proclaimed the First Crusade at Clermont, France in November 1095 and thereby unleashed one of the most spectacular examples of the spiritual force in history. The response far exceeded his own expectations. A wave of enthusiasm spread over western Europe, spurred on by wandering preachers like Peter the Hermit, which sent tens of thousands of crusaders pouring eastward, most of them to their deaths, to liberate the Holy Land from the infidel. Many motives inspired them, but the original catalyst was spiritual, and the ostensible goals, symbols, and battle cries of the age of the Crusades continued to be religious in character.

Four and a half centuries earlier, the Arabs burst out of their peninsula to create a caliphate stretching from the Pyrenees to Central Asia and the Indus. The cities fell swiftly: Damascus (635), Antioch (636), Jerusalem (638), and Alexandria (641). Meantime, the mighty Sassanid Empire was conquered in two battles by 642. In 673, the Moslem Arabs were besieging

Constantinople, and in 711 one great victory over the Visigoths opened Spain to occupation. Islam, the word meaning submission to the will of Allah, had become and would remain a world religion.

Often portrayed as a dramatic example of a religious force in world history, the whirlwind Moslem advance gathered momentum from other sources as well. The catalyst *was* spiritual in the sense that Islam unified the warring tribes into a fraternity of looters upon which religion still rested lightly. Religious zeal did not dominate the first waves of invaders, the big incentive being the booty of rich cities and subsequent tribute from conquered peoples. To no small extent, increasingly poor conditions in parts of Arabia spurred tribal migration, the whole movement in this sense being a part of the *Völkerwanderung* (migration of peoples) of the age, which included that of the Germans, Slavs, and Turks.

Earlier Moslem success owed much, in a negative way, to an earlier religious development, the resolute resistance of Syrians and Egyptians to ecclesiastical domination from Constantinople. Their struggle to maintain cultural and social identity found expression in the religious form of monophysitism, in espousing Christian doctrines different from the Greeks; being therefore persecuted, many of them welcomed the Arab invaders, not yet much disposed to seeking converts themselves. Soon the Arabs fell victim to the same phenomenon, for the conquered Persians of the Sassanid Empire presently turned Shi'ite, thereby sharply differentiating themselves through a separate religious sect from the conquering Sunnite Arabs. In North Africa, where the Donatist Christian heresy had formerly found a stronghold, the Kharijite sect of the Moslems took root, especially among the Berbers, as a means of maintaining regional and ethnic identity.

Religion thus became a vehicle for movements being generated by a number of other social forces. Within the context of the times, in which most ideas came clothed in religious guise, the natural public expression, the rallying cry, for restless rebels was religious. Throughout much of history, religion provides a convenient outlet, an ostensible cause, for developments born out of a miscellany of reasons and temporarily binds together otherwise diverse elements.

How much did the influence of the church mitigate the brutal violence of an age of castles and walled towns? Religious suasions on the raw natures of medieval warriors, the effects of imposing a set of rules upon their conduct, can scarcely now be measured. Nor can the modern observer see clearly enough into the average manor of the age, vulnerable to exploitation by the military aristocracy, to estimate spiritual successes in encouraging a solicitous, charitable attitude toward the less fortunate. Religious influences in channelizing personality drives and in making the community liveable are usually taken for granted.

Early Christians frowned on wars and deplored military service. The medieval church tried, with only limited success, to establish the so-called Truce of God, whereby fighting was forbidden on certain days and in certain seasons. More successfully, the Peace of God encouraged people to band together in preventing desultory violence within the community itself. Perforce, finally reconciled to the existence of war, the Christians fought the Crusades as Holy Wars against the infidels, and some Christian campaigns against the Spanish Moslems took on the same character.

Starting with the Benedictines in the sixth century, monasticism performed many services beyond the purely religious and in the process nurtured European civilization. Monks served functions other than being spiritual leaders, teachers, and missionaries; in fact, the Benedictines were supposed to do seven hours of manual labor a day. Monastic groups maintained the best farms, drained swamps, cleared forests, and helped to colonize the land. In the eastward expansion of the Germans, the Cistercians, spreading out from their original monasteries, set up a network of agricultural establishments in the wasteland, improved farming, and became skillful cattle raisers. Without the labored copying of manuscripts and their careful preservation, much less knowledge of the classical world would have survived in the West. In the masculine world of the times, convents offered unmarried women security, occupation, personal goals, and the means for leading worthwhile lives.

A church hostile to capitalism prohibited usury and thereby theoretically prevented capitalistic enterprise in economic affairs, but it manifestly accomplished little more than perhaps to delay the rising tide of capitalist ventures in western Europe. Italy, homeland of Catholicism, also became the original homeland for vigorous, organized capitalist commercial and banking ventures. Early in the Middle Ages, the Jews of western Europe, with no such religious restraints, had been able to take over, along with Greeks and Syrians (the old Phoenicians, once again—or still—following the ancient trading routes), the role of traders. Not permitted to own land, the Jews necessarily put their property into movable goods, into trading articles and money; they developed a commercial network stretching through the Middle East and southern Russia all the way to China.

Christianity's lack of animism may have opened the way for Europeans to develop modern science and technology, to learn how to control nature's forces. That is, as long as the physical world was envisioned in terms of gods and goddesses, the practicality of tampering with these forces did not occur to the human mind. To set up a water driven mill could be considered a sacrilege to the god of that stream, and when a bridge or dam was built, the local water deity, in early times, had to be appeased by the sacrificing of a human being, often a child. Once having escaped animism, the more emancipated of the Christians began, with excruciating slowness at first, to harness the energies of nature.

Our age is now too secularized for most of us to be able to appreciate fully the role of the religious in the formative stage of European culture or the European Christian mind. Perhaps we catch a glimpse of the truth only when seeing how those monuments of medieval life, the cathedrals, even yet bulk large in the middle of European cities. We inevitably undervalue the role of the spiritual in the minds of our forefathers, whose ideas were formulated within a religious framework, and find it difficult to penetrate genuinely into their thoughts, values, and feelings. Their other motives blur into the religious, and matters are not helped by so much of the written evidence coming from the clergy, naturally presenting its own viewpoint and thereby distorting the real picture.

To understand the strength of the religious throughout the long story of humanity, even beyond the tenacity of traditional religious beliefs and explanations, the ever-present experience with death must be realized. Epidemics, their nature not understood, swept away vast numbers, average longevity running to not much more than thirty-five years, and young mothers suffered because of the high fatality rate of babies in their first year after birth. Life was indeed a time of testing, and not to see this in the Christian centuries is to rip a partial picture out of its full context.

Disease, misfortune, storms, droughts, and floods all had supernatural origin—how else explain them? The natural science of the ancients consisted largely in knowing how to placate fickle, whimsical gods or spirits and, later, for the prescientific Christian, in invoking protection against the Devil and his demons. So the protecting temple loomed over every town as the epitome of these ages and an important and permanent source of causal motive power in the community, and into it went enormous quantities of wealth and labor.

Quite possibly, the religious viewpoint in the writing of history has itself been one of the most important of spiritual factors. The Hand of God theory, that a Divine Will guides the unfolding pattern of events, dominated interpretations of history during the Christian era up until the past two centuries and as such often decisively determined human responses to specific situations. Secularized versions of it still persist. Reactions against religious forces have also helped to shape the contours of our history. Edward Gibbon, in the eighteenth century, posited his long history of the decline and fall of the Roman Empire on the idea that the triumph of Christianity greatly contributed to Rome's decline and to the coming of the Dark Ages. Voltaire ferociously attacked religious superstitions, and Karl Marx considered religion the opium of the people. These sweeping, monolithic judgments distorted the real shapes of the past as badly as did the more zealous advocates of the Hand of God theory. Some of the most severe strictures against religion have been aimed at the wrong targets, the real culprits being the excesses of the True Believers and the institutional factor in organized churches.

Another religious phenomenon remains to be explored, one that, reconsidered, has vital relevance for contemporary historical processes. Alongside the Renaissance, the Reformation, and the origins of modern science went a grim, macabre sideplay of witchcraft and witch hunters. This mania was in full swing by the end of the fifteenth century and, despite a temporary ebb, intensified after 1560, not subsiding until after about 1660.

Once believed to have been a residue of medieval darkness, it seems, in fact, to have started when the church tried to stamp out ancient pagan survivals in the mountainous areas of the Alps and Pyrenees. (Anyone who has experienced the moods of the uncanny, drifting mists in an Alpine mountain forest will understand the villagers' persistent clinging to pagan vestiges.) According to Hugh Trevor-Roper in *Religion, the Reformation and Social Change,* the persecution originated with the lower clergy among those working on the "social frontier," and who were trying to enforce conformity on people like the mountain folk, who were different. The persecution spread to the lowlands and, with the uncovering of scapegoats, provided a focus for the socially frustrated. The witchcraft mania, as well as the rampant antisemitism, fed on the social tensions of the period, and then, in the time of the Reformation, attained heightened ferocity with the outbreak of religious wars after 1560. Catholics and Protestants were equally zealous.

Numerous erudite investigations into witchcraft resulted in the publication of manuals and encyclopedias, the first of the latter being the *Malleus Maleficarum (Hammer of Witches)* in 1486 compiled by two Dominican monks. A papal bull two years earlier had deplored witchcraft in Germany. This learned activity accumulated much "evidence," a whole new mythology for the True Believers of the age, enough to convince many scholars and important personages whom one would have expected to have known better. To be sure, some evidence came from individuals being asked the appropriate leading questions while being tortured, hence likely to admit anything, but others confessed voluntarily and in great detail. Modern psychiatry explains this on the basis of mentally disturbed people adopting the tales, symbols, and explanations of the times. Meantime, equally disturbed persons might have adopted religious symbolism of a "good" kind and be considered holy men and women.

So, for about two centuries, the witchcraft mania persisted. The Devil, whom Preserved Smith once referred to as "an imported luxury from Asia," received full credit for "earthquakes, pestilences, famines and wars." He also caused crops to blight and milk to turn sour. Assisting in the good work were the witches, who flew on sticks to conventions held in numerous well-known places, and there participated in unholy Sabbats. The Devil, as a goat, dog, cat, or ape, presided over this parody of the Mass.

Finally the mania ebbed away, terminated partly by the end of the religious wars and partly by advances in natural science and philosophy, which persuaded the learned that they had been wrong. Before this, however, skeptics of the whole business themselves suffered, sometimes, ferocious persecution during the long reign of terror. The witchcraft mania, unfortunately, is not an isolated phenomenon, periods of collective psychological aberrations recurring repeatedly throughout the past. Never lying very far below the surface of the ordered, rational society, it can spread in times of crisis and trouble, feeding on people's worries and preying on selected scapegoats.

Chronic antisemitism has always been one version of it. The psychological parallels to the witchcraft mania in the Christian Millenarians of the medieval and early modern are obvious enough: a world dominated by evil tyrannous power of diabolical intent, an age of acute suffering by the faithful, the coming victory of the Saints, and the establishment of a New Jerusalem. To repeat from Cohn, "[S]tripped of . . . supernatural sanction, revolutionary millenarianism and mystical anarchism are with us still." This century has witnessed the Nazi mania culminating in the crematoriums and the liquidation of people belonging to, from the Communist viewpoint, "unnecessary" social classes.

Religious social forces need not be limited to the traditional organized bodies of believers in the supernatural. Many events of the twentieth century can be partly ascribed to ideology suffused with religious emotions. Communism, fascism, and ultranationalism all recruit basically religious emotions, appeal to this dimension of the human personality, and, in this sense, our century may be fully as religious as those of the medieval.

The True Believers—the name is taken from Eric Hoffer's book of that title—express themselves in exaggerated versions of the characteristic beliefs and symbols of each age. They have manifested themselves in the various religious faiths, often as persecutors, saints, and heretics, and in the more recent secular mythologies their convictions and compulsive drives make them as conspicuous in today's newspapers as in the pages of history. The True Believer may be the hero or heroine sacrificing his or her life for the cause; in terms of loyalties, he or she displays the virtues in history. Institutions use true believers as examples for others, be it church martyrs, national patriots, or party members executed by a hostile regime. In contemporary affairs, they are devoted champions of righteousness if on our side; otherwise, they are manifest nuisances or villains.

Though possessing psychological characteristics commonly associated with religion, the True Believers perhaps now require a separate label. In their frenetic nature, devotion to some mythology, and obsession with a purported "enemy" in the community, they seem, as a real or potential presence, an independent social force in themselves. This abnormal collective psychology—whether manifested as paranoia, schizophrenia, or something else—seems to be a constant in history, whatever the combination of human biology, environmental circumstances, stresses, and herd contagion that generates it.

17

Forces in History:
Institutional

"Furthermore, we declare, state, define, and pronounce that it is altogether necessary to salvation for every human creature to be subject to the Roman pontiff." When Pope Boniface VIII made this statement in his *Unam Sanctam* (1302), one of the most audacious and sweeping claims to supremacy in all human history, he was asserting more than a religious dominance—it was also institutional.

Urban II proclaimed the First Crusade on religious grounds, but other motives also entered the picture. An appeal from Emperor Alexius in Constantinople for help against the Turks raised hopes that the schism between the Catholic and Orthodox churches, which had become formal in 1054, might be healed. Strong papal leadership in the Crusades might also help the papacy win the continuing investiture struggle with the emperor in Germany. In these and in the papal struggle against the pretensions of the national monarchies, the popes sought to enhance the institutional power of the church and, more specifically, of the papacy itself.

By the thirteenth century, the Roman pontiff commanded more revenue than the Western monarchies combined. A vacuum of secular power had long since made the Bishop of Rome also temporal ruler of the city, a state of affairs duplicated in many other towns in Italy and Germany. Burdened by administrative duties, clerical authorities all too frequently permitted institutional imperatives to take priority over spiritual considerations. The Franciscans began as one of the most spiritual groups imaginable, but later even its administrative organization began to assume primacy, as the advocates of institutional needs became more assertive.

At first doing the traveling themselves, medieval merchants later settled down at permanent bases and sent out their representatives. Important commercial houses planted branches in other cities, and the increasingly organized businesses began to use bills of exchange, marine insurance, and detailed methods of bookkeeping. Famous banking firms in such cities as Florence seemed, for a time, to deal on equal terms with the kings of France and England. The economic motive was primary, of course, but also their operating procedures were becoming increasingly institutionalized, some of the motives and practices being derived from the needs of organization.

During the thirteenth century, the Italian city-republics began drifting toward rule by one person. Intense internal strife brought a general craving for an end to discord, and the endemic wars with other states, requiring a permanent strong leader, contributed to this trend. Most usually, the development began with the appointment of a neutral "city manager," a so-called *Podestà*, for a single one-year term, but eventually someone, usually a military leader, established a permanent dictatorship.

In 1100, the king of France held so little power or land that even nearby feudal lords sometimes escaped his control. By the time of Louis XI (1461–1483), the Crown levied taxes over most of the country without the necessity of securing regular grants from the Estates, possessed enough revenues to maintain a standing army, and held the power of decree. Once the Crown had attained a substantial level of revenues and created the nucleus for a bureaucracy in the time of Philip Augustus (1180–1223), the process of centralization developed its own momentum as royal officials became a vested interest on behalf of the Crown; by strengthening the monarchy, they also strengthened and enlarged their own scope of activity. Again, the institutional factor was at work, the steady aggrandizement of power, at successive stages, in order to perform the functions of government properly.

This institutional factor in history tends to manifest itself in any vital organized social group as an innate tendency of the leadership to strengthen its control over the rank and file and to expand the group resources externally. In order to perform the assigned functions, those in charge perpetually feel the need for more power both internally and externally, whether in the form of money, arms, paper forms, or other resources. A natural vested interest exists in the success of the office, institution, and group that confers status, prestige, and power upon those that serve it. As the leaders or officials seek to aggrandize their base of power, a momentum develops in which organization needs often take priority over the original functions for which the office or institution was established in the first place. External dangers have a tendency to accelerate centralization in a vital organization under able leadership, to furnish the justification for a strongly disciplined membership and the concentration of decision making at the top.

Another facet of the institutional factor can be found in the so-called balance of power, which results from rivalries among a group of autonomous political units. A detailed history of Italy in the period of the Renaissance reveals a certain pattern in the otherwise confusing series of alliances and wars. The popes and the kings of Naples were usually political enemies, while the Florentines often feuded with Rome and supported others against it, including the emperors when they came to Italy. Hence the Florentines and the kings of Naples were usually on friendly terms. Completing the picture, the Venetians and the Milanese often allied with one side or the other, while the Venetians and the Genoese continued their private conflict.

A balance of power occurs as a uniformity or regularity throughout much of history. In the ancient world, Egypt, Babylonia, the Hittites, Assyria, and the states of Syria, Palestine, and Phoenicia lined up repeatedly, some or most of them on one side or the other in similar sets of alliances. From the time of the Thirty Years War (or earlier, for that matter), European countries customarily balanced one another in an equilibrium of alliances.

Manifestly, the popes and the kings of Naples were not enemies because they generally happened not to like each other personally or because they always supported opposing ideological or religious causes. Nor did the mercantile republic of the Florentines and the Neapolitan kingdom of large landed estates ally because they had much in common. Neighboring states tend to become enemies, and states with a common enemy contract alliances. The British or French fought each other repeatedly, then became allies in the twentieth century because the Germans seemed to threaten them both.

Americans long detested this concept of the balance of power, which obviously led to wars, militarism, and the domination of weaker states by the stronger. In World War II, the Americans helped destroy the military power of Germany and Japan, only to discover that apparently they had to step in and do their jobs in both Asia and Europe in order to protect themselves. A new balance of power emerged, as did an American military establishment—to be duly condemned in the same terms Americans had formerly used on others.

A balance of power has been a grim fact of international life wherever rival autonomous groups have appeared. The response of the state to external or internal danger is one of the forces in history, one that must be recognized and reckoned with in order to understand why things happen as they do. Moralizing away the institutional factor has usually been impossible because the alternative is even worse. If no balance of power exists, a country may be in grave danger of conquest, and if the institutional factors within a state weaken, the consequences may be anarchy or reckless exploitation by the strongest. Tragically, these have often been the hard realities of history.

Institutional factors seem to exercise overweening influence in the coming of the European Age of Despots. A coherent historical pattern, originating in institutional forces, emerges out of the increasing stifling of earlier parliamentary forms, the creation of absolutist monarchy, the preferences for a hierarchical society, the shifting balance of power, and the espousal of mercantilism in the economic sphere.

Two of the principal beneficiaries, as well as stimulators, of the institutional factor are the military and the bureaucracy. They do the work of the state and need a well-ordered community for their own services to be successfully implemented. The military is one of the most conspicuous and the bureaucracy one of the least visible elements in the pages of history.

Military necessities may set a very deep imprint upon a community. Charioteers, corps of mounted archers, and medieval knights all imposed heavy burdens upon their respective communities; in fact, the requirements of the military seem to have decisively molded the shapes of their societies. A series of wars usually produces a powerful armed force whose maintenance becomes a matter of utmost importance for its officers and which entails the backing of a disciplined populace. Any community in an especially vulnerable position is prone to incubate a strong military establishment. Among the German states, Brandenburg-Prussia and Austria, both located on the exposed eastern frontier, built up the most potent military aggregations, while in China, in periods of disintegration, the strong local political units generally emerged on the border near the nomads. Assyria became a renowned military state in the ancient world largely because its location in upper Mesopotamia made it vulnerable to incursions from the neighboring and never completely subdued tribes of the hill country; the stark choice lay between maintaining an alert military stance or being destroyed.

Military establishments in the early modern period also helped mold the shapes of the community, the primary motive force in the emergence of the Age of Despots quite possibly being the needs of the armed forces. Standing armies and weapons involving gunpowder must have imposed expenses proportionately as great as the earlier forms of warfare. In some cases, military considerations largely dominated statecraft, and instances can be readily recalled in which a potent military passed completely beyond the control of the people and treated the community merely as a base for its own activities.

Very probably, a majority of humanity's rulers have come from the warrior class, accustomed to command, psychologically qualified to keep order, and trained to defend the community against attack. In Rome, the praetorian guard often chose the emperor and enforced his accession to the purple, while in Baghdad the caliphs presently became the puppets of a similar soldier elite. In Renaissance Italy, the condottieri of mercenary troops frequently seized power. Though civilian rule ultimately became the practice in the more advanced European and Anglo-American countries, generals still predominate among the presidents of Latin American nations and have quickly come to the fore among the newly independent African states.

Despite the squandering of lives and wealth, not all judgment of the military should be negative: military requirements have often been responsible for advances in technology and in the economy; moments of peril may compel the dropping of obsolete practices; when community solidarity becomes mandatory, the military often provides it. In the contemporary world, when a civilian government botches the job, it is usually the generals and the colonels who must try to clean up the mess; sometimes military officers have instituted programs of necessary reform, which civilian regimes seemed unable to carry through.

Bureaucracy makes only brief appearances in most history books. Though its presence is assumed as the very backbone of an organized state, very little is written about it because hardly anything seems more dull, colorless, and uneventful than these dogged pen-pushers and wielders of paper forms. Officeholders at this level do not lend themselves to the historical narrative at all, unless as the anonymous villains in the background who frustrate genius and bring splendid projects to squalid conclusions.

Not that it is supposed to work that way, for in its inception modern bureaucracy represented an improvement wherein written rules would protect the individual from the arbitrary tyranny of superiors. Inasmuch as the modern state requires rational planning, the imperatives of its proliferation are undeniable. The bureaucracy services the modern community, keeps the records, does the official communicating, and implements decisions from above. Historians owe a debt to officialdom for preserving governmental records in the archives.

Bureaucratic mentalities shape the course of events by intrinsically favoring continuity, disliking change and flexibility, and contributing ineffable quantities of inertia to the historical processes. Government officeholders also power the thrust of the institutional drive, seeking centralization and outward acquisitions of more resources, and, eventually, often being more interested in their own vested interests than in the functions they supposedly perform for the community.

Certain unlovely traits have, historically, distinguished bureaucracies with poorly trained personnel. Lacking judgment or perspective and fearing the censure of their superiors, clerks have clung rigidly to the literal letter of prevailing rules and regulations. Rules intended to protect the individual from whimsical overlords have themselves became whimsical. Officials sitting at desks have a tendency to confuse paper forms with the real world and to overestimate grossly their effectiveness in guiding human behavior. The realm of the clerk is a world in itself, made up of routine and ritual, impersonality, hierarchy, and proliferating precedences, whose opaque terminology and intricate procedures frequently block communications between rulers and ruled. Bureaucrats can frustrate any amount of reforming zeal at the top simply by being themselves.

Trevor-Roper's comment about the officialdom of Catholicism in the sixteenth century, "an apparatus which . . . absorbed energy, consumed time, and immobilized property, without having any necessary connection with religion . . .," applies equally well in numerous other instances. John Jewkes and associates assert in *The Sources of Invention* that "originality begins to fight a losing battle with the forces of ossification" as the controlling hierarchical organization develops "traditions and respect for precedence and authority." Crane Brinton in *The Anatomy of Revolution* suggested that major revolutions start as a quest for more freedom and conclude with stronger state structure, hence, by implication, an enlarged bureaucracy. William H. McNeill closes *The Rise of the West* by musing over the probability that, barring the dislocations of more great wars, the proliferating bureaucracy will slow down or halt the present era of rapid change.

One other institutional influence should be mentioned, the relationship between the prevailing governments and the fine arts. Some of the finest art of the Renaissance derived directly out of the sponsorship of the princely courts of the time, the patrons who had the wealth for ostentatious and cultured living. The Medici, particularly, bring to mind the cluster of geniuses patronized by them. Later, the royal courts expended wealth extravagantly in the building and sustaining of Versailles, Sans Souci, Peterhof, and other palaces; these playgrounds for the courts, with their paintings, sculpture, gardens, and other furnishings, constituted a sort of cultural major league in which the members of the royalty competed with one another in the splendor of the artistic achievements they possessed.

Early in the dawning Age of Despots, Machiavelli expressed the institutional viewpoint with cynical realism in a book, *The Prince,* intended as a manual for rulers. He insisted that a prince must not be deterred by moral considerations from serving the best interests of the state. Hardly anyone claims to admire Machiavelli, and he apparently did not particularly like this viewpoint himself, but, having become disillusioned by the failure of the Florentine republic, he felt that weak government or anarchic conditions were worse. His essay represents an early statement of that form of statecraft known as *Realpolitik,* in which policies of state operate in a sphere of their own, which has its own logic and laws of behavior undeterred by the moral code of the individual.

The elucidation of institutional factors, and especially of the history and nature of bureaucracy, is primarily associated with the name of Max Weber. He depicted the rationalization of the modern community and believed that the principal struggle of our age occurs between bureaucracy and democratic government. Weber also challenged the Marxist doctrine, insisting that its omission of institutional factors vitiates its whole argument: socialism, far from freeing mankind, builds up a top-heavy omnipresent bureaucratic apparatus that stifles liberty.

Some individuals tend to be allergic to institutional factors, which are inconvenient to reformers, whether liberal or Marxist. If some other kinds of uniformities, such as the economic, are abused by being overdrawn, reformers often prefer to pretend that this category of social forces does not exist. Many a modern crusade after a triumphant start has ended in the two swamps of military vested interests and bureaucratic red tape.

18

A Handy Checklist: Multiple Causality

Some time ago, an article in a newspaper unveiled the sensational news that the decline and fall of Rome "resulted not from high living but from eating and drinking from lead utensils."

The quickest way to spot an unabashed illiterate in historical matters is to note his or her handling of causality. A monocausal explanation, often based upon the latest fad, stamps the perpetrator as a novice, ignorant of historical processes. In this case, the dictum seems offered in total obliviousness of some fifty other suggested causes, some of them still quite credible, and the fact that high living has not been considered an adequate answer since the beginning of this century. Glibly proclaiming Number 51 as *the* reason and obtusely presenting a long obsolete explanation as its current alternative, once again reveals the chasm between the historians' knowledge and the fatuous elementary-mindedness of some of our sources of information.

Not much credence should be given to commonly used explanatory words that, more closely examined, turn out to be nonexplanatory. What does a writer mean by saying that a country fell because it became soft and overcivilized? If the writer calls an empire "exhausted," does this refer to the human stock, material resources, finances, or a loss of will power? Words like "degenerate" and "luxurious" used in a causal context offer only specious explanations by verbalization.

Basic historical processes necessarily involve a multiple causality in which a number of reasons are operative in any given historical situation. In the past four chapters the Crusades have been observed, successively, in terms of geographical, economic, religious, and institutional factors, no one of which alone provides a satisfactory picture. Each category suggests a number of further possibilities, for instance, the sharp differences in the economic motives of the Venetians and the landless knights or the interplay of various institutional rivalries. The four categories do not retain the same proportional influences in the different Crusades. Additional factors may also be operative, including the technological aspect and the sheer spirit of adventure that sent many crusaders on their way.

Categories of this type can be highly useful to a student as a handy checklist in searching for explanations. Each should be tested in any given case to see whether it will to some extent fit the circumstances. With increasing experience, the categories become reservoirs of suggestive possibilities, adaptable to successive areas of history when encountered. In approaching the material in this way, a student is using a simplified version of the historian's own technique.

Each category can suggest one or more exploratory hypotheses in looking for explanations in major historical developments. For the Italian Renaissance, the economic sphere yields the old, standard correlation between the rise of the middle class in the cities and the ripening of their urban culture into traits supposedly characteristic of the Renaissance. The religious immediately recalls the subject matter of much of the art of the period and also raises the question whether the somewhat earlier religious revival centering about the Franciscans and the Dominicans may have contributed to it by quickening the sensibilities of the age. Geographic considerations suggest that some of the so-called Renaissance traits actually commonly characterize many Italians of any age. Patrons supported and encouraged the artists, in part an institutional matter of prestige and status.

Missing pieces may be suspected. Renaissance ideas, their origins and diffusion throughout western Europe, remind us of the existence of an as yet undiscussed category of social forces, the ideational. To it also belongs the question of maturation of individual genius and why a most unusual galaxy of great individuals flourished in a short time period within a small geographical area. Then, too, do the arts perhaps have their own kind of historical evolution, an intrinsic process of development in art forms themselves? All of this, without worrying about the suspicions of some historians that the Renaissance may, after all, be somewhat of an optical illusion or that the ideas claimed for the Renaissance are merely popularizations of concepts worked out earlier.

Applying the economic category to the Age of Explorations yields a rich harvest of motives, ranging from the desire for gold to the attempt by people on the Atlantic seaboard to eliminate the intermediary merchants in the spice trade by going directly to the Far East themselves (or to increase the supply because the old routes no longer met the demand). Multitudes of souls overseas awaited the Christian missionary, while the national monarchies, once given practical reasons, possessed the material means for mounting expensive expeditions. These factors made Columbus's voyages an effective discovery, in contrast to the earlier visits of the Norsemen, and so did the development of better sailing vessels, as well as the use of compass and astrolabe, other reminders of the technological category of social forces.

Manifestly, a number of causal elements must be considered in almost any imaginable episode. Those fifty causes for the end of the Roman Empire, however, contain many that have become outdated. If one opens Donald Kagan's *Decline and Fall of the Roman Empire,* which contains a collection of related essays, one finds, among others, the following causes: (1) depopulation; (2) Christianity; (3) moral degeneration; (4) drain of precious metals to the East; (5) exhaustion of the soil; (6) abandoned land becoming swampy and mosquitoes bringing malaria; (7) extremes of wealth and poverty; (8) the replacement of the old martial

Roman stock by the descendants of imported slaves; (9) "pitiful poverty"; (10) state socialism, a "workshop of forced labor"; (11) a decline of rainfall in the fourth to sixth centuries; (12) an end to compulsory military service, the Roman soldiers being replaced by barbarians; (13) and the crushing load of taxation.

Some of these insights reflect the impact of successive contemporary events upon several generations of historians, who then projected these upon the past. Others, like Huntington's rainfall theory, were exciting theories, which for a time seemed to open up new vistas and which were made to explain too much. Some have been refuted by evidence uncovered by other historians while testing the hypotheses. Whatever the individual case, no single cause is ever likely to offer a convincing explanation for the fall of Rome. Carlo M. Cipolla, in his book on the nature of decline, has listed a number of currently acceptable symptoms: desertion of the least attractive jobs; a high standard of living leading to excesses; the increase of bureaucracy; growth of military expenditures; a vast amount of public consumption; and a great growth in taxes.

Lead poisoning may, in fact, have been one of the *numerous* factors involved, and, for that matter, "high living" may indeed have some correlation to decline. Cipolla has suggested that a high standard of living at the peak of a country's fortune, a seeking for "abnormal sensations and unnatural experiences," is a symptom of success, which will, sooner or later, be followed by a reversal of fortunes. That is, to argue that high living *causes* decline is a bit like saying that trout fishing is best when apple trees are in bloom. Apple trees have no effect whatsoever on trout, but spring does produce both apple blossoms and flies, and trout do regard flies as a delicacy.

Having ascertained the probable causal elements in an historical situation, the next problem is the question of priority, how to weight causes that seem to have a genuine bearing on a development. One useful approach in testing for causal elements is to omit, successively, the possible factors. By imaginative reconstruction, the historian can in this way hope to separate the decisive or dominant factors from those peripheral in influence.

Returning to the case of the Crusades, the question may be asked whether an increasingly vigorous Europe would have erupted anyway, without the religious motive. The answer can scarcely be an unhesitating negative, recalling the Norman conquests in southern Italy and England, a brief Norman thrust into the Balkans, and the number of Franks going to Spain to fight the Moslems there in the period just before the Crusades.

Would the Crusaders have successfully conquered the Holy Land, or ever gotten there, if other motives had not bolstered the religious motive? How long could the Crusaders have held on without the commercial motives of the Venetians and the Genoese? Did the merchants sully an originally pure enterprise, in contrast to the faithful Christians dying for their faith? Were the Crusades helped or hurt by those feudal lords who grabbed land for themselves? Did these worldly people corrode the inspiration and thereby cause it to fail in the long run? Or would the whole enterprise have collapsed earlier or have never manifested itself if these forces had not been activated by the religious catalyst?

A different perspective frequently yields additional causal ingredients. For instance, examine the Crusades from the viewpoint of Baghdad or Egypt, applying the "fall of Rome" criteria. After enjoying a lengthy period of superiority, the caliphate had disintegrated, leaving only relatively weak local forces to resist the invaders. The crusaders, seen from the Moslem side, are the ancient Peoples of the Sea all over again, joining in the rapine. Against a strong caliphate or without the military advantage of the mounted knights of the French, any such invasions would have been bloody fiascos.

Knowing what did happen may not fully reveal the dimensions of a specific situation; it may be necessary to ask, given the factors at work, what *might* have happened. In this way, the variables can be distinguished from the regularities. The latter derive out of the larger background and, incessantly exercising a potent influence, seem to guide historical developments in certain directions over a period of time. Rarely is any given situation, seen in detail, predictable, but in a cluster of contemporary episodes, the regularities impose a trend or tendency. An equation of causal elements never quite repeats itself exactly, and a complex of similar factors does not produce the same result twice because of the interplay of variables. Regularities themselves, rarely measureable, vary in potency and so do their proportionate impact.

Variabilities are also introduced by the unpredictability of specific personalities and the presence or absence of strong leaders. Past experiences of those involved, always a variant, largely determine the initial human responses to unfolding events. *Timing* may be crucial. And finally, the fall of the historical dice, the consequences of sheer chance.

Another approach to sorting out the priority of causes is to isolate the *immediate* reasons that set a sequence of events going. Into the normal course of events, the continuing routine of a community, comes an intrusion, an unusual catalytic factor, which stimulates a series of dramatic episodes: the preaching of the First Crusade, the voyage of Columbus, Luther's battle against indulgences. Finally, another question must be settled: whether an immediate cause functions as a genuine impelling force, or whether another catalytic factor sooner or later would have precipitated roughly the same sequence anyway.

Historians go through an approximation of this procedure in handling their materials and then, intent on getting on with the narrative, usually settle for "sufficient cause," that is, limit themselves to formulating a credible explanation.

For the beginner, learning the possibilities in certain historical situations and shaping satisfactory explanations out of accepted regularities, variables, and immediate causes is a matter of experience, perhaps to some extent comparable to a chess player learning to choose appropriate responses or gambits according to the position of the pieces on the chessboard. Something important, however, may have been forgotten during the preceding discussion. The sixteenth century Europeans thought the Africans backward, it will be recalled, and it seems historically true that the Europeans did find the West Africans in a condition less felicitous than that of a hundred years earlier. Why? What is the causality here?

Without knowledge about African history, the foregoing checklist of categories and procedures is not very helpful; the ultimate answer may be the same as that of the Europeans, that the Africans were simply backward. That is, a lack of sufficient evidence compels an elementary answer or perhaps a solution taken from an a priori system of history unrelated to the facts of the case. Those who do have some knowledge of African history would point out that the discovery of America reduced European commercial interest in Africa, that the gold of America made acquisition of that metal in Africa less imperative, and consequently the economic base for the West African political empire had dwindled in strength. Then, in the same period as Cortez and Pizarro, Juber Pasha, a Spaniard turned Moslem, led a Moorish army against the weakened Songhai empire. It was destroyed, the trade routes to the Mediterranean were disrupted, and the Africans who had hitherto collected the gold lost their lucrative contacts.

Similarly, anyone who lacks a sufficient knowledge about China and attempts to explain why the Chinese, long ahead of the Europeans, failed to develop a modern economy and technology will automatically produce an elementary or a priori answer.

All of this serves as a reminder that the procedures for handling multiple causality depend entirely upon the evidence, upon available detailed data. Social forces and causal components are not broad, general concepts that can be shuffled about at the pleasure of the historian. They are shorthand devices for representing a multitude of data of various kinds, and the evidence itself determines their usage. Unless this is borne in mind, the concepts are all too likely to become the masters rather than tools of our historical-mindedness. Far from being concocted for the occasion, the concepts have been proposed and thoroughly tested in the primary sources by professional historians, and their basic validity derives from the authority of historians having full access to the original evidence.

19

Cleopatra's Nose: Chance

Everyone knows the standard story of Christopher Columbus's first voyage to the New World. His crew became increasingly restless, threatened to mutiny, and finally he had to promise that the expedition would turn back if no landfall occurred in the next three days. Then, with the time nearly elapsed, the lookout saw a distant flickering light in the darkness. Suppose that land had not been sighted, and, after perhaps pitching Columbus overboard, the crew had turned around and headed back to Spain. Would the Americas have been discovered?

Obviously. The necessary factors were operative: the need for a new route to the East, national monarchies capable of mounting transoceanic expeditions, ships and navigation devices capable of getting explorers overseas, and gunpowder to keep them there. European fishermen may already have been busy off the Newfoundland banks. Portuguese vessels going around Africa would sooner or later have been blown off course to the west, if, indeed, this had not already happened. The times were ripe.

If Luther had followed his father's wishes and become a lawyer instead of a monk, would a Reformation have occurred? Well—it might not have been called a Reformation, the church could possibly have temporarily survived intact, the ultimate shapes of things might have been different, but, again, the times seemed ripe for an historical movement of reform.

Given a lack of strong government in some parts of Europe, did the rise of commerce virtually ensure the emergence of city-states? Would some form of Western European expansion have occurred without Pope Urban's crusade? Would the United States have become involved in World War II without a Pearl Harbor? In these three cases, very probably.

Some events or developments have a feel of inevitability about them. The cards seem stacked for a certain outcome, the dominoes arranged to topple. Those of any perception who lived through the 1930s could sense a certain inevitability in the steps to World War II in Europe, an uneasy awareness of Greek tragedy inexorably unfolding. Our contemporary technological transformation compulsively generates its own momentum, each step forward leading to the next.

Such cases tempt the observer to think in determinist terms, to believe that powerful causal forces beyond human control determine the course of history. The mighty sweep of history and the deep currents that seem to run through it present an exhilarating panorama, one that insidiously challenges human intelligence to set up sharply contoured patterns and then fit men and events into them. A set of uniformities may implant such conviction of predominant influence that the observer elevates them, virtually, to the level of predictable laws of history. It can become an inebriating game. Once conviction hardens the pattern to dogma, its possessor can readily adapt the resultant prefabricated answers to all important questions.

Several determinist schemes have been encountered earlier, including Buckle's theory of geographic factors, the economic pattern devised by Marx, and St. Augustine's version of the Hand of God. Almost any attempt to find ultimate meaning in history will result in a determinist solution, and statements beginning with "it was inevitable that . . ." or "history teaches that . . ." partake of this quality. A fatalist by temperament is apt to discover some specific pattern of inevitability that makes sense out of it all.

As someone has said, occasional swigs out of this bottle probably serve as a useful corrective for those who assume that historical figures actually can exercise completely free will in playing their roles. Though individuals need not necessarily be only pawns of powerful social forces, surrender their personality to some vaulting world process, they are constantly subject to such suasions, and oftentimes the compulsions become irresistible. Room for maneuverability, however, can usually be found within the conflicting confluence of the impersonal factors, the interplay of fallible human personalities, the inefficiencies of institutions, and the intervention of chance. These impersonal social forces and the tidy meshing of historical patterns, so majestic and overpowering when seen from afar, seem much less convincing when more closely scrutinized.

Probably Paris offered the most logical site for the French capital, but had not the Capetians found Paris the most useful location for themselves, some other town would have served equally well. If Russia was to be unified in early modern times, geography must very nearly have predetermined that unification would come from the area in central Russia where a network of river tributaries provided transportation. It need not have been Moscow—half a dozen towns had the qualifications—but Moscow happened to be ruled by a succession of strong princes with a minimum of internal dissensions. The Spanish capital should probably have been placed at Seville or Cordoba, but Philip II, flouting natural geographic and economic considerations, established it in Madrid.

When the approximate boundary between Catholicism and Protestantism after the period of Reformation is compared with the ancient borders of the Roman Empire in western Europe the similarity is striking. Those peoples whose ancestors lived outside of the empire to a startling extent turned Protestant, while the inhabitants of the countries where the invaders had been absorbed usually remained Catholic. The parallel becomes even more exact if one remembers that Germanic invaders permanently altered the ethnic character of some areas inside the old Roman frontier—England, the German portions of Switzerland, and to some extent also Alsace. Can the parallel be the consequence of chance or coincidence, or had a thousand years of time still not obliterated certain important differences between Roman and non-Roman peoples?

Northern Europe accepted Protestantism with near unanimity, but the actual circumstances of the change varied drastically from one country to another. Free towns made the change by something like a popular mandate, as did some Swiss cantons, but princely decisions dictated the switch in numerous German states. The Swedes turned Lutheran in conjunction with a war of independence, while the Danes did so after unseating the same king who had earlier lost Sweden. A secularization of military religious orders brought Lutheranism to the eastern shores of the Baltic. England's fate rested on the will of Henry VIII and then Elizabeth, while the more vocal and vigorous elements of the Scots a little later overruled the sovereign to turn Presbyterian. Many methods and circumstances, but, like iron filings magnetized, they all seemed to respond to a common impulse. Albeit the components involved in the decision varied greatly, the breach nevertheless occurred. Were there sufficient factors in common between Zürich, Scotland, Sweden, Brandenburg, and East Prussia to cause this result, or does the contagion of successful example in itself explain it?

If the latter, why did not the earlier successful revolt of the Hussites stimulate such a movement? Had events not taken their course in Germany, would the Calvinists nevertheless have asserted themselves a little later? Were the dominoes, the causal factors, all set up, and sooner or later somewhere in western Europe would an episode have started them toppling anyway? Would the Reformation have occurred without the invention of the printing press, which made possible the rapid spread of the Protestant message?

Causality in a major development may only look quite clear when viewed in perspective *after* it has happened and when it is cleared of the debris of the rest of that contemporary scene. In the case of the Reformation, an observer now sees religious motives at work; the role of the economic interests of merchants, artisans, and princes; the institutional factors prompting the break with Rome; and the existence of comparatively rapid communications. Viewed together, these motives give an impression of massive compulsion, of a majestic series of social energies driving events to their predestined conclusion, but, seen from the standpoint of a particular person or episode, the viewpoint may be quite otherwise.

Consider, for example, the position of Charles V, the Holy Roman Emperor. An intelligent man in a dull sort of way and temperamentally a moderate, he did the best he could in a situation not of his making. Many pressures played upon this pivotal figure in the European political framework of the time. Suppose that the Habsburg habit of acquiring real estate by marriage had not resulted in Charles V becoming king of Spain and that he had been able to formulate policies on the basis of central Europe alone. The emperor, either willingly or at first unwillingly, could have put himself at the head of the badly needed reform movement in Germany, with the enthusiastic support of large elements of the population, and in the process materially strengthened the power of the central government as well. Consider the consequences if the pent-up forces had been channelized in this direction: perhaps another general wave of church reform, like the Cluniac, or even—preposterous as it may seem—Martin Luther, basically a most conservative man and a rural reactionary within the Catholic context, going to Rome, another Hildebrand becoming another Gregory VII.

Would the Anglican Reformation have occurred if Charles had not been the nephew of Catherine, the queen of Henry VIII, or if Catherine had agreed to an annulment? That is, Charles would presumably have exerted no pressure on Rome to refuse an annulment of the marriage, and under the conditions in Rome at the time and with the high stakes involved, the annulment might, however reluctantly, have been granted. Would the Reformation in England then have come later, bearing in mind the subsequent growing strength of the Puritans?

In a parallel situation, the Huguenots failed to make France a Protestant country. But suppose that a Huguenot king had ascended the throne of France, someone who might then have adopted religious policies like those of Henry VIII or Elizabeth. Oh, but this *did* happen—Henry IV came to the throne as a Huguenot and eventually turned Catholic. Why the difference between the two countries?

If England had remained Catholic, would the Irish have turned Protestant as a way of expressing their identity and their hostility to England? If so, some historians might, in fact, be proclaiming that the Irish temperament made their acceptance of Calvinism inevitable!

Suppose that Spain, increasingly dominated by the aristocratic-clerical outlook of the Castilian plateau, had not been the agency whereby America first came into the orbit of Europe. The riches of America poured into the coffers of a Spain whose policies, among those in western Europe, were least adapted to the circumstances of the times; its rigid, outdated outlook, thanks to this wealth, placed its imprint, especially in the Catholic Reformation, on a western Europe increasingly characterized by an active capitalist bourgeoisie. In terms of the time, the Spanish outlook was alien, incapable of articulating the new spirit and, as in the case of the Dutch revolt, at war with the dawning age. Had Columbus, having exhausted the possibilities of Spain, actually sailed for the king of France, what then would have been the shapes of later European history?

Numerous other "ifs" have been suggested: if Prince Henry had been older than his brother, Frederick the Great; if Emperor Frederick III of Germany had not died so soon; if the chauffeur of Archduke Francis Ferdinand had not backed his car at Sarajevo. Edward Carr has wondered about the history of Russia if Trotsky had not gone duck hunting, become ill as a result, and thereby missed the funeral of Lenin. Albert Einstein once stated that God did not play dice with the universe, but how else explain that random cosmic particle which, by altering the genes, introduced hemophilia, so it has been surmised, into the family of Queen Victoria.

The title of this chapter derives from a famous essay by J. B. Bury in 1916, which in turn was based on the words of Blaise Pascal: "Had Cleopatra's nose been shorter, the whole face of the world would have been different." The episode refers, of course, to Marc Antony's infatuation with Queen Cleopatra, though one may also very rightfully doubt whether Cleopatra's nose—"full wanton lips under a thin curved nose"—had all that much influence upon the actual situation. Nevertheless, the element of chance does vary from the case of an undoubted fluke all the way to situations where chance only determines the specifics in a development that otherwise seems virtually inevitable. Apollo 14, waiting to blast off for the moon in 1971 after every conceivable contingency had been foreseen and every calculation made to the full extent of human ingenuity, was delayed for a while by a chance rainstorm that wandered over the launching area. Perhaps advocates of determinism should take more cognizance of Murphy's law: If something can go wrong, it will!

These chapters deal largely with the major developments and long-term patterns that make up the standard fare of a survey textbook in history. Focusing on a short-term event may shift the emphasis remarkably. Take, for example, the famous episode of the sinking of the Titanic. Geoffrey Marcus in *The Maiden Voyage* lists the following reasons for the disaster: (1) the ship was moving too fast for prevailing weather conditions; (2) the icebergs had drifter farther south than usual; (3) had the ship reached the area in daylight, the iceberg would have been visible; (4) it could still have been seen in time except for the fluke that its dark side was to the ship, which apparently entered a haze shortly before reaching the ice; (5) unbelievably, the lookouts lacked binoculars; (6) if the watertight compartments had actually been watertight, the ship would not have sunk; (7) ice warnings from other ships had not been forwarded to the bridge by wireless operators harrassed by the large number of private messages being sent by the passengers. Had any one of these factors not been present, the disaster would not have happened. Nothing seems inevitable in this skein of causality, in a set of circumstances occurring only once in a century, as a ship's officer said, but an eventual major accident due to chance factors, given the hectic competition among passenger liners, would seem statistically probable.

In the words of Butterfield, "[A]ccidents and conjunctures and curious juxtapositions of events are the very stuff" of the historian's narrative. Chance may be nothing more than human error or the result of human irrationality. Quite possibly it may not be chance at all for those with a thorough understanding of psychology. The intervention of an unknown factor or unexpected contingent element may be attributed to chance. Or the word may simply be a way of saying that so many factors bear upon an incident that the consequences are completely unpredictable.

Much depends upon the coincidence of contiguous causes, the happenstance of a particular juxtaposition of factors. Though the general direction may have been set, such ingredients determine the specific details, as well as the erratic consequence of the interplay of social forces. History does reveal patterns in the long-term consequences of major social energies at work, but to try to identify these uniformities in the details of specific events poses vexing difficulties. Leon Trotsky's dictum that historical development occurs through the "natural selection of accidents" shows sensitive historical insight.

Other considerations enter into the picture. For instance, massive social energies may be there to be released but require a stimulating catalytic episode to set them in motion. Not so released, the configuration presently shifts, the potential forces finding outlet in another direction or perhaps eventually dissipating.

Social energies, to be implemented, must generally have vehicles for expressing themselves. The impersonal forces are meted out, guided, channelized, or contained by organizations or institutions of some sort and by the individuals who lead them. Social forces do not always find expression in adequate vehicles, an existent institution being enfeebled or its practices too ritualized to react to a novel situation. Where vital, these vehicles of power are themselves subject to institutional factors that involve their own welfare and that thereby corrode or distort the original forces. Human planning, or lack of it, and responses to novel situations in which past experience is not instructive, all contribute to the fortuitous aspects of causalities.

A brief recapitulation of causal factors may be helpful at this point: (1) an awareness of social forces and other elements that may be influencing the situation; (2) a "feel" for the comparative effective influence of various factors in the particular situation; (3) the vehicles or instrumentalities, such as institutions or organizations, whereby the social energies are to a greater or lesser extent expressed; (4) the specific channelizing of the energies, how and by whom, and the resistance to them; (5) the catalyst, the immediate source or trigger that sets events moving; (6) the timing and juxtaposition of factors at the time. Beyond these lie the dice of chance and the personalities involved. Not that historians necessarily formally analyze the evidence by these specific steps, but unless they have trained themselves to make some disciplined survey of the causal elements, their own explanations may lack credibility.

20

Luther Hits the Jackpot: The Individual

Medieval cathedrals still loom over their European cities as monuments to the spirit of an age, the achievement of many decades, sometimes centuries, of collective community labor. A closer inspection reveals the individual artist, emersed in the common organized effort, expressing himself or herself in the contours of a particular face, the posture of a figure in the cathedral, or the humor and horror of a gargoyle—the work of an individual leaving something of himself or herself for posterity. Though their names have vanished and their years have been forgotten, nevertheless the personalities call to us across the centuries, "Look, we *lived*. Our days were as vital as yours!"

Future generations presumably will know our achievements in technology, that they were the work of this age, but the names of individual contributors, the inventors, will seem unimportant. Even now, relatively few persons could list those people who developed the automobile, airplane, radio, television, and space vehicle. Nevertheless, these were devised by individuals, however much posterity may see impersonal forces and organization plans molding their actions.

History, after all, is populated by human beings. Episodes in the past may, in a sense, be compared to the cathedrals, the individual triumphs and tragedies being imprinted, not in stone, but on the moving scroll of historical time. Some have been imprinted deeply enough for them to be still visible in records, more are only vaguely apprehended, and most are now forever beyond perception. The defeat of the Armada or the Battle of Lepanto may appear in a textbook only as a happening, like a cathedral seen as a whole, but studied in detail the individual faces, and then personalities, reveal themselves in the fierce light of conflict. When seen through the microscope of detailed episode, the individual presence reaches us, insists on being seen, in the authentic, living vigor of a human being.

One record of human history can be found in the virtually endless lines of rulers that have governed—or been made to seem to govern by the powers behind the throne—in political states all over the world. Among others, they include the impressively lengthy line of Chinese emperors, over 330 in number, Egypt's approximately 230 pharaohs stretching for three millenniums, Roman Caesars and popes, and the caliphs of Islam. Although representing much more, they were each an individual in history, their human qualities convincingly demonstrated in the colorful array of nicknames bestowed by their contemporaries. A few earned the epithet of "the Great" or "the Good" or perhaps even that of a saint. Lines of rulers, which afflicted schoolchildren before concepts of teaching history changed, look less dreary when the nicknames are scrutinized: Edgar the Peaceful, Ethelred the Unready (or Redeless), Charles the Bold, Louis the Stammerer, Charles the Fat, Charles the Simple, Vsevolod Big-Nest (Big Family), Ivan the Terrible (more accurately, the Dread), Suleiman the Magnificent, Selim the Grim, Selim the Sot. The history of Romania, home of Dracula, might make exciting reading, considering the nicknames of some of its princes: the Terrible, the Lame, the Tyrant, the Bad, the Cossack, the Monk, the

Bad (another one), the Turk, the Disowned, the Impaler. Moslem rulers also bore descriptive names: Akbar (great), Mahdi (Messiah), Hakim (sage), Mansur (victorious).

Until recently, most history came compartmentalized in the separate reigns of successive kings, an arrangement accentuating the importance of the personal factor in historical processes. The end of a reign spelled the end of a chapter. "The king is dead—long live the king!" meant a new beginning, with all of its hopes, dreads, and uncertainties.

Anyone doing much reading in the histories of India, Iran, China, or Egypt learns to expect the consecutive appearance in a dynasty (though sometimes with one or two minor figures sandwiched in between) of the Founder, the Conqueror, and the Magnificent, followed, often, by a deterioration of quality. The Founder displays the Henry Tudor type of characteristics; the first successor, able to rely confidently on the newly entrenched establishment, has the power to impose the hegemony of the state on surrounding territories; while the resultant strong and competent government enables the third and spendthrift ruler to ornament the court, the capital, and to do sundry other public works. The Saul-David-Solomon succession illustrates this. Scarcely regular enough to be considered a uniformity in history, the tendency does raise the question of whether the obvious external circumstances surrounding each of the three leader types suffice to explain the sequence or whether biological inheritance of ability predisposes a dynasty to the regal equivalent of from shirt sleeves to shirt sleeves in three generations.

In cases when a ruling family produced a longer series of able leaders, the state tended to enjoy a period of unusual prominence. The Osmanlis, maintaining unusually high talents over an extended period of ten sultans, built up a small Anatolian emirate into one of the world's great historic empires. Enough strong men appeared among the Muscovite princes to enable them to become the rulers of a unified Russia. Sweden's Vasas produced several extraordinarily vigorous, if not always sensible, men, who made Sweden, despite its meager resources, into a great power. Similarly, the Hohenzollerns of Brandenburg-Prussia.

After the middle of the sixteenth century, the Osmanli quality dropped to a level often below mediocrity. An overextended empire? Institutional rigidity? Conditions in the rearing of Osmanli children? Genes? Or a combination thereof? Genes or circumstances at court may account for the cases of obviously abnormal psychology in the ruling tsarist family of Russia. Why did not the Vasas, who usually refused to miss the fun up in the front lines in battle, curb their warlike attributes? And why did the Hohenzollerns seem to produce an alternating succession of masculine extroverts and sensitive men of culture—genes, generation gap, or circumstances?

Historians sometimes ask what might have happened in history if a given historical figure had been different. Allan Nevins in *The Gateway to History* wondered about events if Philip of Macedon had had a son like Oliver Cromwell, or if Cromwell's son had shown the qualities of Alexander the Great. He also asks whether England would have passed under Norman rule anyway without the existence of William the Conqueror, and whether Saul of Tarsus, better known as St. Paul, made all the difference in the beginning of the rise of Christianity.

Suppose that Edward VI had been a healthy young man physically and had perpetuated the Tudor dynasty, thereby eliminating James I and Charles I, whose inability to understand the nature of English politics helped bring on the Puritan Revolution. Denis Brogan asks what would have happened if Louis XVI had died before he became king and if, instead, the much more intelligent brother, Louis XVIII, had become king in 1774. Trevor-Roper recalls the famous Macaulay query: would Ignatius Loyola, placed at Oxford, have led a secession from the Catholic church, while a John Wesley, located in Rome, have founded a society for the Roman church?

An historian must always wonder whether the personalities of Martin Luther and Leo X made up the decisive component in the outbreak of the Reformation. Did the break require a bullheaded, obstinate man of conviction, or were his other characteristics more important? (Luther himself believed that the Reformation would have come anyway, and that his "steady doctrine" prevented more radical and violent developments.) Place either

John Calvin or John Knox, equally stubborn men, at Wittenberg, and consider the possibilities. Was Luther truly a Great Man, or did he happen to be the one who, historically speaking, stepped up to the slot machine at the right moment just when the thingumajigs were going to release the jackpot?

Or Leo X. Did his personality determine his reaction to Luther's complaints, or would almost any occupant of the office at that particular moment have been obliged by institutional factors to make the same response? How much room for maneuver or personal decisions does a pope now have, considering the precedences of over 260 popes and many church councils, the established routine of the office, and the pressures inherent in an international institution with over half a billion members?

Many different personal considerations enter into the equation of any given historical situation, such as that of Luther and Leo X. The best formula is *the right individual in the right place at the right time*: an individual with the right attributes for a given situation, such as the military genius of Napoleon, the ability at organizing a rebellion of Lenin or Trotsky, or the capacity of a Prince Henry the Navigator at his "Cape Kennedy" for preparing the way for transoceanic navigation. Louis XVI apparently had the right individual as his first minister in Necker, then fired him. Barbara Tuchman quotes Bismarck, "We can only wait until we hear the footsteps of God in history and then leap forward and try to catch on to His coat-tails."

Many persons have died unnoticed because they were the right persons for a time that did not occur, possessed a genius not needed at the time by their communities. No doubt, numerous potential Pattons, MacArthurs, and Eisenhowers never had the opportunity to display their abilities. Artists and musicians have shriveled for lack of an appreciative audience. One may wonder about the possible career of the great black baseball player, Satchel Paige, given the opportunity to play in the major leagues in his youth.

George Kubler has suggested that artistic achievement is at least partly a matter of the right individual at the right time. He differentiates between six kinds of artists: precursors, *hommes à tout faire* (universal men), obsessives, evangelists, ruminatives, and rebels. These different types, he says, flourish best, fulfill their potential most completely, in circumstances encouraging the talents of their particular temperaments.

Do the times create the right person? Morton White quotes Thomas Carlyle, who believed in the Great Man: "Alas, we have known Times call loudly enough . . . but not find him when they called!" Whatever went wrong with the plans of General Kurt von Schleicher, who was supposed to stop Hitler's accession to power? The historian may wonder if a strong leader at the head of the League of Nations, instead of Joseph Avenol, in 1933-1940, could have helped to stem the drift toward another war.

Perhaps the circumstances nourish the full potentiality of some persons, summon forth their full strength, when, without the challenge, they would never have developed these abilities. American presidents have been said to either grow or swell. King Frederick William I of Prussia may have been a coarse, beer-swilling bully, but he also responded to the frontier-state imperative of Prussia by creating, for good or for bad, Prussian militarism and the Prussian bureaucracy. As such, he may well be historically more important than his son, Frederick the Great. An often-cited example of the human factor in history is the role of the Roman emperors; one after the other, from at least Diocletian to Theodosius, they "shouldered the burden of a tottering world" and thereby performed the nearly impossible job of holding the empire together longer.

Personalities themselves do make a great difference; William of Orange, Henry IV, Gustavus Adolphus, and Elizabeth I all possessed special qualities enlisting loyalty. The history of the British Isles might have been rather different if Mary Queen of Scots had not been such a female sort of female.

Knowing when to quit, recognizing the limitations of one's own power, is of the utmost importance. Martin Luther did, but not Boniface VIII. Bismarck knew when to stop, but not Charles XII, Napoleon, or Hitler, unless, in fact, the latter three had set forces in motion that made it impossible for them to halt. Sometimes, however, sheer persistence pays off. Churchill, after a glamorous start, spent a quarter of a century as the wrong person in the circumstances, then became exactly the right person at the right time in World War II. The younger Lincoln experienced a long series of defeats. Frederick the Great held on to the bitter end and kept his conquests. So did Hitler, but . . .

A leader needs to have a sense for what is possible, and must be a master at proper timing. Surrounded by many factors, such a person is rather like a poker player who receives successive hands in a card game as circumstances change and who must know when to play, when to pass, and when to hedge the bets.

Luck is of the essence. Charles X, grandfather of Charles XII, is said to have gambled against the odds on a water invasion route to Copenhagen staying frozen and thereby won the three southern provinces for Sweden. If the story is true, the margin between being a hero and a bum was as thin as a few inches of ice. Count Berchtold, foreign minister of Austria-Hungary in 1914, gambled on a small war with Serbia after the assassination of Archduke Francis Ferdinand and dislodged the landslide of World War I.

Occasionally, someone comes along who gains his successes by breaking all the rules of the game, as witness Alexander the Great, Napoleon, and Lenin. Were they great enough to see through the petty obstacles of the time or just lucky? Nikita Khrushchev became master of the Kremlin this way but seems to have lost power, basically, for the same reason. History is littered with the names of those who by breaking the rules only broke themselves.

Fame in history is a strange thing. Hardly anyone remembers the name of Colonel Richard Nicolls, conqueror of New York City (1664). Suppose Lincoln had *not* been assassinated in 1865 but that Woodrow Wilson had been killed in 1919. Or that Hitler had been killed by a bomb in the autumn of 1941 while at the peak of his conquests. Some say that John Kennedy's assassination elevated his fame beyond his achievements. Sometimes a leader makes fateful decisions and still remains a secondary historical figure. Elector Frederick the Wise of Saxony offered Luther the indispensable protection that ensured the early survival of the Protestant cause; earlier, he had refused the German imperial crown, thereby giving it to Charles V and unknowingly closing the door on alternative policies at the beginning of the Reformation.

The extent to which the individual may be a causal factor remains moot, but the Great Man sometimes turns out to be a political device, as, for instance, in the cult of Lenin, whose omnipresent portraits and statues in the Soviet Union compare closely to the large number of figures of Christ in a strongly Christian community. Lenin no doubt ranks as an event-making man but was scarcely *that* great. The reverse side of this practice can be seen in Khrushchev blaming Stalin personally for evils in the Soviet system, the usual method of freeing "the system" from blame by placing it on persons.

How, then, does the individual fit into the broad social forces discussed in the preceding chapters? Looked at from the standpoint of the determinist, human beings seem to be animate particles of the great impersonal forces, their attitudes and actions predetermined by the milieu. Adam Smith's "Economic Man" worked on his own behalf, serving his own interests, but the cumulative self-interest of the many also improved the material conditions of humanity. Karl Marx held that people "enter into necessary relations which are independent of their will" and thereby set up the class struggle, the intrinsic functioning of the capitalist system, and the seeds for its ultimate destruction. An historical figure achieves success by serving as an instrument for these forces, while one whose behavior is not in accord with the resultant powerful trends ineluctably experiences frustration and eventual failure.

Unfortunately for this inviting theory, the economically influenced person is also altogether likely to be simultaneously influenced by religious and institutional factors and especially by traditional beliefs that may not coincide with economic motives. Luther, as a Religious Man, was undoubtedly guided by a spiritual Hidden Hand, but several nonreligious factors greatly assisted Luther in hitting the jackpot, plus, of course, his own vigorous fist giving the machine some hard thumps to help matters along.

Beyond doubt, the fate of individuals greatly depends upon forces beyond their control. Compare the prospects of a person who went into railroading in 1850 or in 1950 or a Russian manufacturer in 1880 or in 1912. Often the successful person learns to recognize the essential environmental forces, then leads in the natural direction of development or, lacking this astuteness, just happens by luck to hit upon the right trail. It is worthwhile remembering the prefect in the Parisian mob during the 1848 disturbances who suddenly discovered that the crowd was moving off and exclaimed, "I am their leader. I must follow them."

Between the two extremes of determinism and free will, the extent to which individual leadership exercises influence in historical processes can only be a matter of opinion. Sir Lewis Namier, after many years of work on the subject of the history of eighteenth-century England, contended that he could find little evidence of rational planning; he believed purported foresight to be nothing more than patterns imposed by posterity's hindsight. In many historical situations, the participants are the victims of forces stronger than themselves. And yet Henry Kissinger, a noted historian long before he became secretary of state, once declared that though he formerly had thought of history as largely run by impersonal forces he had learned in his diplomatic career "the differences that the personalities make."

Anyone who has ever served as presiding officer of an organization will recognize the basic situation immediately, any source of action circumscribed by prevailing opinion, precedences of predecessors, factional dissidence, and a succession of problems not necessarily congenial to his or her talents. In such circumstances, he or she is seeing from within and experiencing a tiny model of what, writ large, has been the most customary position of the individual in history.

IV

MORE BASICS

21

Change and Continuity: The Gradualist Approach

"When it is not necessary to change, it is necessary not to change." In these words John Kennedy, a few years before becoming president, expressed one of the oldest feelings of mankind, for the necessity of change surely must have been greeted much more often with dread than with anticipation throughout the past. Humanity has quite regularly begun its marches into the future by facing backwards.

During the long ages of belief in a perfect beginning, that an existent order of things had been originally divinely ordained, any deviation was necessarily deemed to be a corruption rather than an improvement. It is therefore less paradoxical than it may seem that so many of the major alterations in history originated in purported *returns* to former conditions, as *restorations* of what allegedly had already been changed.

Martin Luther's Reformation began as an attempt to reform the church by removing medieval accretions to the supposedly original practices, and the Calvinists sought to restore their conception of what the early scriptural church had looked like. Moderates who resisted the Stuarts claimed to restore the traditional English polity as it had functioned before the Stuarts tried to strengthen the Crown at the expense of the parliament. Machiavelli conceived of change as a renewal or renovation, the typical attitude in the days before a belief in progress began to popularize change.

A desire to restore things as they were "in the days of King Edward the Confessor" characterized the mood in many other places than England. Chinese reforms often came disguised as a return to an ancient Golden Age. The name of Charlemagne stands at the head of the list of Holy Roman Emperors, although at the time the pope only crowned a Roman Emperor for the West, a restoration. Adolf Hitler imposed Nazism upon Germany, but during the first years many Germans rejoiced in the ostensible return to the German symbols and outlook that existed prior to the defeat in World War I and the Weimar Republic.

American rebels began their revolution by appealing to the rights of Englishmen consecrated in the seventeenth-century upheavals in the mother country. As C. Vann Woodward has stressed, American radicals have usually couched their arguments in favor of a return to a true faith. Once in power, rebels often will justify themselves by claiming to have restored original conditions; John Locke's defense of the Whigs in 1688 had been preceded in the Netherlands by Hugo Grotius's contention that the Dutch, by revolting against Spain, had preserved liberties deriving directly out of earlier popular assemblies.

Another form of change originates from within the framework of the permissible. Cultural or ethnic differences find expression within religious faiths through heresies, as in the aforementioned cases of the Shi'ites and Kharijites of Islam. Many a group of rebels sponsored a royal pretender, who, in the days of dynastic legitimacy, might advance a righteous claim to the throne and thereby carry his or her supporters to power. The German underground against the Nazis came largely from the people on the right, those with unimpeachable claim to nationalist orthodoxy, while the Hungarian revolt in 1956 started as a demand that true Communism be implemented.

Change behind the facade of the unchanging has been one of the most common forms. Anglicanism came to the English, allegiance to Rome ceased, and the monasteries were dissolved, but the local church, for the average person, did not seem much altered. Lutheranism started much the same way in Sweden, even to the point, as in England, of maintaining a claim to the apostolic succession of the bishops. Hirohito still presided over his country after World War II, even though the Americans imposed numerous other changes upon the Japanese. Augustus was Roman Emperor and so was Theodosius, but the office in the meantime had taken on the external attributes of an Oriental despotism. The British have been past masters at pouring new wine into old bottles, retaining older institutions and older formulas in order to make the new palatable. In the United States, a stable political system has provided a framework of continuity for unceasing economic and technological alterations over the past century and a half.

Very often an institution changes so gradually that a single generation may be unaware of its occurrence. The French still maintained the three medieval estates until 1789, though, as a result of an evolving society, they no longer made much sense. Earlier, the French monarchy had assiduously maintained a facade in the handling of the nobility. Far from abolishing the social class or the increasingly obsolete titles, the kings often compensated the aristocracy for loss of real power by, if anything, rendering their outward appearance even more magnificent. The nobles kept their social status, their prestige, their etiquette and manners (even elaborated upon them), while being assigned working positions in the state that often amounted to sinecures and mere ornaments of the court.

Columbus returned from the discovery of America to announce a familiar idea, that he had reached the Indies, then, when subsequent voyages destroyed this illusion, he still tried to crowd the new evidence into prevailing philosophic notions about the earth. Only after about twenty years could Europeans discard the preconceptions and accept the truth. Trevor-Roper writes of later medieval Europeans digesting antiquity "not in one great bite but in several nibbles interrupted by slow periods of silent digestion." The human mind in general seems to nudge slowly into a novelty, gradually accustoming itself to a change and only when the change seems no longer frighteningly strange being prepared to accept it.

Our own age, with its many-faceted, rapid alterations, has brought a profound revision in people's attitude toward change, still often fearing but also demanding, it. The new has become desirable because it is presumed to be better. Politicians, caught between rhetoric and practicality, frequently contrive clever optical illusions, publicly working for drastic changes while vigorously applying the legislative brakes in private. French politics in the Third and Fourth Republics seemed to operate on two levels, one conservative and the other, the rhetorical, full of radical clichés. Socialism emerged as the ancient state paternalism in new dress; often new names are put to old practices, which are then proclaimed to be change.

Rapid alterations in the past seemed most likely to occur in areas where traditional behavior had not yet been established. Quite possibly, the Industrial Revolution picked up momentum in England first, rather than in France, primarily because fewer regulations existed or, at least, had ceased to be rigorously enforced. That is, new possibilities opened up in an area relatively unfettered by existing regulations or entrenched precedences. Americans, until recent decades not as restrained by older traditions and bureaucratic regulations as the Europeans, outpaced the twentieth-century world in technological development. Viewed against the earlier slow pace, modern mass media and forms of transportation evolved with amazing speed because of the freedom to improvise and experiment.

Politically, in both the United States and the United Kingdom developments have tended to go through a few years of accelerated change followed by periods of consolidation and

greater continuity. For various reasons of economic circumstances, temperament, or tradition, their citizens have lined up on
the side of change or continuity in any given situation, thereby
producing a flexible equilibrium. Eventually, the gradual growth
and decline of specific social groups in the community have
altered the equilibrium, or other factors have caused a shift in
attitudes in some of these groups. Special crucial events, like the
Great Depression or the black revolution, may provide the catalyst for the onset of a new period of unusual change. In each case,
those advocating reform have prevailed for a time after the breakthrough, then, as dissatisfied interests were placated and others
became frightened at threats to their welfare, the equilibrium
swung back in the direction of conserving that which was good in
the existing society.

A period of notable change has occurred in the United States
about once in each generation, approximately every thirty years,
while in Great Britain the cycle seems to stretch over about forty
years. Within a framework of continuity in which alterations are
constantly underway, the processes of change periodically attain
unusual potency and momentum, then after a few years subside.
Transitional evolution eases the sufferings of change, makes it
possible for people to absorb the necessary alterations one step at
a time, and thereby avoids the greater ordeals of cataclysmic
upheavals.

Perhaps the politics of the Anglo-American countries have
mirrored with special faithfulness a natural sequence in historical
change and continuity, their political framework allowing the
social forces in the modern community to express themselves
most faithfully. Perhaps, too, a belief that this is the natural order
of things has itself helped to mold the habitual practices in
Anglo-American democracy. This specific cycle, however, should
not be universalized into an historical political uniformity. It
seems to fit the Anglo-American countries reasonably well, an
area in time and space where certain approximate social forces in
common have shared in molding the shapes of history. Institutional factors associated with the state and church long remained
weaker than those on the continent of Europe. Furthermore,
relative freedom from *external* interference may have rendered

the cycle atypical, that is, the sequence in the cycle functioned with unusual freedom because it was not seriously distorted or shattered by outside intervention.

As nineteenth-century historians became increasingly aware of the accelerating incidence of change in their communities, they began to articulate the shapes of time in terms of gradual evolution. Within the flow of time, historical forms were assumed to be in a state of perpetual transition. British political institutions have offered classic illustrations of this so-called gradualist approach.

Both the English parliament and the cabinet system emerged, unplanned, out of a set of molding circumstances. Parliament came into existence with the appearance of a House of Commons alongside the older assembly of nobles and high prelates. Over a period of about fifty years in the first half of the fourteenth century, many of the characteristic features of these institutions assumed enduring forms, some adapted from earlier practices and some improvised out of necessity. Relations between parliament and king were gradually regulated as a succession of conflicts forced more specific definitions of their respective prerogatives, but the continuity of practices derived more from the sanction of prevailing habits than from statutory regulations.

Great Britain's cabinet system also emerged by a process of trial and error, by a combination of preserved traditions and improvisations. This sequence arose, primarily, out of the need for a central directorate, responsive to Parliament, in a period of "weak" rulers. It, too, developed rapidly for a few decades, then subsequently much more slowly. Later still, the British evolved the Commonwealth out of their empire and, in a sense, also handled the decline and fall of their own world empire in the same way. British leaders had consciously adopted the gradualist approach as the one best conforming to and most effective for contending with the realities of their community.

These examples deal with the simple linear evolution of single phenomena. Manifestly, any line of evolution is likely to produce diverging forms or a succession of these until the effect is like that of a family tree, numerous related forms branching off into increasingly varied characteristics. Historical explanation involves a knowledge of the genetic background of the subject in question, how it evolved from its origins through a sequence of shapes to its present form, as well as its relationship to kindred, divergent forms.

A language student soon becomes aware that Latin, French, Spanish, and Italian share many words in common and that a knowledge of one of them expedites the learning of others. Similarly, English, German, Dutch, and the Scandinavian languages possess a large number of shared words. Knowing one Slavic language automatically provides some working vocabulary in the others. Occasional words also recognizably recur in all three groups of languages: "no," "non," "nein," "nej," and "nyet," though in Greek "nai" means "yes." A sprinkling of related words survive, in fact, all the way across Eurasia to the borders of Burma.

For the curious, these fragments out of a cross section of many modern languages may pose a great mystery, the pervasive presence in the contemporary world of something that cannot be explained in terms of today's contours. About two hundred years ago, scholars intrigued by these relationships began searching for explanations and in doing so found the answers in the origins and the "becoming" of things as they are today. In their quest, they helped to develop the conceptual tools of gradual change, evolution, and the family tree of relationships.

According to one commonly accepted theory now, the ancestral Indo-European language, or a group of them, was being spoken five millenniums ago somewhere in the steppe region near the borders of Europe and Asia, perhaps north of the Caucasus. Another theory has these languages originating on the plains of central Europe. Whatever the case, during the following 1,500 years this group of languages was carried eastward by invaders of the Middle East, Iran, and India, as well as west and south over much of Europe. Henceforth, the new languages evolved over the centuries, ramifying into numerous separate tongues by altered pronunciations and by the borrowing of words from the vanishing local vocabularies.

Out of this long evolution and divergence emerged the family tree of the Indo-European languages, the primary subdivisions being such groups as the Romance, Germanic, and Slavic, plus the Celtic, Greek, and others. Most of these have subdivided again into the present national languages, which, in turn, have proliferated into a number of regional dialects. Some major branches, like the Hittite, vanished long ago; others, the once important Scythian group of the Iranian languages for example, scarcely survive. Lithuanian and the priestly Sanskrit of India seem to deviate the least from the ancestral core of the family of languages. The evolutionary process of divergence continued, at least until the coming of radio and television. English, planted overseas, began to send out offshoots. An American student learning Spanish as spoken in Mexico will be startled by the Spaniards spitting out "th's" in Madrid, if learning German will be nonplused with the Barvarian of a Munich *Bierstube,* or may even encounter difficulties with English in some quarters of the British Isles.

In the perceived development of the family tree of Indo-European languages lie qualities to please the aesthetic sense of a true gradualist: unplanned, spontaneous evolution flowing through the sweeps of time and a continual slow movement of transformation being molded by varying sets of circumstances. Only through a process of becoming and the resultant genealogy of changing forms can the present-day relationships among the languages be fully understood.

A family tree of the churches duplicates the phenomenon, wide diversities amidst the fundamental kindred similarities. The early medieval church, by reason of difficulties of communication, varying languages, and doctrinal differences, slowly diverged into groups looking, respectively, to Rome (Catholic), Constantinople (Orthodox), Antioch (Eastern), and Alexandria (Coptic). A fifth, the Celtic, or Irish, was snuffed out, but several other smaller offshoots survived in the Middle East. A second series of branches appeared in the Reformation period out of the Roman Catholic: the Anglican; the Lutheran; the Reformed, or Calvinist; and the so-called Radical churches. The latter three quickly subdivided into national or doctrinal groups, while the Methodists eventually sprang from the Anglican. In time, the Orthodox divided into national churches, and the Christians of

Ethiopia separated from the Coptic of Alexandria. Finally, a whole series of modern branches sprouted out of Protestantism, especially in the United States and England.

Various differences in doctrine, ritual, vestments, church edifices, Holy Communion, baptism, and governance can of course be explained by means of the concepts determining the practices. However, the full picture emerges only against the historical background of origins and reasons for divergence, the sources for modifications, adaptations to circumstances, and responses to obstructions; any living institution bears forevermore the residual imprints of derivation and formative experiences. Explanation through the tracing of genetic relationships is an inherent part of historical-mindedness.

22

Grooves of Habit:
Forces of Tradition

The earliest known written records on the continent of Europe, dating from about 1200 B.C. were uncovered at Pylos in the Peloponnesus shortly before World War II. These clay tablets mostly contain inventories of wheat and barley, olive oil, spices, wine, farm animals, furniture, and military equipment, plus listings of the working personnel of the kingdom. This is the fresh rosy dawn of European civilization in the Heroic Age of the Greeks, the era of Agamemnon, Helen of Troy, and Achilles, and who are in the center of the stage as the curtain goes up on recorded European history? Some grubby bureaucrats!

Noticeably, too, the tillers of the soil already seem to be second-class citizens, visible mainly in the form of government statistics. Bureaucrats and peasants, along with those keepers of the traditional, the clergy—perhaps their unexciting presence, customarily on the side of continuity, helps to explain a strong partisanship on behalf of change in our own century.

Many individuals now tend to be strongly in favor of either

stability or innovations, predisposed to prefer in various matters one or the other. As noted in connection with the Anglo-American political cycle, the difference of opinion between advocates of reform and advocates of the status quo forms a significant element in recent historical processes. A more conservative person, the strong believer in continuity, fears change, alarmed, perhaps with reason, that his or her security and niche in the community will be jeopardized. Modifying the rules of the game is always risky. Few communities in the past possessed enough material resources for everyone, and those people who did gain an advantage concentrated on retaining it. Surrounded by the poor, and, seeing only too well the misery of poverty, they defended their possessions, using tradition to enshrine privileged positions and the status quo.

As for the abjectly poor, too busy scrounging for a mere living to join in any marching battalions of rebels, their attitudes have usually been the despair of advocates of reform or rebellion. Hoffer has written of the "conservatism of the destitute," who live in too much "awe" of the world to dare risk change and whose "dangerous life" offers too thin a margin of safety to gamble on anything that might upset familiar ways of feeding their families.

Conservatives of True Believer intensity may become virtually pathological in their belief that any tampering with society will bring the landslide of revolution. Understanding neither the nature of nor the necessity for continual adjustments in the community, they will caricaturize advocates of reform in the most extreme terms. A rigid mind of this kind—and most minds, be it remembered, were rigid in this sense throughout most of the past—will regard change as wicked, or heretical, or foreign, or revolutionary, depending upon the time and place.

Proponents of change run all the way from inventors or artists trying to get a novel creation accepted to those obsessed by a nihilist passion for destruction. Some of them do not necessarily occupy a superior moral position, for their reforms may be merely calculated, recognized or not, to tilt the power in their own favor at the expense of the conservatives. More extreme believers consider change as good in itself, just as extreme conservatives feel the same way about the status quo, neither side concerning itself much with specific problems or practical measures. Reformers, too, will caricaturize their opponents and misunderstand worthwhile reasons for resistance to certain reforms. Advocates of innovations and stability all too often close off debate by consigning each other to the Outer Darkness. Both sides thus suffer from the same weakness, may be equally self-centered, and thereby weaken their own causes by not understanding the interacting role of change and continuity in historical processes.

Reformers often underestimate the power of the will to continuity, and, failing to make allowances for the fears of their opponents, advocates of worthwhile alterations may build up sufficient irrational resistance in their opponents to frustrate their own plans. Wrenching changes leave large elements of the people bewildered, yearning for a return to continuity and a healing of wounds. After the Puritan and French Revolutions came Restoration periods. The Russian Revolution of 1917 was followed after a time by a return to traditional Russian nationalism and an essentially hierarchical society. An overly abrupt overthrow of the German monarchical system in 1918 left part of the populace unreconciled and the more ready to delight, at first, in Hitlerian ceremony and militarism. Nostalgia for the good old days can still be a potent force, as witness the long popularity of "Forsythe Saga" or "Bonanza" on television.

French history over the past two hundred years has been strongly influenced by the alternating domination of advocates of change or of continuity. The French Revolution set a "pendulum" swinging left and right, between periods of radicalism and conservatism in which the pendulum tended to swing too far. By contrast, traditions among the British have alleviated fear of change, eased the transitions by their reassuring impression of solidity. Soon the changes are themselves incorporated into the body of traditions in the same way that dissident groups, attaining a share of power, undergo absorption into the establishment. Used in this sense, traditions serve as a bridge to the future.

Watching a pope, accompanied by the papal guard, being borne into St. Peter's Cathedral on a litter, the spectator senses almost palpably the living existence of something far greater in dimension than the life-term of an individual. The pageant touches a deep instinctive chord, a poignant awareness of possessing a property owned by everyone, regardless of religious background. Here is the embodiment of one of humanity's supreme achievements, the nearly sixty generations of the Christian experience, and one of the bedrocks in the ceaseless, bewildering flux of happenings. Whether found at St. Peter's, the Wailing Wall in Jerusalem, the Blue Mosque in Istanbul, or an oriental temple, an immemorial spectacle evokes an exalted veneration for the universal saga.

This is what tradition, collective folk memory, is all about, a sense of an added dimension, a taming and yet inspiring conviction of being a vital part of something far greater than oneself. The world of tradition and accompanying institutions exists on a different time scale than the life-span of the human being. The Haggia Sophia in Istanbul, though no longer used as a cathedral, has stood for forty-five generations, and the French state, counting from Clovis, dates back equally far. When the Israelites left Egypt, the pharaohs had already governed their people for a period of time as long as the period from the fall of Rome up until now.

The dimensions of the traditional can be compared to an individual walking in Manhattan, the street level measureable by the contemporary scale but the bulking skyscrapers the equivalent of the time dimensions of states and institutions still existing. In this sense, we have always walked in streets surrounded by huge buildings—human stature dwarfed by greater dimensions. Tradition is not simply something out of the past; it forms a conspicuously tangible part of the environment. Earlier generations had no great preoccupation with Now, the line between past and present being virtually irrelevant, and in a very real sense they were living in their own past.

Would the Jews, Greeks, and Armenians have survived so long without rich tradition? Did the memory of earlier achievements spur their repeated rejuvenation and the new flowerings of their peoples? A viable minority will carefully maintain special traditions, and the more fiercely it is threatened, the more vigorously it will defend its own heritage. Colonies transplanted to other lands have sometimes tended to adhere rigidly to traditions brought with them to a point where, by comparison with the traditions of the original homeland, these transplanted traditions have become archaic. Traditions help support cohesion and morale within the circle of an elite, a loss of faith usually being considered a sign that the dominant group is losing its will to rule. A general erosion of prevailing values and beliefs within a community may well portend a major upheaval.

A collective instinct for survival spurs the maintenance of traditions long after they seemingly lose relevance. The Yankee farmer of New England remained a model for industrial America, and Old Testament prophets extolled the virtues of the shepherd in the hills rather than those of the farmer or town merchant. The heroic legends of the Mycenaean Hellenes continued to be told in the later urban era of Greece, and the industrializing Japanese still cherished the warrior samurai.

Peasants were great conservators of tradition. True peasants in general reverenced the land and nature, regarded work on the land as a higher calling than commerce. Their way of life made experimentation dangerous; always at the mercy of the weather, the peasants required their own lore about nature and traditional practices in order to keep on good terms with whatever higher spirits governed the growing of their crops. Agrarian circumstances demanded stability, which in turn meant adherence to custom and communal routine, as well as to a peaceful, ordered society. Peasants usually did not question the superior position of rural overlords as long as they performed their services properly and humanely.

Robert Redfield writes that the peasant community in itself was "incomplete," needed ties with town life, from which came the greater cultural traditions of civilization; these were mixed with local memories and tales, transmitted orally from generation to generation and in which the peasants took pride. In addition to the fellowship of the nearest town marketplace, the priest provided ties with centers of culture; more recently, other urban figures have appeared, the teacher and the lawyer, the omnipresent tax collector and the bureaucrat.

Peasant folk were not without recourse against injustice.

Strong family ties, much more far-reaching than those in modern cities, helped to maintain a network of personal relationships among the villagers of a district. Given a harsh overlord, peasants were often masters at noncooperation. Peasant uprisings, which their lack of leadership, organization, and effective arms doomed to failure, punctuate periods of general unrest.

Within the framework of politics, they have usually been considered conservative and tradition-bound. More accurately, people on the land were genuinely *different*, did not fit historical shapes or political stereotypes devised in the cities, and were themselves usually politically indifferent within that context. The inhabitants of the countryside, in our general histories, remain virtually mute, though they must make up at least four-fifths of the populace throughout the ages of recorded history. They did not write history, rarely recorded their doings, and therefore appear mostly as seen through the eyes of city people and clergy. One suspects a gross misunderstanding in both their frequent depiction as ignorant louts and in their occasional portrayal as the noble savage by writers and political thinkers. (After all, most of our ancestors must have been tillers of the soil.) Lynn White, writing about the medieval peasant, comments that such a person was normally "a lively and enterprising fellow, quite unlike the tragic caricature of combined brutishness and abused virtue." At their best, they were practical people, prudent, sober, and pious.

Only fairly recently have historians begun to explore the peasant past in depth, and most generalizations about them as yet are premature. Much more remains to be worked into the context of general history: differences among peasantries of different regions; diffusion of plants and animals in local variations; the coming of technological innovations; various modes of landholding, serfdom, taxes, and corvées; and, in the more immediate past, capitalist influences, emigration to cities or overseas, and peasant political parties.

Those scribes who were attending to the business of King Neleus and King Nestor at Pylos undoubtedly had numerous predecessors elsewhere. When they were building Cheop's pyramid in Egypt nearly five millenniums ago, someone must have been standing there counting the stone blocks one by one, as well as the bread, radishes, and onions for the workers. And when the genius in Erech (maybe) devised the first wheel and triumphantly paraded the first wagon, heaped high with manure for the fields, down Zalul-Nebo-Marduk Boulevard, some bureaucrat probably came pelting down from the ziggurat tower to clamor that the building regulations for sledges had been violated. (Had there already been ziggurat towers, that is!) The lineal descent of bureaucrats starts, at least, with the beginnings of recorded history and continues, though not quite unbroken, to the friendly campus registrar's office.

Tradition and continuity serve the convenience of government best. Once a routine has worn deep the grooves of institutional habit, officials can pursue their jobs with the least anxiety. Unpredictable change can be vastly upsetting for officialdom as new problems must be coped with and new routines devised. Bureaucracies are the great vehicles of continuity, and as such it must be seriously doubted that any of the great empires of the past could have survived without the stiffening backbone of minor officialdom. A major element in enforcing conformity, officials quashed disorders, incipient revolts, bright ideas, and contrary-minded mavericks; while stifling elements deemed dangerous to the community (or themselves), they also frequently frustrated creative thought, original ways of doing things, and the aberrant conduct of genius.

It need not be so. Frederick William I by setting up the first large-scale bureaucracy of the modern national monarchies thereby obtained the means for a series of drastic changes in the direction of centralization. His well-trained officials functioned like clockwork and with the discipline of an army. In our own century, bureaucracies have also been used as instrumentalities for enforcing changes decided upon by the government.

Strong rulers can do this—temporarily. Then the routine sets in. Clerks in the lower bureaucracy, afraid of making mistakes, adhere to the letter of the regulations and limit themselves to typical ritualistic behavior, while, isolated from the reality of the living world, they try to reorder that world in accordance with office procedures. The mind of the bureaucrat conflicts with other social forces in history, snuffing out weaker forces for change, and more vital forces take weird and contorted forms in evading the network of intricate regulations. Filtered through a strong bureaucracy, processes of change and continuity undergo distortion with the piecemeal changes, relatively spontaneous alterations as problems occur, becoming less likely. When reform does come, it is apt to be a sweeping convulsion, aimed more at scapegoat personnel and the current structure of a given bureaucracy than at the problems demanding solution. Eras of stability tend to last longer and produce fewer minor innovations, whereas times of change are apt to be violent and more upsetting to all elements in the community.

Though assigning the bureaucracy, with cheerful malice, to the Outer Darkness, a final grudging admission must be added, that the modern community could not function without this machinery of officialdom. Its great fault lies in being peculiarly prone to excesses of its own virtues, and society has never learned how to use this necessary tool without being blighted by its negative compulsions. Individuals who do not understand the workings of bureaucracy will be forever bewildered by certain things that keep happening to them.

Finally, lest we overlook somebody of unexcelled importance, there are the mothers and grandmothers of the human race. Through the ages they have watched their menfolk, overgrown boys with hunting-band hormones still popping, trailing off in martial array intent on making masculine history, war or rebellion, and generally succeeding in creating mostly havoc, suffering, and woe. Mothers, anxious for the welfare of their families, and grandmothers, compulsively knitting together the generations, have usually prayed, oftentimes in vain, for the security of a peaceful and ordered society.

23

A Brighter, Immaterial Sphere: Ideas

A student may at one time or another have drawn a book out of the library and found that a preceding user had repeatedly underlined sentences in it as presumably containing the high points of the account. Perhaps an alert reader may also have noticed that the penciled thoughts by no means corresponded to the author's own direction of argument and that in fact this knavish despoiler of public property had left only an indication of his or her own ideas as they appeared in this book.

Ideas are difficult to handle. Even the idea of ideas seems blurred, ranging from logical, conceptual statements of relationships to amorphous thoughts reflecting little more than feelings or personality drives. The imperious presence of a dogma in the mind, the careful, measured weaving of a deductive statement, the glib repetition of half-understood clichés, all of these cohabit the realm of ideas. They do not usually come singly; a number of them tend to be associated together in the mind, to appear in clusters with perhaps one dominant insight at their core.

Students perhaps most usually identify ideas with the concise, distilled summary of someone's philosophy as found in textbooks and encyclopedia articles, "starved and false image[s]" (Barzun and Graff) conveyed by a few explanatory sentences. Or perhaps they associate them with the deductive and inductive thinking taught in a class in logic. Presumably, they possess conceptual content and serve as images or a sort of mental shorthand of reality. Though scientists have gone to great pains to create forms of ideas conveying precisely the same meanings to all minds, they otherwise come alloyed with varying shades of meaning for different people.

In general, in contrast to the memorization of textbook learning, we actually understand an idea only by experiencing it, that is, by coming into personal contact with circumstances like those out of which the idea sprang. It may be an insight stimulated by everyday life or the vicarious experience of movies, television, or a novel, but, unless we are content to leave it as a string of words, we must enter into an idea, make ourselves at home there, and become familiar with its cluster of associations. An idea in a book that already contains meaning for the reader instantly takes on life. An individual tends to seize upon those that express his or her own mood and circumstances and add a personal flavor to them, while being aware of other ideas only as opaque book learning or perhaps as someone else's wrongheaded notions, without grasping their cogent significance.

Ideas become our own property as we read or hear them articulated in a form that agrees with our own experiences or the experiences of those we trust. Our particular set of cherished insights may seem to identify us and to prove our superiority over those of less discernment. The human mind is sadly limited; we all tend to have cookie-cutter mentalities that carve out of actuality only those shapes that coincide with our prepossessions. A group of insights may become so convincing that we universalize them, feel that all rational, righteous individuals must surely share these illuminations. Sometimes these insights grip us so compulsively that we turn into fanatics, True Believers, and reject any contrary evidence. Possessing ideas, we are then possessed by them.

Skill in the handling of thought processes requires much practice. Most of us are strangers in the field of ideas, clumsy and awkward in their usage, and are therefore obliged to endow them with dogmatic texture. A budding student intellectual may experience a rapture, like first love or a religious conversion, in his or her first encounter with a burst of illuminating insights. They seem sacred, compelling in their conviction of rightness, a veritable philosopher's stone in ideas that provides the golden security of truth. Nevertheless, this partakes of ideological alchemy, the reverse of the practice of the mature thinker, who automatically assumes that any broad proposition can only be tentative, must be modified and then modified again. To cling to an initial set of ideas for any length of time reveals an intellectual novice and closes the mind to the natural succession of illuminating insights through which comes greater wisdom. The owner of many ideas is possessed by none.

Ordinary people, writes Lukacs, believe ideas to be in a "brighter, fragile, immaterial sphere" in an ascending hierarchy of truth. Used in political ideologies, they may also reduce human beings to labels or send them to crematoriums. Understanding the role of ideas must surely be the most difficult in all of the historical processes, but by knowing how our own minds work we may come closer to a comprehension of their place in history.

The role of ideas has been subject to the customary elementary forms of handling, and historians themselves must often out of necessity engage in deliberate oversimplifications. Sometimes the history of ideas has been written by the "pack rat" method, an outline of thinkers, titles of books, and "starved and false images" of insights; the organization is likely to be chronological and by country. Processes of change and continuity may be shown only on the crudest level as little more than a continuing accumulation of knowledge and ideas, an approach approximating the chronicles version of political history.

Perhaps the Great Man theme makes more sense here than in most other areas, inasmuch as the creative ability of the genius must surely be a major ingredient in any history of ideas. Nevertheless, any genius must articulate the viewpoint of his or her age or of an age aborning, otherwise the message and the talents go unrecognized. To strip a great individual of contemporary fellow thinkers and the spirit of the times is to mistake the towering peak for the whole mountain range of which it is a part.

Perils of oversimplification abound in the tracing of the story of a Great Idea. To assume an idea to be an autonomous entity, a thing in itself, cramps its real nature, and the genealogy of descent from one thinker to another does not present all of the picture. An idea derives originally out of an historical situation as a response to specific circumstances and may be partially shaped by contemporary antagonistic concepts as well as by other obstructions to its acceptance. Any dominant concept comes imbedded in whole congeries of ideas and notions; to describe the triumphant march of a Great Idea, if not carefully done, can be the equivalent of regarding a "cult of progress" story as complete history.

The Master and Disciples stereotype is an institutional form of history used by the followers of a movement. Shorn of much of the intellectual context and many of the currents of the time, the master stands forth as the fount of truth from which through the disciples, the uncorrupted dogma comes down to its present custodians and to the devoted, who faithfully sacrifice for the cause. Outside of the fold wander the heretics, who have fallen into error, and the benighted who dwell in the Outer Darkness.

Present-mindedness and moralizing tend to figure largely in elementary handling of ideas. Most of us are quite literally prisoners of our contemporary intellectual world, translating earlier ideas into versions recognizable now. We gratefully seize upon seemingly familiar insights in a cluster of ideas, thereby distorting the emphasis and tending to judge past ideas according to present beliefs. Naturally, our generation needs to know the origins of the currently prevailing thoughts. In so doing, however, the cult of progress often insidiously tempts us into searching out the genesis of the present "advanced" beliefs, as minted by a great person or by a great cause. This closes the mind to what actually was going on at the time, obscures an idea's evocative and compulsive character for its own contemporaries, and many of the concepts of history consequently remain foreign to us. On the contrary, someone, great or not, whose ideas happen to approximate current beliefs wins attention, or an earlier thinker gains repute now because current developments spotlight one segment of his or her work, not necessarily that which he or she cherished most.

The direct influence of ideas on events can easily be exaggerated. To assume that ideas alone can persuade anyone, except a True Believer and presumably some intellectuals, to a certain course seems naïve. To assert that a series of speeches actually moves events, without first considering the other historical processes at work, is equally naïve, the equivalent of attributing an episode to a monocausal economic factor or a great person. Profound changes, declared Butterfield, are not necessarily achieved by the use of logical arguments. Namier derided the supposed effectiveness of ideas in history. Louis Gottschalk tentatively concluded from his extensive studies that ideas are "products rather than producers," more effect than cause in their age.

Not that the debate over the influence of ideas has been this definitely resolved, for it is difficult to imagine any sort of human activity without the presence of ideas. Persuasion may be the key that unlocks the door to action but only if the key happens to fit that particular lock, the existing circumstances of that moment. Ideas obviously bind human minds together and make collective action possible. They permit the setting up of goals and act as guides and spurs for the individual, however much intentions may be obstructed or distracted in actual practice. At the least, an accurate evaluation must consider the interaction of ideas and circumstances—human beings trying to reproduce faithfully the images of actuality in their thoughts while also striving to reshape reality in accordance with their vision.

To deny the long-term influence of the world's great religions, in their intellectual content, would surely be preposterous, as would any glossing over of the impact of nationalism, the cult of progress, the concept of evolution, and the beliefs of liberalism. Many a debate has raged over the specific role of ideas in historical processes. Hippolyte A. Taine argued that the ideas of the philosophes caused the French Revolution and in the process warped French development irredeemably. Gerhard Ritter roundly maintains that the French revolutionary leaders copied Rome, England, and the United States, did not understand any of them, and that France never recovered from the damage. The outmoded ideas of Three Estates, an "inherited conceptual scheme" (Franklin Ford), were still afloat for some time after the French Revolution. A chapter in itself are the influences of Marxism, thoroughly nineteenth century in origin and spirit but applied to a number of societies not basically nineteenth century in nature at all.

Should the principal bearers of ideas, the intellectuals, be considered a distinctive group in history, the equivalent of other groups that influence events as they serve their own interests? Through their mastery of the "brighter, fragile, immaterial sphere," they have undoubtedly always known how to defend themselves and exercise leadership, especially if their ranks be broadened to include the intelligentsia, the rank and file of the clergy, journalists, teachers, and bureaucrats.

The printing press opened up new scope for their talents, and by the eighteenth century the intellectuals, in a secular noninstitutional form, had become an important historical force in their own right. New means of communication in the present century, as well as the growth of schools of higher learning, have vastly expanded their opportunities. Most intellectuals would very likely reject the notion that they constitute a social group, preferring to see themselves as speakers for various sectors of the community; some tend to envision themselves as superior observers of the situation and therefore as more clearsighted and objective. Once essentially the bearers of tradition, intellectuals today would most likely consider their role as being one of stimulating society, of fermenting changes and helping the community make necessary adjustments to changing circumstances. Their most congenial role undoubtedly is that of a Victor Hugo or a Boris Pasternak, as a beacon of light shining over dark tyranny. They are also apt, according to the pungent comment of Bernard Norling, ". . . to assume that the nonintellectual masses are heavily influenced by the cerebrations of more intellectual types" who try to lead humanity to their own kind of utopia.

Eric Hoffer, quoted repeatedly in these pages because of his contrary opinions, has expressed a far less flattering view of their role and of their class interests. In his *Ordeal of Change,* he charges that "on the whole" the intellectuals, disdaining the practical and useful, as mandarins, scribes, and bureaucrats, have often helped to stifle worthwhile changes. In societies dominated by intellectuals, traders perform their work as "a sort of subversive activity," scorned and closely supervised; in fact, he claims, scribes tend to regulate and dominate the traders off the face of the earth. Hoffer attributes the amazing American economic achievement primarily to the fortuity that for the first time in history a people enjoyed the freedom to develop its physical resources without strangling controls being imposed by the intellectuals. Others have added the accusation, in recent years, that intellectuals tend to be chronically alienated from their societies, regardless of the nature of the community and the political system in which they live.

24

From Megaliths to Printing Press: The Diffusion of Ideas

Diffusion, as an historical process, has long offered spectacular opportunities for the mythmakers at the street level. In the nineteenth century, attempts were made to trace worldwide cultural traits to a single origin in the Egypt of the pyramids, and the wanderings of the seemingly ubiquitous ten lost tribes of Israel were traced to some astonishing places. Virtual cults emerged espousing the land of Mu and the sunken continent of Atlantis as sources for the beginnings of the early historic civilizations. Space travel, of course, has opened up another exciting vista, the diffusion of civilization by means of extraterrestrial beings in flying saucers.

Based on more sober factual evidence, artifacts, domesticated animals and plants, and goods of various kinds were obviously being diffused long before the beginnings of recorded history. Early contacts seem to have occurred between the hydraulic civilizations of the Nile, the Tigris-Euphrates, the Indus, and China, but the extensive irrigation works of the Andes must surely have had an independent origin. One of the most bitter arguments in the whole field of history has long raged between those who believe that the American Indian developed in isolation from overseas influences and others who deduce from some similarities that diffusion was also involved even here. Radiocarbon dating of the widespread megalithic structures along the Atlantic coast of Europe set off another heated debate in the late 1960s. Such structures, long assumed to have been stimulated by copying the stone constructions of the Mediterranean area, now appear to antedate these presumed models, hence the megalithic edifices must have been invented locally. (Unless, indeed, the technique of radiocarbon dating is still faulty.) Is it possible that such a practice developed quite naturally and independently in Western Europe, the Mediterranean, Polynesia, and the Americas when Neolithic peoples reached a certain stage of development? Or the practice of heaping up earth mounds, exemplified by the American Moundbuilders, found in many parts of the world?

To talk only about diffusion is to focus on one aspect of a larger process. The cultural seed must find suitable soil in which to germinate and grow. Whether an innovation originates by diffusion from somewhere else or by independent invention in that society may be less crucial than whether the local circumstances are ready for the adoption and usage of that particular novelty. Whatever its source and original shape, an innovation will speedily be molded by its environmental influences.

Ideas diffused into a milieu somewhat different from the place of origin usually undergo subtle shifts of meaning, being adapted to the new environment in order to be accepted. Novel ideas undergoing large-scale intellectual diffusion can best be absorbed in terms of what is already there, that is, the new concepts can be most easily understood by blending them with ideas already known; in the process, the nuances or even, sometimes, the basic meaning changes.

Luther's ideas, diffused to other regions, soon meant many things to many people. Renaissance art north of the Alps changed greatly in character. French ideas of the Enlightenment that were accepted in Germany tended to become a compromise between the old and the new, *reason,* for instance, sometimes looking suspiciously (at least to this observer) like an Enlightenment word for the older Lutheran justification by faith! Islam underwent changes in Iran, and the peoples of Southeast Asia, greatly influenced by both India and China, altered their cultural imports until they seemed virtually indigenous. Russian revolutionaries accepted Marxism and continued to use its terminology while simultaneously permeating this ideology with specifically Russian and Russian nihilist traits. Marxist ideas, diffused to various communities, diverged into Social Democracy, Russian Communism, Maoism, and Titoism, to mention only the four most conspicuous versions.

The spread of ideas accelerated rapidly and pervasively once the possibilities of the printing press began to be understood. Nevertheless, the amount of diffusion prior to this in the Middle Ages should not be underestimated. University professors and students wandering from school to school, clergy being transferred from one place to another, the incessant traveling of large numbers of pilgrims, the movements of merchants, the Crusaders, the missionaries who carried Christianity to Germanic and Slavic Europe—the list of the carriers of ideas is a long one. (Nor is the Master and Disciples motif as crass a caricature when applied to ancient times.) An earlier example of "brain drain" occurred when many learned individuals migrated from Athens to Alexandria under the aegis of Ptolemy Soter (305–283 B.C.), a loss from which Athens never recovered, as intellectual leadership of the ancient world passed to Alexandria. Greeks again emigrated as a consequence of the events of 1204 and 1453, this time from Constantinople, with Padua being the major beneficiary, but later also Oxford, Prague, Heidelberg, and others. The making of gunpowder and perhaps the idea of printing were transmitted from China during the days of the Mongol Empire, brought to Europe most likely by merchants traveling with caravans across the steppes of Central Asia. The caravans evidently also brought the Black Death, but that is another story.

Not that the older method of moving ideas to new places by

moving oneself ceased with the coming of the printing press. In the sixteenth to eighteenth centuries, many individuals were forced to migrate because of the religious controversy and its side effects: Flemings, Jews, North Italians, South Germans, and Huguenots. Trevor-Roper in *The Crisis of the Seventeenth Century* describes how the Reformation, the sharpened attitudes created by religious conflict, reduced tolerance for moderates of any kind and also produced a larger bureaucracy of people lacking sympathy for or insight into the needs of commerce and industry. By the time of the Reformation, large-scale industrial capitalism had developed in a number of cities, from Venice, Lucca, and Milan in Italy, through Augsburg, up to Flanders and the great seaport of Antwerp; Lisbon, as a result of the developing Portuguese commercial domain overseas, also became a center. Then, says, Trevor-Roper, between 1550 and 1620 the techniques of capitalism were carried to new locations, Amsterdam being a prominent example, when some of the leading capitalists migrated in order to escape increasing religious, political, and bureaucratic restraints in their original homes. Antwerp suffered greatly in the Spanish war, and, when conquered by the Duke of Parma, many Protestants moved, especially to Amsterdam. Some Jews, expelled from Spain and Portugal, also settled in the Netherlands and elsewhere in the North. Subsequently, the expulsion of Huguenots by Louis XIV brought a similar migration of human energies and ideas.

By revolutionizing communications, the printing press to some extent permanently altered the whole nature of historical processes. Knowledge stored on paper had hitherto remained the property of a small class of people, a type of learning generally regarded by the populace as sacred or magical. The press permitted the rapid spread of ideas to a larger group of people, the bourgeoisie, and eventually to the villagers by someone reading aloud before an audience. It also introduced that catalytic agent of modern times, the publisher working for a profit by publishing contemporary writers; ideas to some degree ceased to be the property of institutions, the church particularly, and a free market in ideas became possible.

From this point of view, the Protestant Reformation saw the

first of that modern phenomenon, a public opinion molded by the printed word. Although a few contemporary writers had been published by about 1500 and such men as Erasmus and Guillaume Budé found a reading audience, David T. Pottinger says that "still no one perceived the real power of the press until Martin Luther started to use it to further his religious reforms." His printers, making good profits, were happy to cooperate, and in those days before copyrights, other publishers speedily exploited the possibilities. By 1524, according to Hans J. Hillerbrand, over a million copies of one or more of Luther's writings had been published, and Luther's ideas had become known all over western Europe.

Obviously, the Europeans were ready for his message. Outside of Germany, Hillerbrand asserts, the communication consisted more in a general stimulus than in any exact reproduction of his theology, the conveyance of a mood and "what people took him to say." His general viewpoint roused others, rather than the specific ideas already known to many before Luther, that is, the communication met with such astonishing response because people were ready. As would so often be the case later also, those who early advanced his ideas in other countries—men like William Tyndale in England, Olavus Petri in Sweden, Huldryck Zwingli in Switzerland, Guillaume Farel in France—did so within their national cultural amalgam. Protestantism in various countries therefore displayed differences according to local traditions and circumstances.

Again, the rapid spread of Calvinism from Geneva amply demonstrates the power of the press. At the height of its early diffusion, perhaps as many as 300,000 volumes came off the presses, including Bibles, pamphlets, Calvin's own *Institutes,* and psalters. They flooded over the frontiers, no matter how closely guarded, being sold either openly or secretly by peddlers or in markets. This also helps to explain why Calvinism tended to be accepted by, particularly, the elements of the town population that knew how to read.

The eighteenth century saw, according to Paul Hazard, an "effervescence and a diffusion of ideas so remarkable in its nature, so far-reaching in its extent as to be without parallel" in history. Eventually these ideas permeated western Europe and spread all over the continent, and, as in the Reformation, the printing presses were instrumental. By the middle of the century something like the modern situation prevailed, a public able and willing to buy books, and a regular publishing business of well-established firms. Despite censorship and various repressive measures, a type of communication and diffusion had developed, particularly in England, Holland, and France, which no longer depended upon institutions or patrons. Ideas were for sale, could be purchased on the market, and from then on to the present this important agency in itself helped to mold events.

A growing reading public created a steady demand for lives of the saints, devotional books, and fairy tales, and also for almanacs, stocked with all kinds of useful information. School books continued to pour from the presses. Reflecting the interests of the period, religion provided the greatest amount of published material, but in the eighteenth century works in history, political science, and natural science increasingly rivaled the religious works. As such, they catered to the intellectual needs of bourgeoisie and nobility, though in France a multitude of societies and reading groups sprang up for the purchase of books and often for reading aloud before the illiterate villagers.

Perhaps the emphasis on reason in this century can be better understood if viewed in the light of this activity, based on the insatiable curiosity about the natural world and the excitement of successive advances in science, mathematics, and technology. Humanity had discovered a whole new perspective and an excitingly successful approach to knowledge. The facts arranged on the printed page seemed to give an assurance of validity, of secure acquisition of sound knowledge. No wonder that one symbol of the century is the encyclopedia, epitomized though not originated by the French Encyclopedia: if knowledge could be properly discovered and systematically arranged, so it seemed, humanity would then hold the key to the future, be able to plan and build a better future.

Other aspects of diffusion pertinent to its role as an historical process involve communications within a group, the conditions that make minds receptive to novel ideas, and the changing texture of an idea as it wins mass acceptance. A division into schools of thought tends to characterize the history of ideas; for example, the modern philosophers come grouped into schools of Rationalism, Idealism, Utilitarianism, Pragmatism, and others, while literature passes through such eras as those of Classicism, Romanticism, and Realism. In brief, each school articulates its own spirit and insights, a number of thinkers developing kindred viewpoints until a general configuration of ideas becomes characteristic of the group. A succession of shifts of emphasis may occur during the lifetime of a school of thought, each change opening up new problems to be resolved.

Ideas that eventually typify a school of thought or an historical period such as the Enlightenment often seem originally to be "in the air" in an inchoate way, a certain prevailing mood, climate of opinion, or *Zeitgeist* (spirit of the times) begging to be expressed. Those who have sensitive antennae to pick up this mood and successfully articulate the new fashion in ideas are likely to become the admired thinkers and writers of their period. A few creative minds first formulate the new intellectual fashion, but unless many other persons happen to be thinking along the same lines, searching for answers to related questions, these few would not find an audience. Occasionally, someone like Sir Francis Bacon or Giambattista Vico will put forth ideas whose full implications must await a later audience, but, like the individual role in history, an idea usually must be the right idea at the right time and place, "an idea whose time has come," in the words of Victor Hugo.

Typical ideas and modes of expression spread from the leading figures to secondary individuals and to the literate populace. Schools of thought in the modern world usually seem to have a life-span of, at most, three generations, after which the possibilities within their focus of attention become exhausted and any further challenge to first-class minds is lost. The climate of opinion may be altering, preparing the way for a new approach and a new galaxy of geniuses for articulating it. A preoccupation with trivia and formality, rigid copying of the earlier masters, seems symptomatic of decay, along with a baroque plethora of expression and increasingly strained attempts at restoring a vanishing relevancy.

An idea believed to be new is far more likely to be an old idea accoutered in new terminology, restructured to appeal to the contemporary generation. Over the ages, certain themes appear and reappear, reworked, applied in different contexts and with altered emphases. During our own century, styles and fashions in modes of thought in literature and philosophy seem to change rapidly and with almost kaleidoscopic variety, reflecting the swiftness of social change, the ease of communication, and the rapid boredom of a public suffering excessive exposure to each fashionable school in turn.

Ideas used by institutions or popular movements must be reformulated or simplified in order to be understood by the rank and file, thereby losing much of their intellectual content. In a coarsened or vulgarized form, they then take on the texture of dogmas or doctrines, slogans or battle cries. Popularized ideas used by mass followings may reflect meanings rather different from those of the original propagators or be used for purposes other than those intended by their creators.

Within an institution itself, several levels of meaning usually coexist according to uses and intellectual capacities. Established institutions of long duration, such as churches or the Communist party, tend to develop a certain hierarchy of ideas, the intellectuals, interested in ideas themselves, weaving their skeins of theology or ideology, while an elementary creed or certain dogmatic doctrines suffice for the rank and file. The notion of the average person that ideas come in an ascending hierarchy of truth may well still reflect ancestral experiences with institutions. Conflicts within the organization are often based on minor abstract points, issues that do not challenge the dominant dogma itself but serve as rallying points for factional rivalry. In the period of decline, of ebbing popular support, a dogma may deteriorate into a pure fetish, zealously defended by the vested interests as a symbol of their attempt to preserve themselves.

Certain circumstances will intensify the zeal of the holders of ideas. Those ideas accepted by relatively few but fervent persons tend to harden into dogmas. A milieu hostile to ideas may also engender dogmatists in sheer self-defense, as in the case of the Russian intelligentsia of the later nineteenth century. Within a school of thought, a certain momentum, an inner logic of development, seems to drive some adherents to an extreme version; an important idea will attract its quota of the obsessed, those who become True Believers. Then, too, a certain premium on the increasingly sensational may exist, that is, leaders must assume an ever more extreme position in order to attract or hold public attention. A condition of violent controversy in the community will cause the antagonists to revamp ideas into weapons, into battle cries and dogmas. Religious wars have been peculiarly savage because each side believes itself to possess the true ideas, as in the Protestant and Catholic Reformations, where the sharpening of attitudes, the increasing dogmatism, the hardening of theological battle lines weakened the position of the moderates. A similar hardening of positions, a going to extremes, occurred in the French Revolution.

Another form of selectivity may also occur, the actual grouping of believers in particular places or organizations, which then, in an organized form, may play a role in history out of proportion to the numbers involved. Many Calvinists flocked to Geneva, while less ardent souls moved out, thereby creating a concentration of the devoted. In the French Revolution, the more militant joined the Jacobin club, while the less zealous departed, thus mobilizing an energetic core of revolutionaries.

25

The Genesis
of New Ideas:
Science

Christopher Columbus, it will be recalled, was able to discover a new continent but could not bring himself to discover a new idea. Having announced that he had reached the environs of the Far East and being trapped in the contemporary belief in an Island of the World that did not contain the Americas, he long ignored mounting evidence to the contrary. Squirming and twisting to escape the obvious, according to Edmundo O'Gorman in *The Invention of America*, Columbus finally came to the conclusion that he had found the Terrestrial Paradise, something that could be fitted into the prevailing pattern of concepts. Genuinely new ideas can be excruciatingly difficult to accept because they may necessitate a realignment of the prevalent framework of knowledge.

Those of Magellan's men who survived the circumnavigation of the earth, eighteen of them, learned that they had lost a day while going around the world; not understanding the reason, the men did formal penance for having celebrated the church festivals on the wrong dates. These sailors had participated in a great and novel work, but, being children of their time, traditional beliefs continued to dominate their behavior. Butterfield describes in his *Origins of Modern Science,* upon which the following account is largely based, how even Leonardo da Vinci and Galileo experienced great difficulty in understanding certain ideas now easily learned by a grammar school student; men like Bacon or Harvey on certain matters "remain stranded in a species of medievalism."

Not that these men possessed less intelligence, the problem lay in the very wealth of their learning. In the Aristotelian framework, they possessed a dovetailed series of explanations for natural phenomena by no means simple or naïve; the writings of Ptolemy and Galen also set forth considerable knowledge about the heavens and the human body, respectively. Early modern thinkers saw what they had been taught to see by the ancients, and the new explanations, so very obvious now, were rejected because they did not fit the then prevailing scheme of things. The genuinely new ideas, perceived and developed only with the greatest of difficulty, were long delayed in acceptance because they involved basic reorientation of intellectual structures.

These scholars had, in the thirteenth to sixteenth centuries, been students going to school with the ancients, recapturing the lost learning of the classical age. Agonizingly difficult anyway, a realignment seemed to entail, in a very real sense, the rejection of their recent, hard-won achievements. In addition to this psychological obstruction, a vast amount of intellectual underbrush virtually suffocated new growth. The witchcraft craze and a "morbid predilection" for allegories and symbols intermingled with scientific gropings. Chemistry still functioned largely as alchemy, astronomy served as the handmaiden for astrology, and scholastic thinking became increasingly convoluted. Out of this kind of matrix emerged modern science.

Furthermore, the very concept of scientific law, so natural today, first had to be formulated. The scientists started with the

Christian belief in an orderly universe, its shapes and forces created by God, and attempted to search out the design constructed by the Master Workman. Though the West had believed since the days of the Babylonians that a Supreme Deity had formulated certain "laws" for the natural world, the actual modern conception of laws governing the natural phenomena originated only in the latter part of the sixteenth century.

No sudden breakthrough occurred in the early rise of modern science. No one person had the genius to present a clear outline of the concepts and methods, which emerged by stages with infinite difficulty and much encumbered by baggage from the older ideas. The origin of the modern conception of the solar system, as described by Butterfield, illustrates this very well. Everyone knows that Copernicus took the great step of proposing the heliocentric (sun-centered) theory that the earth revolved around the sun; he thereby became a "first" in the chronicles of science. However, Copernicus did not dismantle the ancient concept of celestial machinery; he retained the Ptolemaic system, including the idea of a series of crystalline spheres making up the canopy of the heavens, and only rearranged it in order to reduce the number of inconsistencies. This "retiring canon" did not set out to stage an intellectual revolution; he merely discovered that many of the older variations and inconsistencies could be removed by postulating that the earth also moved. Copernicus stepped into a debate underway ever since the days of Ptolemy himself, who, in fact had also considered the possibility that the earth moved but had been dissuaded by Aristotelian physics.

The temporary appearance of a new star in 1572–1574 and the passage of a comet through the presumed crystalline spheres shook the faith many had in the old system. Tycho Brahe, another astronomer, collected much supporting evidence in favor of the heliocentric theory, while all the time refusing to accept the theory himself. Brahe's successor, Johann Kepler, did accept it, and by the use of the growing body of advanced mathematics provided a more coherent and probable version, which included the planetary ellipses. While doing so, however, he also devoted much of his efforts to proving a universe of geometrical shapes and in seeking the music of the spheres. Both Brahe and Kepler, as part of their official duties, were also supposed to provide astrological predictions, still considered a practical aspect of astronomy by some rulers of the time. These "sleepwalkers," Arthur Koestler's term for them, discovered modern scientific truths while simultaneously doggedly propounding other theories that now seem utter nonsense.

Galileo and others, using the newly invented telescope, soon found additional proofs for the heliocentric theory minus the original Ptolemaic structure. Brusquely insisting that the theory did in fact represent the true state of the heavens, Galileo brought upon himself, by what now seems unnecessarily cantankerous behavior, the condemnation of the church. Not until Isaac Newton could benefit from more mathematical advances and additional discoveries in physics was it possible for someone to produce a framework that could fit together the discoveries of the past two centuries.

This whole process required the better part of 200 years, while the ideas of Kepler and Galileo each took, respectively, about forty and twenty years to be generally accepted. Newton's own theory of gravitation, essential to his system, did not spring out of an intellectual void either; other people had worked with it, including Kepler and Galileo, and here again Newton happened to be the right person in the series to complete the long fumbling progress toward the answer.

From the foregoing, it should be obvious that certain elementary forms of scientific history are inadequate. A collection of firsts hides most of the story, for the history of ideas must be one of processes, not only of a series of geniuses and their ideas. Narrating it in terms of Great Men, originally used in a history of science by William Whewell in 1837, omits the supporting cast of others involved in a development, the failures and partial successes, and the obstruction of traditional concepts. These people were also dependent upon the diffusion of ideas, subject to sundry institutional aid or interdict, and stimulated by the debate among various schools of scientific thought. For the same reasons, that other common version of an elementary history of science—the triumphant victories of our contemporary beliefs over other and "wrong" ideas—is equally simplistic.

Early scientists had little interest in improving workshops, metallurgy, or shipping; they were searching for final answers, for some single stupendous discovery that would release and give them control of the forces of nature. Experimentation, so much at the core of later science, was originally the most diligently practiced by the alchemists. Though classical authority may have inhibited discoveries, the struggle to regain the learning of the ancients served as a preparatory school for later developments, that is, the intense intellectual effort involved in attaining the pinnacle of the ancient achievement prepared the scholars to go *beyond* their predecessors.

Since the diffusion of ideas necessarily constitutes an indispensable element in the whole process, the establishment of universities undoubtedly contributed greatly, both in bringing individuals of learning together and in the dissemination of knowledge by scholars wandering from one school to another. A fairly consistent pattern of scientific development started from this time. Leading to ideational fermentation and changing outlook, as well as to advances in the development of the scientific method, the intellectual currents of the age converged most notably at the University of Padua, located in Venetian territory and hence relatively free from clerical restraints. It was no coincidence that Copernicus, Galileo, Andreas Vesalius, and William Harvey were all connected with Padua at one time or another.

As with the realm of ideas in general, the printing press expedited the spread of scientific knowledge throughout western Europe; thus, modern science might have developed sooner if the press had appeared earlier. One basic conceptual obstruction in the beginnings of modern science had been the Aristotelian idea of motion as necessarily requiring a mover, since Aristotle had assumed a state of rest to be the natural condition. Modification of the theory had been started by a school of thinkers in Paris in the fourteenth century but did not immediately win wide acceptance due in part to the slowness and relative ineffectiveness of communication before the printing press.

Later, discoveries could be quickly disseminated, thereby speeding up the whole process. By the late seventeenth through the eighteenth centuries, scientific journals began to be published. The press also permitted the popularization of science, the building up of a substantial body of interested persons, while writers like Bernard de Fontenelle and Pierre Bayle helped to inspire the new mood that would dominate the Enlightenment. Scientific societies and academies appeared, the Royal Society being formally created in 1662 out of a group of people already meeting together, and the Academie Royale des Sciences starting in 1665, both of these supported by the Crown. Wealthy patrons began to support science financially.

Sir Isaac Newton claimed that he discovered the law of gravitation by "thinking about it ceaselessly," but, born a couple generations earlier, no amount of cerebration could have produced this results; first he had to have the analytical geometry of René Descartes and the infinitesimal calculus developed by Gottfried Wilhelm Leibniz and himself. That he was quite aware of his debt to others is indicated by another comment: if he was able to see farther than others, it was, he said, "because I stood on the shoulders of giants." Kepler was able to go beyond Copernicus and Brahe in astronomy because he was abreast of recent mathematical advances. Without these, including the use of decimals, logarithms, and coordinate geometry, further scientific advances would have been blocked. Experimentation remained chaotic until organized and refined by mathematics.

Modern scientists could scarcely move much beyond the earlier achievements until certain other tools had been provided. These, in turn, appeared largely as a consequence of a need for them, a pressing demand encouraging people to work on them. Scientific instruments were devised: the telescope and microscope by the beginning of the seventeenth century, then, in the eighteenth, a good thermometer, the air pump for collecting and isolating gases, the micrometer, and better balances for weighing. Whereas Aristotelian scientists had thought largely in qualitative terms, now the great breakthrough occurred into another dimension altogether, where precise instruments and quantification made vastly enlarged and more accurate observation possible. Somewhat earlier, it will be recalled, the invention of the mechanical clock (now followed by the more accurate pendulum clock) had introduced precise measureable units into the apprehension of time.

A highly suggestive illustration of the specific role of individuals in the genesis of scientific ideas is offered by the formulation of Darwinian evolution in the nineteenth century. Charles Darwin is the heroic figure, say the textbooks, and the date given is 1859.

Why Darwin? Perhaps he came by it naturally through his grandfather, Erasmus Darwin, who believed in a sort of evolution, a generalized concept "in the air" and already being applied in areas other than biology. Charles Darwin had read the accounts of several persons who had perceived a nebulous something at work in nature. He himself incubated the theory from about 1830 until 1858, though he grasped its essentials before 1840 as a consequence of the repeated evidence supporting natural selection and the evolution of species that had been discerned during the famous voyage of the *Beagle*. This data had always existed, though it remained invisible to eyes not looking for it. A sharpening awareness of hitherto unformulated relationships in nature alerted Darwin to this specific area of evidence. He was prepared to *see* it.

So Darwin became the Great Man, an immortal in the history of science. He also had a supporting cast, however, in this drama, especially in the person of his friend Alfred Russell Wallace, who was deeply impressed in Malaya by evidences of the natural selection of species. Their discussions helped them both to clarify the theory. At the end of 1858, the president of the Linnean Society summed up the year in science by saying that no "striking discoveries" had been reported, though epochal papers on evolution by Darwin and Wallace had been read to the society on July 1! Darwin hastily published his famous theory in 1859 because Wallace was preparing to do so, which would have preempted Darwin's own claim to the theory.

These two are not isolated figures. Robert Chambers, an amateur in science, published a book in 1844 depicting a natural creation by evolution. Promptly "shouted down" and heavily criticized by the experts for his numerous minor errors, he was also widely read, thereby preparing public opinion for Darwin. Loren Eiseley in *Darwin's Century* lists several other contributors.

Patrick Mathew bitterly claimed to have been the originator of the theory on the basis of comments published in 1831 on natural selection and "indefinite divergence through time" of species; five years earlier, in an Edinburgh magazine, someone had argued that species change profoundly, an article read by Darwin. Back in 1813 an exiled American doctor, William Wells, read a paper to the Royal Society which "anticipated" natural selection and which was partly based on the already prevalent practice of breeding domestic animals to produce selected characteristics. Several earlier persons had thus verged on becoming the Darwin of the theory of evolution, had come, as Eiseley says, within a "hair's breadth" of the greath theory. This is typical, repeated time and again in science; the fumbling approach, vague perceptions of the truth, partial answers—then along comes someone who articulates it precisely and gets the credit.

Why did Sir Charles Lyell, the most eminent student of species during those thirty years, not become the author of the theory? Having all the necessary information, he seems the logical person. This again brings up a typical feature of the birth of new major ideas, whether in science or elsewhere, the obstruction by currently accepted concepts. Lyell himself had been the hero in triumphantly assaulting the then dominant idea of catastrophism, according to which the undeniable evidence of fossils of extinct species could be explained by fairly recent catastrophes such as the Flood. Lyell believed only in endless changes *within* species, not in the complete evolutionary development, and, as Eiseley says, kept on looking "down the wrong road."

Obtuse as catastrophism may look to later generations, it, too, had represented an advance from the earlier belief in a sudden divine creation of a completed world a few millenniums ago. As a compromise between religious orthodoxy and the early geological discoveries, catastrophism typifies the transitional device commonly used in a period of changing ideas.

Darwin's statement of the theory in 1859 by no means ends the story. Since characteristics could not be acquired, the explanation for evolution by natural selection of the fittest left much to be desired. Someone demonstrated in 1867 that a variation in the species would be obliterated in later breeding, thereby forcing

Darwin into retreat. As it happened, Gregor Mendel in 1865 had proven that mutations occur and had formulated the Mendelian law, an adequate explanation for the variations; the timing was perfect—but Mendel lived in Brünn, and his paper in a local magazine went unnoticed. Not until 1900, by which time Hugo De Vries had independently made the same discovery, did someone take notice of the original article. Then in 1902 came virtually simultaneous announcements of mutations by De Vries in Leyden, E. V. Tschermak in Vienna, and C. Correns in Berlin, all three having faced this problem and all, following the same lines of argument, having come to the same conclusions, an excellent example of parallel discoveries in science.

Columbus could not discover a new idea and Lyell could not believe the evidences of evolution because they did not fit the accepted scheme of things. In astronomy, the planet Uranus had been seen at least seventeen times between 1690 and 1781 by persons not looking for it before Sir William Herschel actually "saw" and identified it as a planet in 1781. Again, the earlier sightings had been obscured by the then current conception of a solar system that left no room for additional planets or asteroids. Eyes opened, astronomers then found twenty asteroids in the next fifty years.

Geologists, in the middle of the twentieth century, possessed no comprehensive explanation for a number of related problems involving zones of earthquakes and volcanic action, the location of mountain ranges, and the existence of mountains and deep ditches in the oceans. Then suddenly the idea of continental drift made possible an overall explanation; everything fell together into a master scheme, including numerous evidences from historical geology.

Manifestly, ideas tend to come in clusters and in their alignment to be dependent upon one another for their credibility. In the history of science, according to one recent major interpretation, these configurations of ideas are dependent upon the formulation of paradigms. A paradigm, a model or pattern, consists of a general statement of relationships that is open-ended, presenting additional problems to be solved.

According to Thomas Kuhn in *The Structure of Scientific Revolutions,* the broad pattern of change and continuity in science is characterized by successive paradigms, which in turn dominate scientific work. Each area of scientific study has had its own sequence of master ideas, a succession of assumptions upon which adherents base their work. Ptolemaic astronomy gave way to the Copernican, and Aristotelian dynamics to the Newtonian. Electrical research "crossed the divide" between 1740 and 1780, physical optics in the late seventeenth century, and historical geology in the early nineteenth.

Following Kuhn's argument, the shift from one paradigm to another is started by the discovery of weaknesses in the prevailing paradigm, anomalies that do not fit the current statement of relationships. Intellectual insecurity leads to a series of modifications, awkward addendums to the paradigm. (In trying to insert accumulating astronomical evidence into the Ptolemaic framework, the scholars had postulated an increasing number of celestial globes in the heavens.) Eventually, after a series of alternative proposals, someone formulates a new paradigm, which gains increasing favor. As in the case of Darwin, several thinkers may have dimly perceived the solution and a number of individuals helped solve the problem.

Kuhn offers the discovery of oxygen as an example. The finding of "air" in chemical reactions precipitated the crisis. First, scientists proposed the phlogiston theory, a compromise solution, but gas samples proved too varied, and the theory had to be dropped. Then Carl Scheele discovered oxygen, not knowing what it was. Joseph Priestley produced several gases, including oxygen, and Lavoisier conceptualized it as a separate element, but Priestley, also "looking down the wrong road," never did accept Lavoisier's answer.

In a conflict between advocates of rival paradigms, the arguments of the antagonists do not meet head on, says Kuhn, they "talk through each other" because they are not arguing about the same things. He asserts that the creators of new paradigms are likely to be either very young or very new to a field, that is, their ideas have not yet been completely molded by prevailing assumptions. Those deeply committed to the old paradigm continue to concentrate on problems derived from it, thereby, as with Lyell, blocking out new perceptions. Kuhn doubts very much that a new paradigm gains acceptance primarily because of scientific *proof;* it may be adopted because it is useful in solving currently crucial problems in that area of science, but its simplicity, neatness, suitability, and the general mood of the age all help it to win approval.

A paradigmatic shift does not necessarily result from cumulative knowledge; it more nearly consists of "picking up the other end of the stick." Based not so much on "raw sense data" as on a change in criteria, a dropping of some old problems as no longer relevant, a "constellation of objects" is transformed from one shape into quite a different shape. However long a realignment of ideas may have been incubating in some minds, the switch, Kuhn thinks, "must occur all at once" to someone. He is tempted to say that when paradigms change, the world changes with them; one sees things in a "different light," looks in new places and at new things. Perhaps this psychological phenomenon may not be altogether irrelevant to interpretations of history either.

26

Modern Technology: Origins and Inventors

Probably no area in history is subject to quite so much moralizing and the good-evil approach as the Industrial Revolution. The elder Arnold Toynbee originally set the pattern by depicting it as a catastrophic event leading to miserable housing, poor working conditions, and exploitation of the workers. Presently, other studies, revealing the background for the changes, portrayed a more gradualist historical point of view. More recently, a number of writers have returned to a belief in the relatively rapid breakthrough, and the debate continues among scholars between the gradualists and those who regard the whole development as essentially catastrophic in nature.

On the public level, an ambivalent attitude persists, the spectacular progress in harnessing nature's foces versus the price paid in human suffering for the achievement. The frustration of Golden Age hopes, roused by the possibilities of modern technology, helps to explain the pessimistic viewpoint, but each generation also customarily exaggerates the sufferings of its own time relative to other ages and tends to look back to the good old days of an idyllic rural village. Beyond any doubt, the early Industrial Revolution brought suffering, but whether more acute or widespread than in preindustrial villages or cities like London remains highly controversial; some historians, to the contrary, see a notable increase in the standard of living. Quite clearly, the ambivalence derives in part, though only in part, from present-minded illusions and other elementary ways of looking at the past. The Industrial Revolution has naturally been peculiarly susceptible to street-level thinking with its violent emotions and political ideologies.

Finding a scapegoat for the failure of utopia to arrive on schedule poses no major problem. The obvious targets are the capitalist and the profit motive, which are charged by critics with the destruction of the good inherent in the advances. Adam B. Ulam says Marx often mistook the "birth pains of modern industrial society" for "the death throes of capitalism," and Marxism has continued to express humanity's resentment and disorientation ever since.

A period of comparatively rapid technological change was not wholly unprecedented. Usage of water power, long postponed, had spread quickly throughout western Europe in the eleventh century. The first known horizontal-axle windmill dates from 1185, and soon after that they began to dot the landscape. By the early fourteenth century, wind or water power was being used in tanning, sawing, crushing ores (or olives), bellows, hammers of forges, grindstones, and producing mash for beer, enough of a development, Lynn White thinks, to justify thinking in terms of an industrial revolution in that period. Then the momentum ceased, but, basically, this was the series of improvements, accomplished mostly with wooden machinery, that would later be replaced by iron, steam, and the factory system. The more recent successes have blotted out recollections of the older technological triumphs, just as the coming of the railroad largely obscured the earlier construction of canals.

One important factor in the timing of industrial revolution seems to be the liaison between science and technology, an inter-relationship that does not become important until the later eighteenth century. To be sure, some contacts had occurred earlier, as in navigation, which involved astronomy, magnetism, and knowledge of the tides. Mining benefited from the study of metals and the development of the pump. From the use of cannon came a study of motion and impetus in ballistics. Scientists, however, usually did not focus on such practical matters, while workshops, shipbuilding, and mining maintained their own occupational traditions. A. Rupert Hall suggests that "practical men were not ready to learn."

Perhaps this explains why, as Marc Bloch expresses it, the age of Louis XIV *wanted* to invent but not much came of it. Hall asserts that the results in no way measured up to the amount of work done; he also suspects that the mechanical spirit of the eighteenth century may very well have been anticipated already in the sixteenth when Leonardo da Vinci, especially, devised on paper all manner of inventions prophetic of the future. The inventions that proliferated in the seventeenth century generally failed because technology was not ready for them.

Both science and technology required further development before their cooperation could be mutually fruitful. Resistance to change stemmed from several factors: fear that machinery would create unemployment, reluctance to venture money on commercially unproven inventions or techniques, the low level of workers' skills, and the secrecy maintained by the possessors of a successful device in the absence of proper patent law. In addition, machinery was not economically feasible until more large-scale production had been attained.

Other broad factors, however, stimulated technological changes. Conditions for water or wind power might not have been favorable where or when most needed, a problem solved by the steam engine. Wooden machinery suffered from the movable parts wearing out too rapidly, the answer being the development of more and cheaper iron. Though the factory system as such originated in the Industrial Revolution, large shops did exist earlier for shipbuilding and the forging of cannon. As for the inventions themselves, Eric Lampard feels that they were not so much "a unique contribution of a heroic generation of inventors" as "novel syntheses" of previous achievements.

England's primacy in pioneering efforts, according to Jonathan Hughes, is explained by, among other factors, the existence of a sympathetic government, a "group of skilled men," contacts between practical knowledge and universities, related industries with interspersed technology, and buyers for the machinery. The national market probably ranked as the largest in Europe, and England had the freest movement of labor. And, compared to the continent, less restrictive regulations hampered the development of new ways of manufacturing.

Viewed from the perspective of world history, the coming of both the scientific and the technological revolutions can be better understood by returning to an unanswered question from an earlier chapter, why the Chinese failed to make the great modern breakthrough. In 1400, the Chinese still seem more advanced than the Europeans in civilization and in the practical arts, as they had been for a millennium and a half. They invented silk, paper, the printing press, gunpowder, the seismograph, the spinning wheel, and casting iron (the latter 1,500 years before the Europeans), and also used some water power. Shortly before 1400, the Chinese were sending fleets of ships larger and more comfortable than the Europeans' to India and even to the east coast of Africa, where Vasco da Gama's expedition would presently appear. At this point, it would seem, the Chinese might well have "discovered" Europe rather than the Europeans penetrating to the Far East. Why did the Chinese series of inventions not gather momentum, and why did the Europeans now pull ahead at an accelerating pace?

To answer most succinctly, China's economy and government should be visualized as a continuation of the hydraulic civilizations of Mesopotamia and Egypt. The necessities for flood control and for maintaining a waterway system for transportation required a bureaucracy, in this case run by the mandarins. Many of the Chinese inventions came precisely in areas directly useful to this officialdom: astronomy, for regulating agricultural activities, in addition to the astrological concerns of the state, and engineering, where need for flood control, irrigation, and maintenance of water transport stimulated advances.

For two millenniums, the most intelligent individuals in China, chosen by literary examinations, gravitated to positions of power and influence in the top bureaucracy. Occasionally, inventions appeared from their ranks, but more usually originated with individuals in various walks of life who were working for a patron or in state enterprises. Under this system scientists and technologists could scarcely achieve coherent organization among themselves for pursuits outside of the administrative and literary interests of the mandarins. Furthermore, being outside of the literary tradition, many of the discoveries were not necessarily written down, diffused, or even preserved.

Subject to external influences only on a small and intermittent level, Chinese advances emerged largely out of their own background rather than being stimulated by diffusion from elsewhere. (Foreign merchants at Canton did bring in some goods from India, Iran, and the Middle East, and the Mongol or Yuan dynasty [1260–1368] temporarily opened more contact with the outside world.) Internally, state enterprises, or at least those controlled by the state, prevailed as the more important projects. China lacked that characteristic social force of Europe in the later medieval and modern eras, the organized activity of merchants and people in business. Missing is the ability of these persons to implement their interests with the aid of the state or, occasionally, despite its authority if necessary. Though numerous, merchants and business people remained always subject to bureaucratic control, liable to confiscatory taxation, and vulnerable to seizures of property; their outlook usually ignored or scorned by officialdom, the Chinese "middle class" failed to achieve the cohesion to become a force in itself. Those who did amass wealth were likely to put it into more socially acceptable activities, into noneconomic uses, and to endeavor to place relatives in the dominant official class.

Political authorities in the Byzantine Empire and the Moslem world also dominated these groups. Only in parts of Europe did private economic leadership and outlook break through into strong influence or control. In China, the basic historical processes leading in this direction did not become effective.

Turning now to certain other specific facets of the historical processes in technology, popular history depicts the early inventor as self-made, usually poorly educated, and often working in isolation against great odds. As John Jewkes and his associates in a study of inventors have amply demonstrated, this is largely a myth.

Intimate ties among early inventors permitted extensive diffusion of scientific knowledge, the company of innovators being a "more closely knit society than is generally supposed." Small groups worked together on the steamboat, for instance a "web of connections" existed between Rumsey, Fitch, Miller, Fulton, Stevens, Symington, Bell, and Livingston; one originator of the locomotive, Richard Trevithick, knew Blackett, Hadley, and Stephenson. The early textile machine and steam engine inventors possessed some education, and the possibilities for self-education through books, scientific periodicals, and institutes should not be underestimated. In Sweden, to cite another example, most of the innovators enjoyed at least some technical education, were also members of a closely knit scientific community, and quite often had financial support for their investigations.

Each invention in turn represents the latest step in a chain of developments, or it results from putting together a number of discoveries. Guglielmo Marconi invented the wireless by combining James Maxwell's electromagnetic wave theory, Heinrich Hertz's transmitter, Edouard Branly's coherer, and Alexander Popov's antenna. The jet engine incorporated the gas turbine and jet propulsion; the diesel electric locomotive came from the diesel and electric traction. To be sure, King Gillette, a traveling salesman, did invent the safety razor one morning in 1895 while shaving, and the ice cream cone was invented on July 23, 1904 in St. Louis!

Similar inventions may be made simultaneously by two different individuals following parallel tracks of logical development. Henry Cort and Peter Onions both puddled iron in 1783, and Michael Faraday and Joseph Henry in 1831 discovered that electricity could be generated by magnetism. Someone named Hornblower, who had independently developed a steam engine, plagued James Watt for years; the Watt and Boulton Company had to go to court to protect their patent. Heinz Gartmann recalls an engineer who, after reading Alexander Graham Bell's description of his telephone apparatus, said that for ten years he had vaguely visualized the same idea but "I was too blind to see it."

Scientific concepts and inventions may appear before becoming practicable, being indefinitely delayed because some of the necessary ingredients are still unavailable. Though the steam engine had existed for nearly a century before Watt, the eventual development of better iron first made his engine useful for industry. The recording machine, theoretically possible by 1900, was held up until electric amplifiers were developed in the 1920s. Charles Babbage developed the principles upon which the computer is based, but a century passed before electronics made it practicable. One invention may also stimulate others, the jet engine forcing an improved metallurgy and hard alloys requiring tungsten carbide tools in order to work them. As with ideas, an invention "whose time has come" will be created by someone who sees the possibilities, though an urgent need does not necessarily bring a prompt solution. Then again, much labor may be invested by someone, only to have another person find the solution unexpectedly.

A chain reaction of inventions ensues as each new discovery, while solving a problem, creates new needs and new challenges. An initial model of a machine or gadget usually inaugurates a new series of improvements, various factors determining which versions of a model will be accepted; thus, the original automobiles appeared using four different kinds of power—steam engine, electricity, compressed air, and the internal combustion engine—and it was the breakthrough of the latter type that made the modern car possible late in the nineteenth century. The steam engine had proved a public nuisance, and electricity not sufficiently powerful or of sufficient driving range to be practical.

Jewkes says that the story of an invention usually is much oversimplified in the telling, described as originating in a logical way and with steady progress toward a solution. The inventors themselves may encourage such a belief, preferring that the real ordeal of much fumbling, false leads, and backtracking be forgotten. As with scientific ideas, they may miss one discovery because they are concentrating on another goal. Many inventions have been accidental, among others, aniline dyes, Duco lacquers, polyethlene, the transistor, and ethyl gas. Jewkes stresses the element of the accidental and the unpredictable in inventions.

In these historical processes, the role of creativity must not be forgotten, for someone, after all, does put it together, does make the "big jump in ideas." Jewkes also believes in the advantages of not being overtrained because it creates grooves of accepted thought, making perception of new possibilities difficult. The "genius breaks the rule" and is rarely an organization person; devoted to his or her own work, he or she is apt to be a poor team member, generally nurses grievances, feels the world is hostile and poses a prickly problem for administrators trying to run a smooth, well-planned program. Manifestly dependent upon other elements in the historical processes, the inventor's spark of creativity is an indispensable ingredient in technological development.

27

Problem Solving: Challenge and Response

Another aspect of the historical processes, that of challenge and response, can be illustrated by the Industrial Revolution. Starting with the early development of textile machinery, a succession of challenges stimulated a series of responses in the form of inventions. Each novel device created a new problem or challenge, which in turn had to be solved, thereby setting up a chain reaction of inventions continuing down to the present time.

Preceding improvements in textiles in western Europe had brought their ingredients—carding, spinning, weaving, and finishing—close to the factory age, and industry in Great Britain, possessing the advantages listed earlier, stood potentially ready. John Kay's flying shuttle (1733), which made possible more rapid weaving, came as a response to the challenge of increasing demand for cloth. However, this very success aggravated another problem, that of supplying the thread for the weaving, since it required the work of four spinning wheels to supply one weaving loom. Some time elapsed before the response to the challenge appeared with James Hargreaves's spinning jenny (1770), whose several spindles speeded up the spinning process. Several more improvements followed quickly, but they created a new problem because the larger machines required a stronger source of power than human muscles.

Richard Arkwright introduced one response with his water frame, run by a paddle wheel. Nevertheless, water power offered only an inadequate solution, production being limited to locations near streams with sufficient current and to times of year when these streams contained enough water. Unfortunately, too, these sites usually lay distant from either the supplies or the market. Watt's improved steam engine, whose appearance on the scene was most opportune, solved this problem. Though invented in the later seventeenth century, the steam engine could not be made strong enough for industrial use until the discovery of puddled iron. The solution to its use in the textile industry depended in turn upon developments in a different line of technology, that of iron.

But how to transport coal from the mines to the steam engine or cotton from the harbors to the mills? Transportation posed a new challenge. An initial response brought the steamboat, which in turn accelerated the digging of canals; and a second solution consisted in mounting the steam engine on carriages or wagons and using the roads. Though off to a promising start, an outraged public snuffed out the latter development by legislating it to death. The most successful response came with the development of rail transportation, putting locomotives and trains of vehicles on "rail-roads."

Challenge and response as part of the historical processes has been repeatedly met in the foregoing chapters without being identified as such. Confronted by mounted nomads, the Persians and Byzantine Greeks created armored cavalry. The inhabitants of central Europe developed an improved plow, horse power, and a better axe in order to cope with their soil and forests. The blacks successfully met the challenges of sub-

Saharan Africa. Living on a strip of land of little agricultural use, the ancient Athenians turned to olive oil, to pottery, and to commerce while procuring much of their own grain from Scythia.

A few additional examples will further illustrate the process. The Venetians, eventually facing insurmountable commercial problems and no longer dispatching their trading vessels to the Atlantic coast, responded by expanding on the Italian mainland. To some extent, Venice became another Italian territorial state, obtaining additional income from landed properties. Also by converting to large-scale textile manufacturing in competition with other cities of northern Italy and the Netherlands, the Venetians remained prosperous for a time. After a while, however, their commercial organizations became too rigid to respond to the challenge of changing forms of business in western Europe, and by the eighteenth century Venice could be considered virtually moribund. Perhaps the situation had gone beyond redemption, or perhaps the "closed, self-perpetuating oligarchy apparently lacked the desire and the ability to devise new methods for new circumstances," as J. H. Elliott expressed it in *Europe Divided 1559–1598*.

The Genoese also had adjustments to make. They had controlled the commerce in the western Mediterranean and, after outcompeting the Catalans, secured a strong grip on Spanish trade. They made the most of their opportunity to share in the Spanish-American trade and, especially in the time of Charles V, served as bankers for the Spanish Crown, while also adding to their monopolies and privileges in Spain to the point of attaining "commanding control" over the Spanish economy.

Toynbee, whose use of the term "challenge and response" helped popularize it, offered the perpetual Dutch battle with the sea as one example. Out of their struggle developed an industrious, hard-working people, he wrote, who knew how to make the most of their opportunities. They turned their enemy into an asset by farming the sea, about one-fifth of the inhabitants being in one way or another involved in the fishing industry. Accustomed to ships, the Dutch also built up their commerce, first particularly in the Baltic in succession to the Hanseatic League and then, as oceanic trade grew, on a worldwide basis; in the seventeenth century, they ruled one of the largest colonial empires in the world. Pieter Geyl, himself a Dutch historian, has, however, declared that too much has been made of this, one factor among several other contributing circumstances.

Sometimes the efforts to adjust to circumstances fail, as happened to the heroic efforts of the Poles in the late eighteenth century. Long disunified by the strength of an individualistic aristocracy and a virtually paralyzed central government, they responded, at long last, by creating a modernized government capable of coping with circumstances. In so doing, the Poles fought a desperate battle, the events obscured by the French Revolution in the west, only to be crushed by the power of Russia, Austria, and Prussia. In a race against time, the Poles lost.

A people may pay a heavy price for failure to adjust, sometimes not even realizing the urgency. The Anglo-Saxons did not follow the peoples on the continent in setting up a strong body of armored knights. Their earlier challenges had come from the Vikings, who were also foot soldiers, and resorting to the response of an advanced military weapon had not been imperative. Then, in the Battle of Hastings in 1066, says Lynn White, the seventh century defending itself against the eleventh was doomed to defeat.

Why do states and peoples sometimes not respond to challenges? What causes "a hardening of the arteries" that makes adjustments increasingly difficult? In some cases, as Toynbee pointed out, the problems may be too severe, illustrated by numerous primitive societies dwindling away when confronted by more advanced civilizations. Then again, the problem may be too novel to be handled properly. The conditions in growing eighteenth- and early nineteenth-century cities yield nothing to our contemporary urban conditions at their worst, bad housing, lack of hygiene and lighting, and inadequate policing. The iniquities in the early factory system, not regulated by societies accustomed to handicraft industry, took a long time to be ameliorated. What accounts, however, for the failure of long-successful communities, such as Venice, to react to new challenges?

Undoubtedly, the sheer momentum of hitherto successful responses is a major factor, a pattern of behavior continuing to be repeated even though changing circumstances render it decreasingly effective. Although no longer the proper response, the routine of predecessors persists in the midst of complacency over past successes. A deterioration in the actual caliber of those in the top positions may occur, or the drive of those who have inherited power may be less energetic than that of those conditioned by the necessities of struggle.

Even in the most vital communities, a considerable time lag usually exists between the coming of the challenge and an effective response. Institutions nearly always react slowly to crises, as the routines of continuity persist. If Leo had taken Luther's complaints seriously. . . . If the British had reacted to the American colonists' complaints sooner. . . . If the Old Regime in France. . . . For those involved, change *is* an ordeal. A response, when it comes, is apt to be partial, implemented piecemeal, and camouflaged by traditional verbiage.

Beyond this, to talk about the community as a whole reacting to a challenge frequently omits much of the story. Within the community, many groups and numerous institutions nourish their own drives and goals, each responding to a particular set of circumstances. Problem solving occurs at all levels. Different groups confront their own specific challenges, and each one's solutions may add momentum or obstruct the response of the whole community to any specific crisis. Among these differing priorities are the imperatives of the military, the routine paper form changes congenial to the bureaucracy, and the special interests of the churches, and none of these groups may be directly concerned at the time with problem solving for the sake of the community as a whole. Economics has its own logic in the laws of supply and demand, the management of economic enterprises, and the calculations of those who handle money. Much depends upon the vitality of the groups equipped to meet the larger crisis and the power of groups whose own interests may be jeopardized by the necessary changes.

An effective reaction largely depends upon whether the elements directly concerned have the power to implement the measures appropriate for the perceived needs. Faced by a menace from outside the community, those within the military capable of seeing the best possible defense must be in a position to assert their will. In economic challenges, the groups concerned need sufficient flexibility within their organizations for changes to emerge. In terms of the direction in which history happens to be moving, those agencies that are creative must be able to express their perceived responses to challenges.

Obviously, too, the strength of vested interests that would be hurt by changes helps determine the efficacy of response. The Anglo-American political cycle, functioning largely on the basis of piecemeal reforms that do a minimum of damage to the vested interests, to some degree reduces last-ditch obstruction to alterations. In other cases, threatened groups may see no genuine alternative to rigid defiance of needed reforms; the upper classes in portions of Latin America have been notorious for this, partly because of older traditions and partly out of sheer fright that change will bring a revolutionary landslide. Institutions, endangered by the threat of change, add their powerful obstructions; their staffs naturally have a vested interest in the survival of agencies that provide livelihood and a measure of individual status and power. Cipolla writes that conservatives and vested interests "cluster about obsolete institutions to help each other."

Failure to respond to a challenge can lead to disaster, as happened to the Anglo-Saxons at Hastings, or it may lead to a long-term condition of stagnation and worsening prospects, that set of comparative circumstances commonly referred to as decline. Cipolla believes that the economic problems of empires in decline "show striking resemblances."

Mature empires, he states, tend to "give negative responses" to the challenge of a stagnating economy. The Spanish seemed to rest on past laurels, to nourish self-esteem by recalling memories of earlier glories, their swollen bureaucracy and huge-tax collecting apparatus working as a positive obstruction. Castilian officialdom entered a period of loss of impetus and initiative. By the middle of the seventeenth century, the Italians were losing one export market after another, while their guilds used their regulations to stop attempts to copy the English and the Dutch. Italy and Spain both underwent "absolute decline" from the 1620s until the 1680s or 90s and thereafter still advanced more slowly than others. Once highly innovative, the Dutch, by the end of the eighteenth century, no longer kept up with advances elsewhere in shipbuilding, textiles, or navigation. The Byzantine Greeks in their last centuries fell steadily behind the advances in the West.

Then, too, a response may indeed occur but to a different challenge than posterity considers important. (Even the tax collector, that millenniums-old enemy of the general public, has personal forms of challenge!) Responsible agencies may be geared to a challenge vital to them at the time, thus the great increase of bureaucracy after the Catholic Reformation was based on a motive both religious and institutional, the need for more administrative control. This new elite of officials, however, lacked comprehension of the business world, and the challenge in that area continued to be ignored. The Chinese mandarins, their focus of attention elsewhere than on the economy and technology, disdained the challenge of the Western "barbarians," the use of the word itself indicative of the problem.

Finally, a challenge too great to be met may stimulate a response of evasion. Some, including Toynbee, would regard the growth of Christianity in the later Roman Empire as a way of finding new goals and satisfactions in a world where material success seemed increasingly unlikely. The millenarianism of the lower classes in the medieval and early modern and extremist political reactions on the apocalyptic level in this century manifestly derive, at least partially, from challenges difficult or impossible to confront on a realistic basis.

The challenge and response theme offers a simplified approach to causality by placing the emphasis on the concrete circumstances attending the solving of a specific problem. Pushed a step further, this becomes basic to behaviorist methodology. Used in other ways, challenge and response lies at the core of *inner-sequence* (internalist) interpretations of historical development.

Inner-sequence assumptions have been met earlier in other

guises, as in the cyclical theories in which some form of inner determinism controls successive phases of an evolution. Users of biological analogies, like Spengler, tacitly assume an inner causality based on a parallel to life organisms in their growth, maturity and senescence. More recent formulations based essentially on challenge and response can be found in the history of science, technology, and the fine arts.

Internalists argue that the appearance of modern scientific thought followed its own pattern rather than being determined by external influences. This pattern they believe to be governed by the forces of tradition, by long periods of piecemeal preparation leading to ultimate breakthroughs, and by the diffusion and fermentation of ideas. Some historians of technology assert that developments originate in a self-propelling series of advances rather than in being primarily molded by external forces. Technology evolves, they say, according to an inner pattern of development in which "a rigid adherence to chronological dates is undesirable and indeed impossible."

In art, too, biological analogies of birth, maturity, and degeneration have sometimes been used. Attempts to find shapes of time in art history have resulted in proposed sequences made up of several or all of the following art styles: archaic, classic, mannerist, baroque, rococo, and neoclassic. Henri Focillon believed that art forms, by the "inherent logic of the unfolding art forms," go through certain stages, experimental, classic, refinement, and baroque, and that the sequence develops internally, quite removed from other contiguous historical developments.

George Kubler's more recent conception of art history is particularly relevant here. A student of Focillon, he sees artistic evolution as consisting of basic sequences that develop in accordance with the solution to successive problems. Rather like the case of inventions, each art problem solved creates new problems, and the existent potential for an "event" does not guarantee that it will actually happen. Each novel form limits the possible succeeding innovations in the sequence, and each stage or position must be occupied before going on to the next one.

In addition to a simplified version of causality, the internalists tend to emphasize breakthroughs and temporarily accelerated responses thereafter, a pattern sometimes veering widely from gradualist conceptions of change and continuity. Useful as the concept of challenge and response in the inner-sequence interpretations may be, internalists seem prone to overdo the sequence as a closed system. They often fail to do justice to other forces in the sum total of the historical community, to influences external to the sequence: stimuli from diffusion and cross-fertilization within the total activity and intellectual currents of the community, the forced draft of demand in another line of development, and the consequences of an internal equilibrium being upset from outside.

28

Internal Wars: Revolution

Like so many historical terms, the word "revolution" has undergone changes in meaning. Originally, it referred to the rotation of the heavenly bodies, the celestial spheres, and, carrying a connotation of supernatural force, was applied in the Renaissance to human events that seemed beyond human control.

During the seventeenth century, the word still meant a return to a natural order of things, a natural order as regular as the rotation of the heavenly bodies. Hence the Restoration in England in 1660 was considered a revolution, but not the Puritan episode, which came under the label of rebellion. The Glorious Revolution, however, was a revolution for those at that time who felt that the events of 1688 had restored the natural order. By the time of the French Revolution, the meaning had altered to convey the idea of revolting against tyranny, of changing the destiny of a people by heroic, romantic deeds.

Popular usage of the word applied to any forcible overthrow of a government, for instance by the military, has blurred its twentieth-century meaning. No one specific definition for authentic revolution will satisfy everyone, and when getting into specifics, several kinds should probably be distinguished. None of the efforts in this direction seem quite satisfactory because the uniformities, as in other areas of history, are not that uniform. Nevertheless, certain ingredients appear to be characteristic: (1) the presence of violence; (2) a breakdown of obedience to authority; (3) a transfer of power in the state; and (4) as most usually conceived, major social changes. Or, in one definition, a transfer of power from one or more social groups to other groups under circumstances of violence.

Different interpretations are held by people who range all the way from those who believe diabolical forces are responsible for these upheavals to the fervent devotees of the cult of revolution. For the latter, revolutions seem good in themselves, sometimes appear to serve in this secular century the older functions of a religious revival, a conversion and cleansing of society. Or they seem a shortcut to the Golden Age of the future. Often uncomprehending or derogatory of other historical processes, the devotees may regard revolution as the only effective agent of change. "Revolution is the locomotive of history, the motive force of the progress of human society," proclaimed a Chinese Communist leader, echoing a similar statement by Karl Marx.

As dramatic episodes in the early acceleration of political change all over the world, the late eighteenth-century American and French upheavals inaugurated the modern series of revolutions. Earlier outbreaks of general political unrest, however, had taken place, one of these being as early as the 1560s. At approximately the same time as the Puritan Revolution in the 1640s, the Fronde in France occurred, a protest against increasing centralization, taxation, and bureaucracy in the Age of Despots. Rebellions also broke out in these years in Spain, Portugal, Naples, and Central Europe, the latter particularly reflecting the exhaustion caused by the Thirty Years War. Even in Russia, the Zemsky Sobor, a partially representative assembly, grew momentarily influential.

The French Revolution, however, lies at the storm center of

a series of disturbances, some, as in Poland and the present-day Belgium, caused by local conditions primarily, while others were ignited by French example or assistance. Presently, the Spanish Americans rebelled against their motherland, the Greeks succeeded in throwing off the Turkish yoke, and in 1830 and 1848 additional series of revolts occurred. Historians continue to debate whether these all form part of a single larger phenomenon, a Western Revolution, or not.

Most experts have considered the French and Russian revolutions the classic examples, those that best typify the nature of revolution and which in turn provided the models, many of the stereotypes, and much of the terminology that prevail in large measure to this day. Crane Brinton, on the basis of a comparative study of these two plus the Puritan and the American, tried to set up, in *The Anatomy of Revolution,* a model of the phases or sequences of developments in a typical revolution. These included a period of criticism by the intellectuals; growing disorder; a peaceful transfer of power; reaction by those ousted and some form of civil war; a period of extremism; and, finally, a return to normalcy, sometimes accompanied by Bonapartism or attempted outward expansion. Certain features of these are worth noting. The transfer of power comes relatively peacefully, more an abdication than a storming of the citadels of power. Most of the bloodshed occurs *after* the transfer of power, as the former leading group discovers the liabilities of loss of power and tries to regain it. Extremists rise to the top within the new group and purge the moderate adherents; as a relatively small, precarious minority, they unleash a reign of terror in order to quell incipient reaction. When the revolution has devoured its own children, the regime eventually passes to those who must seek wider support and who therefore must restore a more normal state of affairs; to this stage has been given the name of Thermidor, after the example of the French Revolution where reaction started in the month of that name according to the new revolutionary calendar.

This attempt at finding uniformities fits the French and perhaps the Russian sequences reasonably well but applying them to others seems to strain the evidence. (Part of the problem is that such an upheaval may evoke support or resistance from other countries, thereby distorting any domestically engendered pattern.) Brinton also believed, as mentioned earlier, that although revolutions start in the name of freedom they end in greater centralization. New rulers tend to be more efficient, often present better solutions to pressing problems, and may still be so fearful of opponents that they maintain more stringent controls than the preceding regime.

No one model can possibly explain fully the nature of revolution. Harry Eckstein has listed twenty-one generalized causes, a variety reminiscent of the reasons for the decline of Rome. Some focus on economic factors, some on intellectual ones, others on political and social structure or general social processes. The reasons range from growing poverty through alienation of the intellectuals, isolation of the rulers, and the appearance of new social classes all the way to excessive prevalence of ideologies. A long war (especially a lost war) may help to precipitate revolutionary convulsions. Different scholars emphasize different parts of the process, no consistent image beyond convulsive changes emerges, and therefore any broad survey of basic processes tends to take the form of a series of generalities.

Modern revolutions require the presence of essentially modern factors, such as improved communications and literacy. Until recently, an urban scene seemed necessary, many people living together, a swift exchange of ideas, and the possibility of effective party organization, as well as the psychological contagion of revolutionary fervor itself. Effective communications and transportation have now, however, also made possible the use of the countryside for mobilizing resistance. Medieval and early modern city-states, where the small areas involved made similar factors effective, sometimes passed through revolutionary episodes.

One of the preparatory elements quite obviously consists of the alienation of the intellectuals. The *philosophes* of the Enlightenment—Voltaire, Rousseau, and others—helped to destroy faith in the old institutions and the habit of obedience, while simultaneously providing justification for rebellion.

Numerous stereotypes of the French Revolution became permanent tools of future revolutionists: freedom from tyranny; the inherent "rights of man"; the noble savage; the cult of the future. Similarly, numerous Russian writers in the second half of the nineteenth century attacked prevailing ideas and discussed alternatives. However, a portion of the intellectuals seem determined to be permanently alienated in every industrial and post-industrial society, and, as such, they usually contribute to on-going change within society, a role not foreshadowing violent revolution itself.

That people rise in desperation against tyranny, that misery causes revolution, these have always been popular notions. Along with the Golden Age of the future, they remain the stock-in-trade of revolutionary leaders. Historians like Carlyle and Jules Michelet (and Charles Dickens in *A Tale of Two Cities*) narrated in full detail both the misery and the tyranny, though even at that time Alexis de Tocqueville was writing that "the French found their condition the more insupportable in proportion to its improvement." Had misery actually engendered revolution, the French, after a century of genuine advances, would have been among the last people in Europe to revolt; the Russian Revolution came after three decades of accelerating material achievements. However, a sharp economic downturn badly hurt some elements in France, and two successive poor harvests reduced the food supply; the Russian suffered the agonizing ordeal of World War I. Therefore, the tendency now is to say that a sudden discouraging setback after steady progress may set the stage for revolution.

Quite possibly, the state of mind is as important as the actual situation, perhaps more so. Where conditions do not encourage hope, it does not occur to people to rise up, but the "revolution of rising expectancies" may bring on an upheaval, the actual possibility of escape producing action. In fact, as Tocqueville wrote long ago, a regime may help to precipitate revolt when it "lightens the burdens and attempts some reforms."

Weaknesses in the regime itself undoubtedly are another indispensable ingredient for revolution. No matter how tyrannical, a competent, resolute government determined to stay in power is extremely unlikely to be overthrown, regardless of how many abuses prevail. An elite ruling class with both appetite and aptitude for power will continue to wield authority, wrote Vilfredo Pareto, until "humanitarian weaknesses" assail the descendants of the tough-minded founders, Pareto undoubtedly drawing this generalization from the events of the Italian city-states and ancient classical history.

Oftentimes, the vested interests in a regime, unheedingly oblivious to their long-term interests, will prevent necessary reforms or adjustments. They may not know how to absorb dissidents, bring them into the establishment. A change of ideas and values, such as the Enlightenment, or the increasing assertion of the values and needs of new social classes may erode faith in former attitudes or positively frustrate large elements. Military disasters also demoralize a regime.

Something may go wrong with the power structure itself, an inner contradiction like a split or disintegration in the elite, its actions henceforth being paralyzed by internal dissension and leaving a vacuum of power in the community. A "healthy" regime always stands ready to use at least moderate force in order to maintain its rule. The weakening of a government reveals itself in lack of resolution and, prior to this, in a long series of abuses, which derive less from tyrannical intent than from ineffective administration. Financial distress of the government, as in France in the 1780s, can be symptomatic.

Bad handling of incipient revolt can also be a symptom. A botched repression not only infuriates but also encourages rebels, as happened in France in 1789 and in Russia in the summer of 1917. It may also serve to set off the revolutionary sequence of events in a situation that has had such potential for some time, whether this be called the "immediate cause," "trigger," or "precipitant."

Eugene Kamenka has pointed out a distinction between Anglo-American and continental European interpretations. On the continent, where governments tended to be rigid in the nineteenth century, economic changes are usually assumed to be responsible for causing revolutions. The English and the Americans, accustomed to economic and social changes within a stable political framework, have been prone to believe the rigid regimes themselves responsible by penning up discontent until a revolutionary explosion occurs. In terms of challenge and response, the authorities fail to respond to changing circumstances soon enough.

Within the pattern of change and continuity, a revolution constitutes a period of temporary, greatly accelerated change, usually preceded and followed by relative stability. The incidence of so-called revolutions may seem to have increased in this century, which has been an era of increasing worldwide transformation and consequent likelihood for rapidly developing maladjustments, but, despite newspaper headlines, an historian, recalling a past that teems with peasant uprisings and town rioting, might seriously question if the present age actually experiences a greater incidence of violence. The difference seems, rather, to lie in a change in the character of revolution, due to the increasing presence of the aforementioned modern factors.

Quite possibly the historian's models of revolution are drawn too exclusively from the classic examples, which within the general long-term perspective of various forms of convulsive violence make up only some of the more complete episodes of what Eckstein prefers to call "internal wars." If this term is used to cover a broader prism of political violence, it designates, to borrow Peter Calvert's definition, "forcible interventions" in order to "replace governments, or to change the processes of government." Seen in this larger sense, internal wars have been classified by Chalmers Johnson into six types: peasant Jacqueries; uprisings by the Millenarians; anarchistic rebellion; Jacobin or Communist social revolutions; conspiratorial coups d'etat; and the militarized mass insurgency along the lines of the Algerians or the Vietnamese.

With the breakdown of authority, one so-called revolution may consist of several successive or concurrent revolutions. The events of 1789 had been preceded by an aristocratic revolt (of which the Assembly of Notables is a part), and the peasants underwent their own kind of upheaval at the same time as the events in the cities. Then came the revolution of the extremists, after the drama of 1789-1791 had seemed to conclude the sequence of developments. In Russia, one revolution occurred early in 1917 with the collapse of the tsarist regime, the Bolsheviks carried through a second one in the autumn, and a third took place among the peasantry. In addition, the various non-Russian nationalities waged their own struggles for autonomy at first and then for independence.

Manifestly, too, the sequence of a complete revolution may be interrupted by opponents gaining the upper hand, as happened in the Spanish Civil War (1936–1939), when a leftist republic was destroyed. Occasionally, a seemingly prerevolutionary phase, either in the stage of sporadic violence or even after a legal transfer of power, culminates in military intervention and suppression of restive elements. Rarely, however, can the "reactionaries" restore former conditions, for the unleashed social forces and altered circumstances compel the new authorities to improvise from an altered set of conditions and structure of power.

In the case of the Anglo-American political cycle, the alienation and the outbreak of sporadic violence may look like the beginning of Brinton's pattern of revolution, but no transfer of power occurs, only a broadening of representation for the discontented within the political equilibrium. For a time, the restive elements weight the equilibrium in favor of more thorough reform. In every such period of change, the extremists, who would come to the fore in an actual revolution, eventually become isolated as the widespread discontent is alleviated both materially and psychologically, while their conduct alienates the moderates in their own camp and thereby accelerates the swing back to greater continuity. A permanent process of change becomes institutionally channelized.

Kamenka maintains that the successful institutionalization of social and economic change in advanced countries has obviated their need for revolution. A number of experts believe revolution unlikely in either a backward country or an advanced industrial state. Nations in transition seem much more vulnerable, the older elite increasingly being unable to control events, while groups representing innovative trends sharpen their demands, increasingly resent antiquated practices and regulations, and eventually gain the strength to strike for power.

What of the role of the military? Manifestly, a loyal armed force can quickly repress the older type of revolt. In both France and Russia, however, the crumbling of morale and desertions played a potent part in the weakening of the government. Charles X had sent part of his army to Algiers in 1830, and Louis Philippe abdicated when his National Guard manifested disloyalty. The Fourth Republic collapsed in 1958 and had to give way to Charles de Gaulle when the armed forces defied government orders. Guerilla warfare in this century evades direct confrontation with military power while simultaneously eroding its morale and confidence. It has been asserted that the machine gun made the old-fashioned revolution at the barricades impossible as long as the military remained loyal, but new means of communication and transportation, as well as the emergence of huge urban centers, have also, in some cases, transformed the nature of revolution into true internal wars.

During this century the military, wherever stable democratic systems have not emerged, has tended increasingly to look upon itself as the embodiment of the nation, as providing government by proxy. Officers of the armed forces, sprung from diverse sectors of the people, may also consider themselves as more truly representative of these elements than are politicians and political parties. In taking power, the military sometimes proclaims a revolution and undertakes sweeping changes of a revolutionary character; eventually, however, the officers, if the changes are to be maintained, must establish a broader base of support in the civil population.

Both popular and scholarly conceptions have been strongly influenced by the Marxist appropriation of revolutionary phenomena for themselves, by their assumption that only upheavals corresponding to the Marxist pattern are genuine revolutions. Most people still think of the French Revolution in terms of the victory of the middle class and of the Bolshevik Revolution as being a working-class triumph. This can only be regarded as an oversimplification in which victors or posterity put their own shapes and labels to the events and thereby greatly distort what really did happen. By demolishing the remnants of manorialism and discrediting absolute monarchy, the French Revolution opened the way to what are called bourgeois regimes, but the leaders at the time, mostly lawyers and other professional people, scarcely represented the core of middle-class activity or motivation.

Simple usage of terms like "capitalist" or "bourgeois" versus "feudal" or "nobility," reflecting excessive influence of the Marxist ideas of social classes and class struggle, does not faithfully reflect the reality of the circumstances prevalent at the time. Much of the wealth in the period of the French Revolution consisted in various proprietary forms, such as land or venal offices, not in direct capitalist, manufacturing, or banking investments. Thiers and Tocqueville believed that in both 1789 and 1848 the revolutions sprang in considerable part from people who wanted state jobs for themselves. The workers provided part of the shock troops for the Bolsheviks in Russia, but the leaders were professional revolutionaries claiming to be acting on behalf of the workers and peasants. Those who became leaders in the party and government officials reaped the ultimate benefits; the working class as such did not.

The question remains open whether a revolution must consist of *lower* classes overturning an upper class along Marxist lines, especially in contemporary societies, which have outgrown the Marxist framework—if this concept ever did reflect the actuality of the real world. Seizures of power by representatives of other classes are, in the Marxist view, counterrevolutionary or reactionary, but a pluralist community, containing so many diverse groups that thinking in terms of social classes becomes inappropriate, might well see revolutionary movements based on neither the traditional upper nor on the lower classes, as seems to be the case with fascism. Few historical processes are as suffused with street-level mythology as those of revolution.

V

THE HISTORIAN'S HISTORY

29

The Century of History: Monks and Prophets

According to the German historian Friedrich Meinecke, the development of historicism has been one of the greatest intellectual revolutions that Western thought has undergone. Historicism as a form of thought emerged in the nineteenth century, along with a number of the conventional shapes of history and the scientific methodology for handling primary-source materials. Though much has altered since then, the fundamental outlook and scholarly techniques in using materials out of the past developed during that century.

Modern historical scholarship, however, may be said to have had its origins earlier, in the seventeenth century, with the methodology of the French Benedictines, who developed techniques for epigraphy, paleography, diplomatics, and numismatics. In 1681, which Bloch calls a great year for the human mind, Jean Mabillon published *De Re Diplomatica*, on how to criticize documents in archives. As history for history's sake, this was the work of antiquarians zealously recovering facts about the past while developing a tradition of critical scholarship.

Enlightenment writers, frequently using history for its relevancy to their own times and as ammunition in their controversies, introduced the vision of human progress and of a coming secular Golden Age. By helping to liberate history from theology, they prepared the way for finding and expressing its own nature in secular processes rather than through Hand of God explanations. Already the difference of opinion in the Mansion of History between the relevancy writers and those who believed in history for its own sake was becoming clearly visible. Because the Benedictine scholars were interested in the past for itself rather than for contemporary purposes, the philosophes scorned them as "les erudits," but presently the historians at the University of Göttingen in their turn began to denounce the abuses of relevancy history perpetrated by the Enlightenment writers.

In the 1800s, called the Century of History by Stephen Toulmin and June Goodfield in *The Discovery of Time,* an era of revolutions, the increasing sense of nationalism, and the flourishing Romanticist movement all helped to intensify a growing awareness of the past. Revolutions naturally attracted attention to history, both because of the dramatic events themselves and as explanations for their occurrence. The impact of shattering experiences swayed spectators and participants alike into enlisting history as justification for the upheavals or for a restoration of continuity.

A growing sense of nationalism greatly contributed to an interest in the past as each national group, with the spread of schooling and literacy, self-consciously focused on its own background; historians often became the "high priests" of nationalism, in the words of Fritz Stern, "revealing to their people its past glories." At a time when railroads, steamboats, and telegraph wires made possible a larger and more cohesive community, this sense of nationalism served a political imperative, helping to replace ancient loyalties to province or city with loyalties to the modern national state. The patriotic story, however, also imposed an enduring caricature on history, unduly dividing it into national segments. The Romantic movement, so much in vogue early in the century, greatly enhanced historical sensitivity. Fascinated by the past and especially the medieval period, the Romanticists studied customs, legends, poetry, language, and folk music and in the process helped to broaden and enrich the time dimension. The resultant inebriating brew of folk heroes and memorable episodes often transformed fact into fancy, but this very enthusiasm stimulated a more sympathetic understanding of some earlier eras and encouraged the historians' scholarly travels into the past.

By the middle of the century, history was ceasing to be considered a branch of literature, though literary historians like Macaulay and Carlyle still prospered. For the public, to be sure, its common purpose continued to remain partly moral, teaching its lessons as had been the practice since the days of the Greeks and Romans. History presumably taught by example, instructing the people of action or the politicians how to conduct themselves successfully. Some writers were now seeking a more ambitious goal, the finding of meaning in the course of the human past, whether in progress, scientific advances, national destinies, or triumphant ideas.

Simultaneously, the intellectual tools for coping with past phenomena were being greatly amplified. A far-reaching advance occurred in the perception of change and continuity. In the middle of the preceding century, the figures in history still acted on an essentially unchanging stage except when catastrophic events might abruptly produce an entirely new stage. Only the actors altered, little cognizance being taken of gradual modifications in physical surroundings, human habits, or cultural patterns. Historians now were escaping this compartmentalized historical time, comparable to a physical world where species do not evolve, as they penetrated to a more authentic past, each area of which, wherever visited, proved to have its own unique qualities. Artists, too, expressed the new awareness by inserting in their paintings architecture and costumes appropriate to the era being depicted.

Johann Herder (1744–1803), one of the earliest to sense

and articulate the flow of historical time, seemed almost obsessed by the ceaseless flux in the stream of time, the endless becoming of all things human. The Romanticists explored and deepened this dimension of human sensibilities, while the aforementioned Göttingen school and historians at the University of Berlin elaborated the evolution of the state and other institutions. Linguistic and legal studies contributed to this emerging mode of thought. In reaction to the abrupt alterations brought by the French Revolution, they stressed a gradual, inherent process of change in the midst of continuity.

In a sense, Hegel systematized the German Romanticist ideas of change in history in the Hegelian dialectic: a thesis generating an antithesis that eventually, after a conflict, leads to a synthesis, which then becomes a new thesis. Originally, the Hegelian concept had some advantages as an improvement over a concept of simple linear progress, but the advent of Darwinist evolution quickly rendered it obsolete. Darwin, as described earlier, popularized a set of related ideas already "in the air," nourished by scholarly minds, and there for creative thinkers to articulate. The gradualist version of history was emerging, satisfyingly parallel to scientific conviction that *natura non facit saltum* (nature does not make leaps).

Many implications flowed from Darwinist evolution, including the idea of the survival of the fittest. Historical evolution could be depicted in similar fashion: historical elements gradually being molded through the selectivity of circumstances into something quite different, some being snuffed out by adverse conditions while those better fitted would thrive. Darwinism also seemed to refute the existence of a single dominating purpose or any ultimate meaning in the universe, whether in nature or human history, and thereby to discredit any comprehensive historical scheme like the Christian, Hegelian, or Marxist.

Another version of evolution and progress emerged in Marxism, a developing or becoming with its core and dynamic in the economic world. As Darwin discovered the law of evolution in the history of organic nature, so Marx thought he had discovered a law of evolution in the history of mankind, finding it in the means of production. He borrowed Hegel's dialectic, an exploiting class being the thesis and the oppressed class the hostile antithesis, these two in successive versions locked in class struggle throughout the past. The "history of all hitherto existing society is the history of class struggle," and revolution is the driving force in history.

Whatever the diversity of their specific interests, Darwin and Marx believed in progress, as did Herbert Spencer, Henry Buckle, and Auguste Comte. Macaulay reflects the typical mood of his age, as V. H. Galbraith expressed it, by indulging in the Victorian assumption that history culminated in his own era, the "Triumphant Act 5."

Meantime, the writers of history had become aware of more varieties of causality in the abundant social energies. The geologists, as they escaped the preconceptions of divine creation and catastrophism, offered suggestive uses of causality; Georges Cuvier, James Hutton, and William Smith at the turn of the century were elaborating the concept of *natural* causality, the molding of the earth's features by the incessant functioning of forces still at work. Men like Buckle and Friedrich Ratzel developed a whole series of geographical relationships, and Mahan later added the influence of sea power. Marx would still be remembered for the economic interpretation of history even if communism and socialism had never emerged as political movements; as Carr expressed it, this made all earlier history seem old-fashioned. Marxism, too, presented an historical scheme, a framework readymade for interpreting history, whose assumption that determinist economic causality partakes of the validity of scientific laws seemed much more intellectually respectable then than later.

Toulmin and Goodfield call the 1800s the Century of History because it saw the emergence of a profound historical-mindedness in many areas of knowledge, not merely in history proper. First, in geology and zoology, the concept of development within the framework of time replaced belief in a static order of nature, then the other sciences, except physics, passed through this intellectual transformation.

If the historical approach revolutionized the natural sciences, the scientific approach also transformed history. This age, with its insatiable curiosity to know, organize, and catalogue all data, tried to do this also with humanity's past. A century that conducted an ardent and successful search for laws in the physical world could find, it was hoped, similar results in the human sphere. Once data out of the past had been assiduously collected and handled "scientifically," broad answers would, hopefully, emerge. In time, some thought, universal laws would be discovered, a great and effective determinist causality in which individuals, variety, and causal factors would all be swept into an overriding pattern.

This school of thought, founded by Comte and called positivism, derived from a complete faith in the omnicompetence of science for the study of human affairs. Buckle, who exemplifies the positivist influences upon historians, wanted them to collect the facts and sift out the uniformities, thus eventually finding the "hidden regularities of human actions in history" and thereby making history a science. Positivism had a strong impact on historians but became much more influential in the formation of those disciplines that now bear the label of social sciences.

That history did not fully lend itself to the approach of the natural sciences speedily became apparent, a primary reason being that the historian deals with human beings, who possess consciousness and varying inner states of mind. Wilhelm Dilthey (1833–1911) in raising this issue suggested that the study of the human being and society required a different kind of science and methodology. Using the positivist pose of detached observation, he insisted, would not elicit true historical data, since historians must necessarily go into the past and *relive* the experiences of those being scrutinized. The inner states of the human mind are reflected or objectified, according to Dilthey, in their cultures, and historians must be able to put themselves into the culture of the time being studied, see the world with the values, attitudes, and concepts of that time, and thus study individuals within their own context. Historical figures confront a choice of courses, and only from within their own cultural context can the decisions be properly understood. Behaviorism would pick up this theme in the middle of the twentieth century.

Leopold von Ranke (1795–1886) became the central figure and patron saint of modern historiography. Already in 1824 he penned the famous phrase that history should be narrated *"wie es eigentlich gewesen,"* (as it actually was). Protesting the misuse of history by Enlightenment philosophes, Romanticists, and philosophic idealists like Hegel, Ranke was reacting against versions of history that had little basis in the real past and did not originate in primary sources. According to Ranke, the weaving of philosophic schemes out of history, the intrusion of the historian's own subjective prepossessions into the narrative, and the making of moral judgments had no place in a history empirical and objective.

The above phrase became, in time, a four-word manifesto for those whose primary allegiance was to the sources. It was also somewhat taken out of context, especially by the Americans, Ranke being made to say more than he actually had. Reflecting the spirit of the scientific age, the Rankeans assumed that historians must be detached observers of their material and strictly limit the making of generalizations, the latter a scholarly taboo that long hampered historians. The shapes of history would automatically emerge from the evidence, so it was believed, as factual material accumulated.

Ranke himself, however, did much more than put down what had happened; he constructed generalizations regularly in his voluminous writings. His emphasis actually lay in the *combination* of primary sources, critical method, objective research, and synthetic construction. Like Herder a Lutheran, Ranke was equally fascinated by the Lutheran concept of God's Creative Order, the ultimate purposes and meanings of which can only remain unknowable but the detailed lineaments of which must be recorded with reverent integrity because each unique event possesses value in itself. In an age of nationalism, Ranke held that each age and nation "stood immediate to God," that all events had importance and significance for humanity.

In this latter belief, Ranke exemplifies that nineteenth-century version of historical-mindedness known as historicism, of which he is customarily considered the founder. At the core of historicism is the belief that everything is comprehended within its becoming, within a "continuous, genetic, causal process" of development. The past consists of an endless formation and transformation in which historical forms appear in an infinite range of varieties, forever changing. Each age derives meaning from its own system of values, each must be accepted within its own context, and the historian must respect its irreducible particularity and uniqueness.

For some time, the Rankean credo was predominate among the scholars in the Mansion of History who made genuine visits to the past. Interestingly enough, their exaggerated reverence for Ranke's empiricism and objectivity—especially the restraint on generalizations—illustrates the history of ideas. Posterity selected and used Ranke's ideas somewhat differently than he himself intended, the thrust of his statement conveniently altered.

Scientific methodology in historical evidence was further refined, particularly, by the historians at the University of Berlin and from Germany transplanted to the United States. In France, Langlois and Seignobos published *Introduction to the Study of History* (1898), a manual for historiography; with considerable positivist zeal, they emphasized the study of documents and verification of facts while ignoring most of the ingredients of historical-mindedness. Henceforth, academic professionals wrote most of the accepted history and did so according to the established canons of historical objective empiricism. Bury's generation repeatedly quoted his overzealous pronouncement that history is "a science, no less and no more," to the exclusion of statements more representative of his thought. As Stern expresses it, the historian became an academic monk in his study, while "the world about him sought him as a preacher."

By the end of the nineteenth century, the controversy between the preacher-prophets and the monks, devoted to a cumulative scholarly study of the past, had long been underway. Viewed more optimistically, a basically fruitful division of labor had occurred between those who journey to the past and those who use history for contemporary purposes.

30

The Twentieth Century: Many Rooms

"Do not applaud. It is not I who speak, but history which speaks through me." Thus responded the noted French historian, Fustel de Coulanges, when, at the end of a lecture, the audience burst into applause.

A typical example of the assumptions at the end of the Century of History: once the data had been uncovered, the facts would "speak for themselves." Historians must keep their own outlook strictly out of the process, avoid imposing prejudices and prepossessions upon the emerging patterns, and not generalize beyond known facts. Working empirically and objectively, they would produce the ultimate historical answers as their cumulative labors converged "along a single line of truth."

Lord Acton, originally one of the more vocal believers in this process, increasingly fell silent, not daring to write because truth was not emerging. Far from producing final answers, even in secure generalizations within narrow limits, the accumulating evidence encouraged an increasing diversity of interpretations, few of them totally provable. Though answers were indeed being found and many errors eliminated, new questions proliferated even more rapidly.

Lukacs has commented that history in its present phase looks on the surface like a social science but in a deeper sense is a form of thought. Over the decades, history and the emerging social sciences have increasingly diverged, the latter retaining much of the positivist outlook, a faith in collecting, assembling, and classifying in order to seek scientifically valid propositions, while the historians have tended to limit generalizations to working tools useful in trying to reproduce the past. Some philosophers in recent years have worried over the apparent irreducibility of history, the continued imperviousness of its form of thought and historical data, to the approaches used so successfully in the natural sciences and which the social scientists have labored to apply in their fields also. Busily pursuing the methodology of their own discipline, the majority of historians have virtually ignored these efforts.

Other factors helped to account for this persistent disregard of the trends of the time, including the chastening experiences of their own craft earlier in this century as a consequence of World War I and the ensuing disillusionment. If history had indeed been speaking, it had served as a false prophet of nationalist destinies and continuing rapid progress; apparently the lessons of the past had been misread, or, just possibly, the past held few valid meanings for posterity. The easy optimism of the preceding century, the Triumphant Act 5 kind of history in which the past is a prelude to our own times, became discredited. As the historians discovered their own limitations and history lost prestige, the public looked elsewhere for prophets. Toynbee, to be sure, was a monk turned prophet, and his popularity indicated a continued general craving for the sweeping historical vision. Having once been led astray, most historians, however, seemed content to let the people listen to other seers, who would, no doubt, in their turn prove false.

The historian's craft had also developed to a level where, in all honesty and integrity, the easy, elementary answers no longer sufficed. More mature concepts of historical processes, the attributes and tools of historical-mindedness developed to deal with a complex world, did not satisfy street-level needs, could not be drawn upon by a public wanting quick answers and the psychological security of final truths. Relevancy writers on matters of current interest and popularizers telling the story henceforth largely served society while the "monks" concentrated on exploring the past.

Our history, says Plumb, is as different from earlier history as modern physics is from that of Archimedes. Historians have continued to refine the interpretations derived out of the evidence from the past, basic changes in the natural sciences have affected the nature of historical thought, the social sciences have repeatedly added new perspectives, and innovative tools are being tested. Numerous problems and crosscurrents are involved: the role of relevancy history; the degree of validity of historical processes; differences between long-term and short-term history; alterations in concepts of change and continuity; skepticism about causality; the reliability of the facts themselves; the permissible scope of generalizations; narrative versus analytical history; relationships with the social sciences and their positivist influences. History in the current century speaks with many voices; though the differences may be too subtle for the average citizen, there are many rooms in the Mansion of History.

The following chapters will be devoted to visiting the rooms in the upper stories of the Mansion where so-called cumulative history is being written. The purpose will not be to train historians in the scientific methodology of handling the materials of the past for purposes of reconstructing and narrating it, nor will much time be spent on the actual content, the substantive results in the numerous areas. This tour of the upper stories is primarily intended to provide a glimpse of the thought processes of the present-day professional historian and encourage some comprehension of the nature of the activities involved.

To return, first of all, to the division of labor between those who work in the past for its own sake and those who seek relevance to the present, each side in the dispute exercises somewhat of a monitory influence upon the other. The latter warn that historians must, for their own survival, be concerned with history's public uses, while the former insist on the maintenance of scholarly standards. Relevancy here means the use of the past to explain the present or to describe the past selectively in terms of topics of current interest.

Quite naturally, repeated protests against what the public often considers ivory tower scholarship are heard. One of the more influential of this kind in the United States occurred early in this century when James Harvey Robinson and others rebelled against "dry as dust" narrative by initiating the so-called New History, an attempt to broaden history beyond an essentially political approach to include a greater stress on contemporary social problems and issues.

Earlier, Friedrich Nietzsche had been one of those protesting the Ranke school of objectivity. In *The Use and Abuse of History* (1874), he claimed history to be necessary for man's "action and struggle, his conservatism and reverence, his suffering and his desire for deliverance" but that the historians had turned an heroic symphony into a flute duet for opium smokers. Great people should be spurred to action by history, not treated as only "visible bubbles" in mass movements; the human personality should not be portrayed as trapped in the becoming of some encompassing world process.

Putting the past at the service of the present, as Nietzsche desired, has its perils, as does seeking final answers in history. Julian Benda, a French writer, once denounced nationalist historians in a book entitled *The Treason of the Intellectuals* (1928) as "men of politics who make use of history to support a cause" and who, in doing so, betray their spiritual ministry. Which again recalls Paul Valéry's comment that such a version of history "gives ... false memories ... keeps their old wounds open ... and leads them into delusions of grandeur or persecution. ..." Another series of historians have read class struggle into every era of the past, on the basis that, visible or not, it must have been there. Historians have often imported past grievances into the present and present grievances into the past.

In the writing on topics of current interest, scholars do not object to relevancy as such, only to the frequency with which the need for relevance may tempt writers into violating both scientific methodology and the basic historical processes as commonly visualized. Writers not historically minded, when dealing with controversial issues, oftentimes lapse into the shoddy devices of the elementary level and display little or no awareness of processes. Over especially heated issues, such as the black revolution or the Vietnam War, elementary thinking—moralizing, the use of the good-evil dichotomy, and the monocausal approach, in continued unblushing array—reemerges. These temptations may be almost irresistible for those concerned with emotionally charged public issues. At the very least, an historian who wishes to be read must be present-minded in his or her communication, not only writing in a fluent vernacular but also orienting the presentation to some extent to contemporary insights. By adjusting to patterns of thinking and stereotypes used on the street, the product may also be distorted. Beyond this, the public does not necessarily much *want* objective history as such, hence one source for the perpetual erosion of historical processes at the street level. Theodore H. White has written that "Americans have a propensity for re-inventing a past in order to serve the needs of the present. . . ." And not only the Americans.

Relevancy history suffers the additional drawback of being short-lived. The very emphasis on matters of current concern means that when these episodes are over and public attention is focused elsewhere, the account quickly becomes outmoded. It also suffers rapid obsolescence because it tends to overplay selected factors at the expense of others, to slight elements of continuity, and to assume continuation of momentum in the present direction, traits which prove embarrassingly glaring once the situation has changed.

Nevertheless, relevancy remains an essential function of the craft, a common workaday use. The principal justification for history, according to some, lies in showing the background for the contemporary world, how the various ingredients and problems came into existence, and the direction of development. To safeguard the collective memory of the community and to utilize it for the better understanding of the problems of each generation constitutes the prosaic task, the core, of the historian's contribution to the community at the street level. Its value becomes most apparent when contrasted to analyses of current situations from which the becoming of things have been amputated: family trees of relationships missing, origins of group or institutional behavior omitted, formative experiences and their subsequent consequences not described. Varying sharply in quality, much of relevancy history is to be found in newspaper and news magazine accounts, in more sophisticated periodicals dealing with foreign affairs and contemporary issues, and as background material in books on matters of current interest.

Strong reactions to the abuses of relevancy may too often drive professional historians into the ivory towers and thereby reduce the proper contribution of history. The historical-mindedness of the upper stories—the product of endless work in original sources and the emergence of tentative shapes and processes—does have relevancy, though often invisible at the street level, by ensuring more respect for all of the contours of reality and more accurate comprehension of how things usually happen than that offered by the mythmakers and their elementary forms of historical-mindedness. Meantime, the necessities of relevancy warn of the need for constant communication between those on the upper stories of the Mansion and those who fulfill public needs by working nearer the street level.

Next, a brief look at the nature of basic historical processes themselves, the means whereby history as a form of thought is conceptualized and articulated. They are not *the* historical processes, for no such certainty seems possible; they are only sketches of commonly accepted processes and shapes used by the historian in what would otherwise be chaotic long-term history. Social scientists consider these processes a poor sort of social science because they are broad generalizations, serving as illustrations and approximate models rather than offering definitive scientific proofs. Furthermore, those appearing in this book happen to be conceptual tools of one quite fallible historian, and other individuals would present somewhat different processes and shapes according to temperament, personal style, and experience. Nor are they necessarily always the Last Word, the latest authoritative conclusions, for Last Words must usually undergo a period of professional testing and digesting before merging into widely used historical processes.

This is quite typical of the historian's craft, in which respect for the unique bans a systematic search for universal propositions and in which processes usually serve as tools for the real goal, increasing comprehension of the past. To be sure, these processes could be amplified to ten times their present length, stated more specifically in various guises, and buttressed with sundry variants of the Last Word. Such a compendium, however, would contain less consensus than controversy. These generalities, some adapted from other disciplines, have been shaped by the experts in the upper stories of the Mansion of History where the historians do not pretend to find final answers, and they constitute, it is hoped, a representative sample of *the historians' current wisdom about how things tend to happen.*

Furthermore, basic historical-mindedness is, essentially, how the historian thinks about episodes and developments *outside* of his or her own specialized area of work. Textbook-level learning in general history is comparable to introductory science in schools, where scientific traditions, protocols, and procedures must first be learned by future scientists, who then go on to develop additional skills in their areas, or to a principles of economics course, totally necessary for a future economist but scarcely adequate in itself as professional preparation.

Shattering news, this, for the literal-minded—for those who crave the security of proven truth—when they first enter the inner sanctum of the historian. Worse is to come. Basic historical processes constitute the warp and woof of long-term history, but a curious thing often happens when the specialist goes to work in the original sources of a specific area. When he or she puts the microscope to personalities and episodes in their full detail, the broader shapes become extraordinarily tenuous or vanish altogether. These conventional shapes perhaps persist only in wisps and traces that, in the midst of other motley evidence, scarcely seem significant enough to be selected as dominating elements in this particular scene, while other wisps and traces may hint at other forces and regularities not yet incorporated into basic historical processes. Or the scene may seem too chaotic, if the unique be cherished, to be subject to patterns at all. Hence the assertions of an occasional historian, like H. A. L. Fisher, that search as he will, he can find no plot, rhythm, or predetermined patterns in history.

Sir Lewis Namier, working on mid-eighteenth-century English history, came to the conclusion that the conventional image in its broad patterns did not fit the data, was more deceptive than illuminating. Jack Hexter could not find the vaunted "rise of the middle class" (nor several other items) in sixteenth- and seventeenth-century England. Historians of the French Revolution have for some time been dismantling the conventional picture, and Alfred Cobban even writes about the "myth" of the French Revolution. Recent studies of feudalism reveal considerable anomalies even in northern France, where feudalism was supposedly the most complete. And Johan Huizinga, trying to pinpoint "rising civilization" in the late medieval, saw the concept escaping him as he tried to apply it.

Here, in the common experience of the specialist, lies a most persuasive reason why history continues to be history, not a social science. Historians, working with the unique in original sources, remain highly suspicious of generalizing patterns and processes; necessary to some extent for both coherence and explanation, the shapes are all too likely to exclude too much and to introduce artificiality into objective reality. The historian, in general, continues to see *happenings* as the true reality and, as the guardian of the collective memory of humanity, to believe that if narrative history did not exist it would have to be invented.

Siegfried Kracauer proposed an interesting alternative in this problem of short- and long-term history, of so-called micro and macro history. Based on analogy with photography, he believed that the "law of perspective" largely determines the perception of historical shapes. He suggested that both macro and micro patterns may be valid, may exist "side-by-side," even though little evident parallel or relationship seems to exist between them.

Thus, we may imagine two people's perspective on a mountain side. One person down below looks up and sees a small cloud floating along the edge of the mountain, while the second person, an artist, is at the cloud level and busy painting a tiny mountain meadow full of spring flowers. Preoccupied with the scene, the artist may be only peripherally aware of the transitory passage of light fog in the air. For the person below, the cloud forms the focus of the picture. Which person's image is the *valid* one? Obviously they both are, and neither one of the two images invalidates the other. In Kracauer's words, the macro dimension seems to be of "another order," to have a "certain autonomy" from the micro level. Furthermore, given fifty artists at different spots on that mountain side, the composite image of those fifty would still not produce the same picture as that of the person below. For that person, the wisps and traces of fog, barely perceptible up there, remain the eventful happening of that moment. That is, the macro historians necessarily limit themselves to delineating episodes and movements still visible to posterity at a considerable time distance, whereas these developments may not seem nearly as significant within the context of the multitudinous events of any given decade.

Suppose that the person below insists upon imposing his or her perceived pattern of mountain and cloud upon the artist's canvas. The artist's reaction would be quite predictable, and in precisely the same way the specialist reacts to those who would write the history of their period in the broad, sweeping patterns of general history. This problem will recur in later chapters.

31

Cumulative History:
Interpretations

A summary account in general history may give the impression of a static record in which the past is a story agreed upon, though in truth this is rarely the case in a discipline undergoing changes nearly as rapidly as the natural sciences. In each of the many areas of history, a number of tentative interpretations, supported by different scholars, are usually being propounded. Interpretations, as basic tools for the handling of historical materials, bear the brunt of professional communications among historians themselves and serve to express successive judgments on how and why events happened as they did.

Usually relatively limited in scope, historians devise their interpretations as the evidence of the original sources seems to require and use such historical processes as may be appropriate. Always subject to further testing when new evidence or perspectives become available, the interpretations remain open-ended without any assumption of a final answer; scholarly knowledge about the past advances through a succession of Last Words. An historian reading a general history does so at two levels, the narrative and the scholarly, duly recognizing the various interpretations, perhaps identifying their creators, and noting which possible versions have been omitted.

For lack of a better term, the not particularly felicitous "cumulative history" may be used to designate the mainstream of professional history. The body of evidence has been cumulative, though the revamping of historical generalizations never ceases, and a newcomer to a special area, inheriting a legacy of interpretations from his or her predecessors, must know their contributions and viewpoints before attempting to improve upon them. The term stresses a working within the framework of the legacy, as contrasted to imposing external a priori assumptions—elementary, ideological, philosophical, or otherwise—upon the evidence.

Voltaire claimed that history plays tricks upon the dead. Others have expressed it another way, that present events cast their shadows backward. Historians can scarcely completely escape the experienced insights and cultural patterns of their own generation, and, consequently, in even the most objective historians an almost unconscious desire for relevancy to the present imprints some of the contemporary contours upon the past.

Butterfield in *The Whig Interpretation of History* offered a classic description of how present contours imposed upon the past distort it. Pointing out that the standard viewpoint of many English historians had been on the side of the Protestants and the Whigs, he asserted that their writings served as a "ratification if not the glorification of the present." The Whig interpretation makes one party more modern, more like the present than it really is, while the other has been made to look like an "obstruction" to progress. Catholics and Protestants much more resembled each other than either was like us, both would "deplore" the twentieth century, the issues in the 1500s were "not of our world," and our issues should not be read into them.

The British constitution, Butterfield wrote, is the product of history, and to name persons and parties as being responsible evades the "whole network of . . . conditioning circumstances."

A "purpose achieved" tends to be a misreading for "purpose marred." Both innovative and conserving agencies, within a tension of equilibriums and the interplay of various factors, helped to create the British governance. That is, the Whig interpretation misrepresents the past, gives an erroneous impression of how historical processes work, and thereby also distorts the view of the present as well.

Because relevancy may warp the shapes of the past, a series of contemporary crises sometimes causes major changes in interpretations. American versions of German history have undergone violent oscillations during this century due to the stormy character of German history itself since 1914; these events have cast their shadows backward upon all of the German past. Americans fought the Germans in two world wars, while the Germans themselves passed through periods of rule by the Kaiser's Reich, the Weimar Republic, and the Nazis, following which they were a partitioned country. During these years, the Americans saw "Five Images of Germany" in succession, to quote the title of a survey of its historiography by Henry Cord Meyer. The original pre-World War I image was of the ancestral home of many Americans, a major world power, and an international leader in science, technology, and the liberal arts. Then the first war brought a reaction of intense hostility and distorted writing about the "Hun" and German militarism. After a period of righting the balance in the 1920s and early 1930s, the Nazi upsurge stimulated a host of books, many by journalists, in which German history was plundered in order to explain the origins of the Nazis. Finally came the image of the West Germans, our *allies.*

These are five images of the total German past, even though the German scene back in 1818 or 1740 or 1044 could not have been changed in the slightest by the drama of this century. Manifestly, the substance of the original sources remained unaltered, and yet, broadly speaking, the writers constructed at least five images of the past from them, depending upon what the individuals saw in the sources and what they disregarded. The experiences of the writers and their generation largely determined the selection of data out of the past, imposed present contours upon the past, and resulted in significant aspects being ignored because they did not fit what seemed important at the time of the writing. In terms of the actual past, some of the resultant shapes were grotesque and jarring intrusions. It should be added that loss of balance and objectivity varied greatly among the writers, but nevertheless this handling of German history demonstrates how interpretations may spring out of current preoccupations rather than emerge from the veritable data about the past.

The Reformation offers another example of how each generation looks at the past through its own eyes. One authority has commented that a hundred biographers have depicted a hundred different Luthers. Gerhard Ritter published a book on Luther in 1928–1929 in which the Reformer was portrayed as a national hero, then, after Ritter had participated in the Lutheran opposition to the Nazis, he found it necessary to rewrite the introduction to the fourth edition in 1947.

Roman Catholics and Protestants from the beginning naturally viewed events from very different perspectives and made history into useful ammunition for their polemics. Enlightenment writers considered bigotry, wars, and atrocities as part of a benighted past in which pointless theological disputes caused unnecessary human suffering. Romanticists found in the Reformation a foreshadowing of their own struggle for liberty, and German nationalist historians adopted Luther as a national hero who led a struggle against foreigners. Nietzsche pronounced the Reformation to be the reaction of "old-fashioned minds" against the Italian Renaissance. With the coming of economic interpretations, vastly expanded sources for nonreligious explanations became available. And, of course, some more recent writers tried to trace German evils back to the Reformation. The "from Luther to Hitler" gambit presented a caricature of processes in the history of ideas, a picture of evil seeds somehow germinating century after century for 400 years, gradually contaminating the thought processes of a whole people until the culmination came in the appalling iniquities of the Nazi period. This, too, was a Triumphant Act 5 kind of history.

Each generation probed into the Reformation in order to explain its own times while simultaneously imposing experienced contemporary contours upon it. As in the Enlightenment, some present writers relegate it to the Outer Darkness; nonreligious scholars, discerning little relevancy to the present, may treat the Protestant and Catholic Reformations, which dominated the lives of several generations, as virtually nonhappenings.

Contemporary significance may even be read into a battle of long ago. Thus, as described by Georges Duby, the Battle of Bouvines (1214) has been successively portrayed as a divine accolade upon the French monarchy, the first victory of the nation, a triumph by a king friendly to the bourgeoisie, and a French victory over the Germans.

Eyes accustomed to seeing certain present patterns will look for these same contours in the past, perhaps finding some in reality and mistakenly perceiving others. Unfamiliar patterns will escape observation, leading to the likely assumption that only the observed shapes constitute the authentic past. Insights born out of experience convey a sense of reality, and so each generation may think it is penetrating to the past when it recognizes there its own perceptions. Recorded insights of earlier generations, born out of their different experiences, may lack reality for their successors, and so each succeeding generation, nourishing preconceived patterns, thinks the current version superior.

Theodore S. Hamerow, summarizing the historiography on Otto von Bismarck, declares that "each successive generation seems to find a new meaning in his career. As our experiences change us, so we change our interpretations of the experiences of others." Brison D. Gooch says of the origins of the Crimean War, "For over a century now historians have tried to explain in cogent fashion how this war originated, but each generation appears to find the previous explanations inadequate."

Each major interpretation facilitates the discovery of evidence congenial to it and simultaneously may block the finding of other data. Soviet historians working on American history do quite well on aspects suitable to their insights—slavery, seizure of

Indian land, the development of American capitalism, the blacks, the American Civil War—while at the same time often missing the living reality of the American scene. In 1935, Beatrice and Sidney Webb published *Soviet Communism, A New Civilization,* a book massively researched and thoroughly useful at the time but completely failing to point out the emergence of a novel elite, the New Class, which was occurring during the time they were working. Their own socialist prepossessions blocked out any perception of this phenomenon, or, if seen, they could not accept the necessary conclusions.

Cipolla's listing of factors involved in decline looks highly valid. These factors also appallingly parallel some present-day circumstances; does his list by any chance seem so right because we recognize the parallel to our own times? These are the hazards of those who travel to the past, of those who, in Carr's words, carry on the dialogue between the past and the present. Obviously more perilous for those deliberately seeking relevancy to the present, these dangers help to explain the original fervor of advocates of objective empiricism and of those who continue to advocate history for its own sake.

Where a dictatorial regime controls the present, the sway of that present over the shapes of the past is vastly strengthened. In the Soviet Union, Mikhail N. Pokrovsky dominated the field of history during the 1920s while his Marxist history of Russia had important uses for the regime. Then in the early 1930s, with a return to emphasis on Russian nationalism, Pokrovsky's schematic treatment of Russian history, and especially his hostile treatment of earlier Russian institutions and leaders, became officially outmoded. Or consider the predicament of Evgenii V. Tarle. His biography of Napoleon, in its section on the 1812 invasion of Russia, carefully avoided giving any credit to Russian patriotism. However, the threat of Japan and Hitler's Germany necessitated the restoration of patriotism in the U.S.S.R., and Tarle's work, aimed at conforming to the original party line, suffered official disapproval. Two years later, in 1938, he published a whole book on the invasion, reversing his preceding position and giving due credit to the national resistance of the Russian people. During World War II, however, the book could be construed as unduly minimizing the leadership of the government or, specifically, that of Joseph Stalin. And Tarle was once again in trouble with the regime.

Though the influence of the present on interpretations happens to be conspicuously obvious, this is by no means the most important aspect of the formulation of interpretations, as an examination of the successive viewpoints on the French Revolution will reveal. Like the Reformation, it drew impassioned responses from both protagonists and antagonists. In a period of growing liberalism, nationalism, and struggle for constitutional government, the Romanticist Jules Michelet wrote descriptions that would ever afterward be the prototype for street-level ideas of revolution: the struggle for freedom against tyranny, the misery of the populace, the victory of the people and of justice. Meantime, opponents, from Edmund Burke on, regarded the revolutionary excesses as reckless destruction of a civilized established order. Some blamed the outbreak on the ideas of the philosophes, some on a plot hatched by the lodges of the Free Masons, and others on the lust for power of those who became Jacobins.

Defeat by the Germans in 1870–1871, the Commune, and the rise of the Third Republic left their imprint. Taine reacted with a "scathing indictment" of the revolution, blamed it largely on the philosophes, and insisted that the French troubles of 1870–1871 went back to the violent wrench of the original upheaval. François Aulard, the father of scientific historiography of the French Revolution and a firm believer in the Third Republic, sought its republican and democratic heritage in the original republic of 1792. Jean Jaurès, a socialist leader, visualized it in terms of class struggle and social revolution and thereby helped impose these shapes upon the popular conception of revolution. Albert Mathiez, a scholar like Aulard, rehabilitated Robespierre as a model revolutionary and leader of a socialist commonwealth while attacking the venality and corruption of Danton as a typical bourgeois politician of the Third Republic.

Russian revolution and the fears of Communism in the West in the 1920s stimulated conservative insistence that the events of 1789 and after had been disastrous. Someone resurrected the Masonic Plot theory. Frantz Funck-Brentano, arguing that the evils of the Old Regime had been much exaggerated, produced a good old days version of idyllic village life. Pierre Gaxotte dwelt on the crimes and horrors of the French Revolution as a warning against more of the same in the twentieth century.

Emphasis on economic questions and a statistical approach have in recent decades added more interpretations, above all in the studies of Camille Labrousse on the background of revolution in eighteenth-century economy. His proof of economic recession in the years before the outbreak of the revolution added an important factor to basic interpretation. Georges Lefebvre, a recent doyen of French Revolution interpreters, made detailed studies of rural disturbances and of the revolutionary crowd and in the process helped destroy the possibility of any sweeping generalizations about the revolution as a whole. The gist of recent investigations, as already mentioned, seems to be that it consisted of a *series* of revolutions or even of a "series of successive minor conflagrations" (Rudé). The bourgeoisie, peasants, and workers, as social classes, have disintegrated into their component parts. Cobban could then write about the myth of the French Revolution and his suspicion that persons who wanted state jobs bore much of the responsibility for the upheaval; Danton, Robespierre, and Roland could have been elected to parliament in England and gotten better positions, but in the Old Regime their careers were blocked—a point of view perhaps reflecting the predominant position of state bureaucrats in present-day communities.

Meantime, in the era of increasing international cooperation after World War II, Jacques Godechot and Robert Palmer led a discussion over the place of the French Revolution in the whole series of disturbances between 1760 and 1849 in Europe and the Americas. Also, Martin Göhring perpetuated a Central European viewpoint that the revolution was an anomaly, caused basically by the failure of the French government to modernize, unlike the governments of Prussia or Austria. No wonder John Hall Stewart, in one survey of the historiography, writes that, ". . . the more historians know about the Revolution, the less they seem to agree about what it was . . . what came of it, and what it really means in Western Civilization."

Each major development sent historians back to the original upheaval with minds conditioned to the revolution in terms of their own decade. Did they write *bad* history? On the contrary, some was superb, as their zeal led them to uncover various facets of the revolution, each contributing to an ultimately more comprehensive picture. Though the role of relevancy is blatantly obvious, the various interpretations deepened the outlook, each foray adding more material and insights until the earlier historical patterns could no longer be tolerated because of contrary evidence. Cumulative history, by the time of Labrousse and Lefebvre, had rendered obsolete the conventional shapes of earlier generations, themselves largely the projection upon the French Revolution of later public controversies. The growing wealth of detailed evidence, overriding experienced insights and shapes of history, mandates a more intimate awareness of what actually did happen. In Peter Amman's words, "ideological bias becomes almost irrelevant," the "marked partisanship" having disappeared.

Genuine advances in cumulative history can best be measured by comparing successive versions of the French Revolution—or of such other controversial areas as the origins of the American Civil War—and seeing the improvements achieved. Massive accumulation of evidence demolishes those conceptual wholes that hide the realities of the details. Many of the handy generalizations or schemes for visualizing the past have been shattered by renewed awareness of various actualities of the past, while myths, useful as tools at the street level, continue to be eradicated from scholarly history.

Historians have not merely been indulging in successive fads, as may be the superficial impression, since the successive interpretations must take into account the reasoning of the earlier ones and, always, the overweening force of the evidence. (Periods of intense emotional involvement may, unfortunately, slow up or endanger the fruits of cumulative history.) Each interpretation opens the way to the discovery of new evidence, and new evidence in turn can destroy an interpretation. One scholar's insights may block out part of the evidence, but many are at work. Cumulative history is the open-ended, tentative product of approximately six generations of historians, each of whose experiences have contributed insights to the body of knowledge, some to be later rejected (rightly or not) and some to be absorbed, perhaps in altered form, into the total picture.

32

The Shapes of Time
Reconsidered

By no means everyone had been satisfied with the gradualist version of change and continuity held by several generations of historians. Between the two world wars, for instance, Sir Charles Oman rejected it in favor of what he called a cataclysmic conception of history. After the second war, Geoffrey Barraclough asserted that he could no longer accept the gradualist assumptions; those who personally lived through the happenings of that conflict and its widespread displacement of peoples, he maintained, "will not be impressed when . . . told that history is a story of continuity, governed by a law not of revolution but of evolution." We have experienced enough discontinuity ourselves, according to him, to have sympathy for the viewpoint of earlier historians, like St. Augustine, for whom the cataclysmic seemed more credible.

Not denying the element of continuity, Barraclough merely stressed the existence of discontinuities, of abrupt upheavals and bursts of accelerated change within historical processes.

Gradualism produces "an illusion of steady flow, which is both at variance with experience and detrimental to all perspective." Some nonhistorians have been so impressed by the acceleration of events, the speed of technological changes, and a sense of abrupt dislocation that past experience no longer seems relevant. According to them, the great leap into the future of our time constitutes a discontinuity so drastic that only a catastrophic version of history makes sense.

Changed concepts in natural science have contributed to the modification of gradualist assumptions. If the Darwinian evolution of the species, the family trees of species gradually diverging, originally suggested a steady flow type of history, the discovery of mutations implied that sudden changes, natural selection through accidents and the abrupt appearance of new forms, made up an essential part of this evolution. Contrary to the old scientific dictum that *natura non facit saltum,* nature *did* evolve by sudden leaps. By analogy, history might have a predominantly continuous character and yet be interrupted periodically by relatively abrupt transformations.

Adding force to this viewpoint was Max Planck's quantum theory (1900) that light waves do not flow regularly; they are more like bundles of energy coming in irregular jerks. The implication again was one of leaps rather than of gradual evolution in natural science. Still another analogy could be useful, this time from earthquakes; a long period of growing tension in the rocks culminates in an earthquake, a sudden violent action or series of actions, followed by another quiescent period during which the tension again builds up.

Eisenstein has pointed out that an altered conception of change and continuity manifests itself in changes in terminology. Such words as "growth," "development," "rise and fall," "decline," and "decay" are replaced by "breakthrough," "breakdown," "mutation," and "crisis"; where eras were formerly regarded as transitional, they are now described in terms of a series of crises. Various efforts have been made to formulate concepts expressing the altered visualization of change, Barraclough himself suggesting "eras of preparation" and "eras of fulfillment." G. J. Renier treated the process in terms of the momentum of habitual conduct, the equilibrium of social forces, and the eventual period of change, which he called "the appointed time." Plumb, in *The Growth of Political Stability in England 1675-1725*, approached the phenomenon from the opposite end, writing that political stability has been "a comparatively rare phenomenon in the history of human society." Nor does it emerge by "slow coral-like growth"; when it comes, stability appears quickly, like water becoming ice. Obviously the concept of gradualism no longer offers in itself a satisfactory tool, though whether gradualists ever considered "steady flow" to be an adequate description must be questioned; it always did carry the mental reservation that in a long-term perspective the temporary deviations would be glossed over.

Several different alternatives have been encountered in the later chapters on historical processes. In one of these, the cycle of Anglo-American politics, the political "pulsations" do not emerge out of rigid political continuity; they only mark periodical accelerations of a change always underway. It will also be recalled that a wide diversity of opinion exists between the gradualist and the catastrophe schools on the history of the Industrial Revolution. Scientific thought, according to some, follows its own pattern, involving periods of preparation and ultimate breakthroughs. Perhaps inventions are here comparable to the successive mutations in a species, a series of usually minute breakthroughs cumulatively producing the appearance of an evolving pattern. Kuhn's paradigmatic sequence also falls into this group. Discoveries take place within the context of the overriding paradigm, but eventually anomalies develop, and a period of frustrating, patching operations and sporadic assays at alternate paradigms follows. Eventually, quite abruptly, a breakthrough occurs with a new paradigm that ultimately wins acceptance.

Kubler's conception of art history has special relevance to the "detection and description of the shape of things" in change and continuity. He finds historical time intermittent and variable, "every action is more intermittent than it is continuous," and "clusters of actions . . . thin out or thicken." The sequences, basic to art history, develop in accordance with the solution to problems. These responses may be far apart, and the time taken to solve the different problems may vary greatly. According to this approach, the artistic scene at any given time is likely to contain a number of forms, several concurrent sequences in which each form evolves in its own time scheme; although to some extent perhaps influencing each other, their development is very largely autonomous. Any given historical period is a meeting place of "chance encounters," or, as Kracauer says, "calendric time is an empty vessel."

Still following Kubler, a sequence may maintain strong continuity over a prolonged period by "replication" (the making of copies or near copies) of "prime objects" (the artistic innovations). An existent potential for innovation does not guarantee that it will happen, and considerable time may also elapse between discovery and practical application, as in the case of oil painting. A breakthrough in technique usually brings an accelerated outburst of exploratory change for a time. Crucial for a shift from "slow to fast happenings" is the possibility for individuals becoming full-time artists. This in turn necessitates community support, which before 1400 came from feudal courts, abbeys, and cathedrals, then, till about 1800, from princely courts and some towns, and, more recently, from large cities and university centers. Tribal societies and provincial towns generate change only at a "glacial" rate.

Robert F. Berkhofer has commented that the patterns of change and continuity "are rarely studied very carefully," and history, he claims, has consisted too much of cataloguing dated events that do not imply change. These do not bring out the existent continuity, necessary for any analysis of change. He, too, suggested the use of sequences, which in turn involves asking five questions: When did something start and stop? What followed what? Why in that particular sequence? Why did it happen when it did? And were some portions of the rate of change faster or slower?

Economic history can contribute useful perspectives on the shapes of time because change can actually be measured, precise patterns traced with the help of valid statistics. Alexander

Gerschenkron, using the abundant statistics available in the area of industrialization, selects out of a number of possible concepts five for special attention. The first, which historians most commonly use, he says, is *constantcy of direction,* wherein a certain development is traced from "hardly perceptible origins" through its pattern of growth. Within a pattern, "wild fluctuations" may occur, but these, in most accounts, have been absorbed into the larger direction of the pattern, thereby giving the impression of steady growth or decline; most theories of progress, he says, "pivot" here.

A second is the *stability of the rate of change.* In an area with voluminous figures on prices, incomes, crops, and industrial output, Gerschenkron finds a high degree of instability. Industry by no means had an even pace of development; it went through lengthy periods of slow growth, then sudden increases or spurts. The "kinks"—leaps, crises, regressions, slow and fast tempos—can be smoothened out to show steady progress, especially when covering a lengthy period, but, he asks, is this good history?

The other concepts include *periodicity of events,* the recurrence of repetitions within a cycle; *endogenous changes,* a homogeneous set of factors within a development; and the *length of a causal chain,* the question of where to start and conclude a development. Discontinuities in the patterns, abrupt alterations, often derive from external factors, such as the tempo of other branches of manufacturing and the help or hindrance of government policies.

Gerschenkron accuses historians of writing too much sweeping history, glossing over the kinks, regressions, and alterations of tempo. By "abstracting from differences and by concentrating on similarities," they create models rather than depict reality. He quotes approvingly the statement of the physicist Ernst Mach that in his field continuity is an "arbitrary conceptual construct" and concludes that continuity in history is also a tool forged by historians, not something inherent in historical matter.

Surely the Bolshevik Revolution must be considered a splendid example of an historical mutation. Prior to 1914, Russia seemed to be moving with increasing rapidity in the same direction taken earlier by Western Europe and the United States. The Russians could see their own future, twenty years ahead, like that of the contemporary industrialized Germany with its parliament and continued aristocratic leadership and then, perhaps thirty years beyond that with a stable parliamentary system like that existing in Great Britain. In 1917 came shattering discontinuity and change of direction. And yet, though in 1920 the revolution looked like a veritable mutation, by 1940, with Stalinism, that analogy appeared less certain. By 1970, the strands of continuity with the older Tsarist Russia—autocratic rule, massive bureaucracy, a basically hierarchical order, intense Russian nationalism, sporadic intellectual rebellion—had virtually eliminated the view of structural mutation altogether. Is the 1920 or the 1970 image more accurate? Or are they both valid in terms of their separate perspectives, that is, had the forces of continuity in the Russian community reasserted themselves since 1920?

Did the French Revolution, packed with a dizzying succession of changes and revolutionaries themselves so convinced of the beginning of a new era that they even started a new calendar, constitute a mutation? Europe returned, however, to an age of monarchies lasting substantially for the remainder of the century. Religious faith revived strongly, usually in orthodox forms after its preceding loss. Romanticism overlapped the whole period from the 1770s far into the nineteenth century. Franklin Ford has listed the permanent changes: in general more centralized and efficient government, a transformation in the military, a greater involvement of people in politics, and the loss of the "appearance of a hierarchy of legally defined orders of men." Can this be described as a mutation or leap?

Quite possibly a future age will judge the nineteenth century to have passed through a mutation in human affairs. It is therefore perhaps ironic that Europeans should have learned in that century to write their history in terms of gradualism. Even now, from the present perspective, the last century seems to have been virtually a Golden Age of steady progress, though this is another optical illusion. Inspected more closely, accelerating change characterizes these decades, change that occasionally breaks into the political sphere; 1815 to 1829, 1831 to 1847, and 1850 into the 1860s were years of relative calm, while 1830 and 1848 witnessed special turmoil. Certainly not mutations, they more resembled earthquakes, violent but soon ended and without any basic transformation.

A series of very different outlines emerge if the century is divided into sectors based on political change, advances in science, industrial development, the spread of capitalism, and eras in literature or the fine arts. Visualizing a single track of development for all of society can be illusory, and one may sympathize with Kracauer's assertion that history does not consist of a single march of time—it contains a march of times, as various elements display different sequences or stages. Minor mutations occur, successive series of them, which sometimes cumulatively amount to more than gradual evolution. This very awareness of perpetual change, seemingly spontaneous and autonomous beyond political planning, greatly contributed originally to the conviction of the reality of gradual evolution.

To regard the *entire* society or community as undergoing a mutation or discontinuity verges on succumbing to the apocalyptic. In nature, changes are assumed to come gradually, visible primarily on the level of useful minor mutations and which, over a very long period of time, profoundly transform the landscape. Similarly, a long sequence of inventions that seem to parallel mutations cumulatively produces long-term major changes; much experimentation in art brings new forms of artistic expression. Occasionally, a cluster of minor mutations or convergent developments or the dysfunction of an equilibrium produce a readjustment of relationships within a community structure.

After the upheavals of the 1930s and 1940s, the governments and politics of non-Communist Europe reverted to their former pattern in virtually all of the countries, a restoration or reassertion of continuity. The postwar world saw decolonization, the Chinese Communist revolution, and the advent of nuclear energy, television, computers, and space travel. Changes enough, but bringing neither the political world revolution nor the nuclear warfare of the doomsday prophets. Where the strands of continuity persist in a resilient world community, the idea of continuity may be considered a conceptual construct, but it also obviously describes something very much a reality in that community.

Gerschenkron believes that, statistically, the long-term curves of change can only be fictitious. In demanding the specific details of actuality, he eliminates the possibility of relatively accurate or at least readable long-term description. However, to abbreviate and smoothen out details into general statements while also, in the long-term sweep, retaining its own level of truth are necessities in general history. Contrasts between micro and macro history become starkly conspicuous in modes of change and continuity.

Hexter could not find the rise of the middle class or the decline of the landed aristocracy, each being an "imaginary construction." Nevertheless, though at one time scarcely any so-called middle class existed, eventually certain elements did consider themselves such and quite consciously supported their own specific interests. Obviously something had happened; they seemingly *must* have "risen," whatever that word may mean, while the once prominent landed aristocracy has now largely receded from the scene.

In these cases, broad concepts of macro history have been imposed upon specific shorter eras, assuming that since the developments did occur they ought to be visible at this particular time. Given an interpretation, some evidence can usually be found to support a facile conclusion that such an interpretation has been confirmed. The curve of change has been smoothened out on the basis of gradualist assumptions of a flowing, pervasive transformation of these particular shapes in history. Many questions thereby go unanswered: Does the middle class grow in numbers? In wealth? In trade statistics? In numbers of holders of public office? Or in the number of people who married into the upper classes? Which elements in this many-faceted entity rise? Or is the term itself one of those "wholes" that obscures more than it illuminates? Perhaps the bourgeoisie did not "rise" because its several elements only coalesced and attained full self-consciousness in the nineteenth century, but historians, needing a shorthand term for certain earlier social forces, found "middle class" convenient.

Once again the micro-macro dilemma emerges as one of the problems of the contemporary historian. Micro history tends to break down the macro concepts, to reduce the picture to the confusion seen by the spectator-participant in historical events except as he or she uses prefabricated shapes, some of which may be helpful and others obstructive.

In moving from an industrial to a postindustrial era, some quarters suggest that the past may be irrelevant for current problems, that contemporary society has undergone such a mutation that past frames of reference have no utility. Most likely, this feeling springs from the same surface appearance of chaotic events, the elusive visibility of macro concepts in the immediate micro scene in which we live. We try to understand the present by seeing in it the shapes familiar in recent decades, a present that also contains origins—usually invisible to us now—of shapes yet to come. Humanity has crossed divides between eras before without history's losing relevancy. It is suggested, however, that historical processes, in the customary sense, will cease to function. But are institutional factors less powerful now than before? Economic drives? The diffusion of ideas? The chain reaction of inventions? The prevalence of the True Believer? The tempo may be quickened and the intensity of various social forces altered, but the components of the historical processes will surely still remain very much operative.

People have always faced uneasily the unknown future. (Han Fei in China some 2,200 years ago was already complaining that former patterns of behavior were not effective anymore because the times had changed!) Some recent statements to the effect that historical patterns no longer apply sound rather as though their authors lack historical-mindedness themselves, their concepts of history perhaps limited to some obsolete shapes and some of the qualities of elementary history. Critics of history sometimes make it easy for themselves by citing historians of a century ago as representative of contemporary practices. Critics may be totally unaware of the nature of basic historical processes; indeed, their notion of the abolition of history sometimes seems in itself a typical elementary version of change and continuity, the vision of catastrophe or apocalypse, an ahistorical, sociological millenarianism akin to the religious Millenarians or the Marxist dawn of a classless society.

33

A Breakdown
of Causality

No agreement has ever been reached, so we learned earlier, on the causes for the Crimean War. A conflict emerging out of rivalries inherent in the balance of power and the collapse of the Holy Alliance, its outbreak has been explained more specifically by economic rivalries, the dispute over the Holy Places, and chronic Russian expansionism in the area. In one sense, the responsibility lay in clumsy (or overly clever) diplomacy. But all of these combustibles can be piled up and still not make the war inevitable. Historians have been wrangling ever since about the interplay of personalities. Nicholas I, tsar of Russia, has been depicted as intent on aggression, while others limit his liability to not understanding British intentions. Louis Napoleon and the British Foreign Office have been blamed, as has Lord Stratford de Redcliffe, British ambassador to the Porte, who exceeded his instructions. To repeat, ". . . contingencies, the purely accidental, quirks of personality . . ." seem more decisive than the background causes in a war about whose detailed causes no two historians seem able to agree.

The February Revolution in France has been called "a result without a cause," subsequently amended by Gordon Wright to "a result far out of proportion to the cause." In three short days, an apparently stable regime, one seemingly capable of surviving indefinitely along the lines of the British government across the Channel, was replaced by a republic. Can it be explained purely in terms of an old king averse to defending his throne with bloodshed, plus his placing the defense in the hands of egregiously poor generals? Broader causes have been proposed: bad crops and a depression, working-class hatred of the new industrial machinery, the unpopularity of Guizot, the political frustrations of the middle class and workers over the limited franchise, and the revival of revolutionary tradition. Are these, any or all, necessary in order to explain the episode, or are they only plausible interpretations dug up after the event by historians seeking broader explanations?

To go one step further, should the causes for the assassinations of Lincoln or the Kennedys be limited to the motives of the assassins themselves or must broader causes be sought in the events and mood of the times?

These particular instances illustrate the perplexing problem of explanation in history. Faith in historical causality reached its peak in the late nineteenth century coincident with the heyday of stressing mechanistic causality in the physical world, but the belief in great and effective forces moving history, which characterized the age, eventually began to crumble as the handling of historical explanation increasingly underwent questioning. The number of possible causes kept on multiplying, like the fifty or more reasons for the fall of Rome and the twenty-one for revolution. As more were suggested, the less convincing they became, since a dozen explanations might be offered without bringing a given episode much nearer an acceptable solution. Problems continued to appear in both the selectivity and the relative impact of any one reason in a group of operative factors.

Excessive use or misuse of certain kinds of causality, most often the economic, reduced their credibility. A lack of balance in selectivity tended to discredit the whole causal approach, as did the attributing of a determinist character to these supposed reasons. Discoveries by psychologists and psychiatrists in the realm of the irrational reduced faith in such causes, since historical episodes could not longer be described purely in terms of rational motivations, decisions, and behavior; outbursts of irrational politics in this century reinforced the skepticism. Some philosophers have, within the context of their assumptions, abolished causality. Meantime, the natural scientists influenced the historians by revising their own concepts. Werner Heisenberg's enunciation of his "indeterminacy principle" dealt a major blow; he found that in the submicroscopic world scientific laws did not fully hold, hence there was no theoretical assurance of undeviating regularities even in natural science. Max Planck's quantum theory contributed to the uncertainty; if light waves do not flow regularly and if they more closely resemble irregular bundles of energy, the causal qualities of social energies also seemed jeopardized.

In cumulative history, the experiences of the historian made earlier assumptions about causality increasingly suspect. When the scholar focuses on a specific event or on some significant episode, the conventional background causes tend to fade away, to lose their power to move events, while the interplay of personalities, the element of chance, and the small localized causes, more accurately called conditions, stimulate and guide the happenings. Broader causalities seem broken up by contingencies, the accidental, personality factors, the conjunction of causal sequences, and discontinuities that may suddenly alter the apparent weight of factors in the situation. The causes as such may seem to make up an interacting whole rather than to be discrete kinds of forces individually affecting the elements within the episode.

Lynn White, jocosely exaggerating, has said that no historian now dares use the word "cause," that we isolate certain ingredients "which seem to exert a 'gravitational' influence upon each other" and which "move in a cluster in the direction of the movement which we are now trying to comprehend."

So, what now? Have the historians, in effect, gotten rid of the basic energies in history, the causality? It may not have escaped the reader that the preceding description of the abolition of causes is itself written largely in terms of causes!

At this point, the perplexed should read some of the stories of Franz Kafka. In one of them, the hero is walking along a road, and odd things keep happening that do not make sense. In another, the hero is on trial but never does find out why, that is, the nightmare quality in Kafka's stories derives in considerable part from his depicting happenings without causes. In reading Kafka, one discovers that a need for causal explanations is part of our psychological makeup, the everyday life becomes impossible unless reasons, right ones or wrong ones, can be used for purposes of orientation. Theoreticians can abolish causality to their hearts' content; it will still remain operative in modern minds and in human affairs.

Responding to contemporary intellectual currents and to their own experiences, the historians have been cautiously modifying their approach to explanations. In place of causes, with their connotations of immediacy and determinism, historians began to talk of factors, implying a diversity of interacting agencies and processes. This did not, in practice, alter matters much, and Hexter has acidly commented, "Thus the human mind progresses—sideways." Recent usage of causality takes several different forms. Butterfield preferred to point out "mediations." Others prefer to emphasize relationships among factors or the potentiality of tendencies within a situation. For some, the word "explanation" avoids incriminating connotations, and these people may limit themselves to providing "sufficient" cause. Probably the most prevalent method, currently, is to depict the "conditions" attending an episode or development.

Butterfield complained about some historians: "What we call 'causes' are made to operate with astonishing immediacy." Causality has not been eliminated in present-day cumulative history, only transformed from general motive forces into devices more specifically adapted to helping historians understand their area of the past. Causes can no longer be visualized as though they were billiard balls making direct tangible impact, as independent forces impelling the movement in a happening like water on a paddle wheel or wind on a sail. They are not the equivalent of chemicals, whose specific elements and/or compounds placed together react with predictable results. Nor should they be thought of as autonomous wholes transmitted and articulated by individuals, groups, or institutions. A cause rarely exerts full compulsion upon an event because too many other agencies are likely to be of influence for any single element to be that dominant. The causal factors themselves form part of the situation, are themselves constantly subject to other influences.

"The progress of science, since Marx, has roughly consisted in replacing determinism and the rather crude mechanism of its period by a doctrine of provisional probability" (Albert Camus). It assists the mind mightily, in moving to newer concepts of causality, to learn to think in terms of *probabilities,* which gets away from both the clutches of determinism and the trap of excessive literal-mindedness. Causal factors can be seen as statistical probabilities or potentialities that may or may not exert influence as a specific situation evokes their forces. The broader causes do not necessarily function automatically; they are potential in a situation whose specific elements may trigger them or provide a vehicle for their expression.

As commonly used, causes are devices or a mental shorthand for identifying various influences, conditions, and instrumentalities in any given historical situation. Quite aside from our psychological necessity for causal explanations, something *is* there, in the form of social forces and motivations, which must be included in the total description; to jettison causes altogether distorts the picture of an historical episode. To eliminate the compulsions operative upon human beings, groups, and institutions leads to a misunderstanding of the dilemmas and responses of human behavior and bestows more free will upon the participants than was really the case.

In cumulative history, some historians, viewing with considerable suspicion the whole business of attributing developments to nebulous causal factors, now prefer to minimize the "why" in favor of "who, where, when" narrative. In stating the antecedents without necessarily implying any causal character in them and in describing the conditions of an event, they assume that they have provided an adequate, a *sufficient,* explanation. "If the facts are true and relevant they are conditions, not causes" (Barzun). The writer explains the *why* by narrating the *how,* by a sequential narrative in which successive events themselves mold the situation and serve to impel further events. Hexter has suggested that "processive" narrative "opens the way to historical understanding beyond explanation."

The behavioral sciences have virtually abandoned multicausal and long-term explanations. No longer primarily sequential, causes are closely interrelated in the explanation, attention being focused on the specifics of certain participants in a concrete situation. The emphasis lies in explaining their actions, their behavior in terms of ostensible motives versus real motives, the cultural pattern in which they live, and the power structure in this particular episode. Since individuals must be understood within the context of the system of values prevalent in their society, the basic concern focuses on discovering the state of the participant's mind, using current psychological and sociological theories. In short, the explanation is sought in the pressure of circumstances that determine the focus and scope of the participant's activities, his or her interpretation of the situation and responses to it; meantime, the historian is also using his or her own perspective in evaluating and checking all three.

Looked at from within micro history, only in a very narrow time and space scope do causal factors sometimes possess credible "intimacy" or exercise a directly observable impact upon the situation. Often, any one of these factors appears so diffused, sporadic, or intermixed with other motivations that its efficacy in a particular happening seems dubious. Dignifying it as a cause may be to impose an artificiality upon the event, to carve asunder something that is true only as a living whole.

Macro history, however, has its own exigencies. Without broad patterns and the energies of causal factors explaining development in history, general history loses coherence and falls apart into annals or stories. To read about the Reformation, the French Revolution, or the outbreak of World War I in a general context without the causation of broad social forces in the background would be to wander in the world of Kafka. No such thing as Economic Man may exist in real life, but the consequences for society of many thousands, or millions, of individuals each contributing rather similar motivations from that part of his or her personality must surely partake of a causal nature.

Specific episodes that illustrate the potent force of a broad cause can, of course, be recalled: national feeling in the "jingoism" preceding the Crimean War, the patriotic "On to Berlin" excitement in Paris in 1870, or class antagonism in Paris in 1848 and 1871. Though less typical of their respective scenes than once assumed, such outbursts nevertheless indicate a potentiality that must be taken into account when visualizing the motive forces in nineteenth-century European history. When certain influences, social energies, and trends appear and reappear in successive segments of an era, even if diffused and intermixed into relative intangibility, surely a uniformity exists for which a label is necessary. Again it is a matter of perspective, of contours that seem to be there in long-term history, which demand identification and insertion into the shapes of the past.

Causal factors remain useful for those who are not experts as a checklist for searching out the components of an episode, as convenient labels for matters more complex, as symbols conveying the complex reality of the past in a necessarily simplified way. To be sure, excessive literal-mindedness in handling these causes, beyond the level of basic learning, often contributes to the clumsy thinking of those using history for purposes other than understanding the past. Experts must retain an awareness of the broad range of possible influences bearing on their subject of inquiry, lest too narrow a vision omit significant aspects for a sufficient explanation; in their own training, scholars risk a lack of balance and an excess of schematization if they fail to acquire a sensitive feel for basic multiple causality. They must come to a more mature level of historical thinking by first assimilating the basic processes of history.

The mental tools of historians have been refined to a level too subtle for the comprehension of the untrained. Typical of a century in which the natural scientists have long since advanced beyond the limit of observation by the five senses, historians' concepts have become sophisticated far beyond everyday usage. Here, in the arcanum of the Mansion of History, the complexity of their subject forces historians to use special thought processes and, as a result, their terms may take on a symbolism rather different from common substantive meanings.

34

Poor, Despised Facts

"Poor, despised facts, they have a hard time. Nobody believes in them. . . ." Henry Steele Commager, in his sparkling book *The Nature and the Study of History*, went on to say that historians with "almost a single voice" declare that no reliable facts exist. And added that "as we look at them they fade away, all but the grin" just as the Cheshire Cat did in *Alice in Wonderland*. Thus far have historians come since the days of Ranke when facts, assumed to be the building blocks of history, supposedly produced truth once the historian had validated and properly arranged them.

Isn't it a fact that Christopher Columbus discovered America on October 12, 1492? Louis Gottschalk has expressed some reservations. What Columbus found was an island, possibly the one now called Watling Island, and he had no correct idea whatsoever, then or later, about the identity of the continent. Gottschalk says the discovery was made by a "group of sailors captained by a man known in English as 'Christopher Columbus' on a date conveniently labeled 'October 12, 1492.' "

Julius Caesar crossed the Rubicon in 49 B.C. Carl Becker long ago quarreled with this perfectly obvious fact. Caesar did cross the river known as the Rubicon, though naturally not, as Caesar understood it, in the 49 B.C. of the Christian calendar. Human beings cross over rivers quite regularly, however, without historians taking any interest in the matter; consequently, additional meanings must be involved in the seemingly simple statement. This one historical fact remains meaningless unless the reader also understands numerous other facts about Rome, its government, and the preceding political events. Going over this stream, the boundary between his own provinces and Italy proper at that time, meant that Julius Caesar became a rebel against the government in Rome, which in turn set off a sequence of developments eventually leading to Augustus becoming the first emperor in Rome.

Charlemagne was crowned Holy Roman Emperor in Rome on Christmas Day in A.D. 800. Or was he? This question has been met repeatedly before. Though being given the imperial title, he most certainly had no conception that he would later, much later, be looked upon as the first Holy Roman Emperor, nor could he foresee the future shapes of that empire or the ideas that would develop about its nature. Furthermore, the participants scarcely thought of themselves as living in A.D. 800.

Facts come associated with other facts, they very often blur over into one or more generalizations, and the meaning communicated often carries unintended nuances in the words used. *Written* records of the past, however literal they may seem, originated in someone's conception of what happened, that is, the actual happenings have been refracted through someone's mind.

Newspaper accounts from the time of an incident may seem to constitute good primary sources for providing basic substantive material. Most persons, however, have seen episodes that have then been duly reported in the newspapers, and they have been struck by the difference between what they thought happened and what was reported in the press. Or they have heard a speech, then later been astonished at its caricature in the newspaper. Journalistic techniques mold journalistic stories, given the need to tell the story with the help of interest-evoking devices, and so the writer's own preconceptions and personal stereotypes mold the story he or she tells. Every student journalist knows that the information does not suffice, that something must be made out of it. An undergraduate reporter recently printed a series of stories, and very good ones, on a certain local situation; privately, he confided that the real problem lay in the personalities involved, but this could not be said. An historian, writing fifty years from now may not know what actual facts lay behind the version that appeared in print. Though we are subconsciously disposed to accept published material as factual, this need not necessarily be safe because, at the least, the actual happening has been revamped in someone's mind and it may have undergone flagrant manipulation in the writing. This caveat applies to much of the material out of the past also.

Now the historian can *watch* the more recent past unfolding in moving pictures, but this does not necessarily mean access to a purer form of source material. The incidents to be recorded by the camera must still be selected, and the story revealed or perhaps contrived. As in the newspapers, the most violent scenes are likely to be presented as the story itself, thereby often warping the whole scene. Nor are television people immune from the charge of "rigging" the scene in order to capture a better, more viewable story.

A totally accurate past, in a perfectionist sense, cannot be recaptured. Even the most elementary facts carry with them additional meaning, assumptions, and transcription into our own ways of thinking. As early as 1910, Carl Becker asserted that the facts of history do not exist for historians until they create them. He and others like Charles A. Beard, reacting against the objectivist assumptions of the school of Ranke, contended that the facts are actually in the mind, taking on meaning only as they exist in someone's thoughts. The very act of creating them introduces the element of generalization into the facts.

A number of historians in recent decades have expressed similar opinions. Carr says that facts cannot be pure because they are refracted through the mind of the recorder. W. H. Walsh asserts that historians never accept them as such; first they wonder whether to believe a fact, and then they ask how much of it to believe. Renier points out that the historian does not so much find facts as events "in complex and innumerable combinations." That is, facts (he calls them "traces," adopted from Langlois and Seignobos) "seldom, if ever, come singly. They appear in bundles." Barzun and Graff say that most of them "come dripping with ideas." Bloch declares that sources speak only when "properly questioned."

To repeat, one fact usually comes associated with others. In the February Revolution in Paris someone fired a shot, the troops started shooting, and a massacre ensued. Apparently the occurrence of a shot is a fact, since everyone seemed agreed about this at the time. As to who fired it and why, we have no agreement and no reliable facts. That a crowd had assembled is a solid fact, but why it had gathered entails more facts. That the overthrow of the government of Louis Philippe soon followed is a fact, but why he quit involves a large number of facts, which, more closely examined, look more like suppositions. The government was overthrown: Is this really a fact? Obviously, a new government replaced the July Monarchy, but the king was not forcibly evicted, he abdicated, and probably unnecessarily. Is this being *overthrown*? Apparently, facts are also contaminated by the choice of words.

The aggression of Tsar Nicholas I caused the Crimean War. At the time, many assumed this to be a fact. Stratford de Redcliffe's machinations in Constantinople caused the war—fact? Lord Raglan was an incompetent commander; true or not, journalists in England made it seem to be a fact. Information seemingly factual at the time may, with later perspective and recognition of other elements involved, seem much too dubious to be so considered.

George Stephenson invented the locomotive. For fourth-grade students, at their level of comprehension, this might well be a fact. College students, however, could not accept it as such without adding a whole paragraph of qualifying information. Which raises a very awkward question, to be considered again later.

In all of these examples something other than pure information enters the picture. A nugget of fact also contains elements of generalizations or, in some of them, may be purely a generalization, whatever contemporary opinion was at the time. Facts fringe over into generalizations; some would contend that, strictly speaking, *all* so-called facts entail generalizing.

So, just as in the case of causality, the facts—the poor, despised facts—have been lost. Or have they? Perhaps we are creating unnecessary problems for ourselves, being perfectionists who are too literal-minded. Quite possibly the problem lies in not having divested ourselves of the nineteenth-century belief in the existence of hard, scientific facts, photographic images of reality. They need not be absolute replicas of reality in order to possess a high degree of usefulness and validity, as long as their limitations are recognized. Nor need evidence be totally rejected for a lack of finality of proof. We do not operate that way in real life, in which complete certainty remains a rarity. Just as the modern mind requires causality and the shapes of time, so it must have the security of a seemingly verifiable environment.

Historians must continue to scrutinize the details of past reality, knowing that their recognitions may be fallible but verifiable to a considerable extent also. Noticeably, researchers in the sources, those in the full stream of cumulative history and the closest to the living past, question the existence of verifiable factual information much less than do philosophers and theoreticians. That facts now seem less simple or reliable than formerly adds zest to the game and enriches the understanding.

To assess their actual importance, a solid piece of information in an historical situation should be deliberately omitted, such as the arrival of the Prussians at the Battle of Waterloo or part of the French army being in Algeria during the 1830 "overthrow" of Charles X. Ignore the qualities of the character of Louis Philippe in the February Revolution or the prevalence of the Napoleonic legend at the time of the presidential election in France in late 1848, and neither episode makes sense. Eliminate the defensive existence of the British fleet in the Atlantic, and the Monroe Doctrine's effectiveness becomes inexplicable.

Facts may demolish interpretations. Pirenne's famous theory that Moslem control of the Mediterranean, by cutting off trade with the east, brought on the Dark Ages in western Europe was riddled by successive discoveries of meager but sufficient factual indications that some trade had persisted. Albert Lybyer, long ago, disproved the idea that the Turks forced the Europeans to discover America by severing the latter's trade with the Orient; Turkish commercial statistics revealed that commerce had continued. Michael Ventris's discovery that Linear B of the Minoan script had been written in early Greek eliminated other theories. David Pinckney, by showing that those prominent in French government both before and after the 1830 revolution came, very largely, from the same background, made questionable the conventional assumption that this revolution elevated the upper middle class into power.

Isaiah Berlin, from the experiences of the researcher, reacted particularly strongly against the loss of faith in facts. He maintained that though the edges may be blurred, nevertheless the objective and the true can usually be recognized within their context. The established scientific methodology of validating facts in cumulative history has, after all, such a remarkable record of sifting error from dependable information that, while recognizing the limitations of facts, they may generally be relied upon. The corroborative witness of many scholarly observers lends validity, while subjective preferences, bias, and suppression of evidence conspicuously obtrude in the work of anyone guilty of these failings.

Some facts are a lot "harder" than others. History contains large numbers of well-known, authenticated facts, as true as human senses can record and perpetuate. Names of historical figures, dates, the general occurrence of episodes, the enactment of laws, these and others, make up the proverbial hard core of information for conventional history. Granted that, as in the case of Columbus discovering America, the writer in micro history may still discover flaws if he or she wishes to be scrupulous, such flaws scarcely invalidate the general account of the happenings. With these mental reservations in micro history automatically recognized, the historian goes on narrating about the past.

The historian works with hard facts and soft facts and every gradation between, disabused of the lurking hope that they may actually be photographic copies of reality. Very many historical facts are buttressed by so many probabilities that the observer has no doubt whatsoever of their validity, though they cannot be indisputably proven. We must not, lacking a photographic quality of truth in the evidence, go to the opposite extreme of assuming that our information is so fragile as to be unusable. (Then, too, different persons may observe different things even in a photograph.)

Probably the word "data" is preferable to "facts," inasmuch as the latter, like "causes," may seem to be claiming too much. Historians no longer use building blocks of facts in the old sense any more than scientists use solid atoms. Evidences in everyday life nearly always amount only to statistical probabilities. In historical situations, if the probabilities seem sufficiently convincing, the data are considered pragmatically usable; cumulative history is constructed on this kind of data, tentative and quite possibly temporary but no less valid for each successive round of interpretations.

35

A Kind of Magnet: Generalizations

Generalizations were supposed to be virtually taboo, it will be recalled, among the more strict adherents of the school of Ranke, emerging only as the facts spoke for themselves. In practice, however, historians continued to generalize anyway, often without realizing the extent to which their own background and use of language imposed certain perspectives, assumptions, meanings, and values on their material.

This difference between theory and practice became one of the more vexing problems for the professional historians. All manner of generalizations could be inferred from the data, but the proof could rarely be demonstrated with any convincing exactitude. Though the pursuit of the Holy Grail of the positivists, the discovery of universal propositions, never appealed to most historians, the question of how much generalizing might be permissible was still left unsolved. The more searching the self-examination of the craft became, the more the intellectual sins of the historians became evident, judged by the credo of the school of Ranke.

Respecting the unique too much usually to venture the broader, more sweeping kind of statement, the historians nevertheless used generalizations out of necessity in order to give meaning to an account, to ensure cohesion, and to communicate their findings to others. Interpretations are generalizations; so are all statements of sequence and of causality, as well as assertions of motivation by historical figures, groups, or institutions. Descriptions of relationships, such as classifications or comparisons, statements of regularities and any other inference from data or depiction of trends and tendencies figure as such.

Beyond this, the evidence itself often contains at least implicit generalizations. Historical terms have clusters of meanings associated with them, while history itself is replete with the usage of groups as entities or wholes and could scarcely exist without them. Any word that involves a comparison implies a generalization: "ever," "never," "often," "always," "all," "few," "some," "most," "many," "customary," "typical," "normal," "best," "first," "recurrent." It is not a question of *whether* to use generalizations, only of *how much,* of how valid the necessary generalizations actually may be in each case.

Louis Gottschalk once proposed the following classification: (1) generalizing only when unaware of doing so (the school of the unique); (2) limiting generalizations to the subject under investigation and only within the setting; (3) generalizing on the basis of trends, to go beyond the material at hand but only to indicate antecedent, concurrent, and subsequent events; (4) drawing parallels and analogies to other times and places (a comparative approach); (5) indicating that the trend might be extrapolated into the future, that is, introducing an element of prediction; (6) propounding philosophies of cosmic proportions, like those of Toynbee and Spengler.

The more sweeping the statement, the less susceptible to a satisfactory verification of probable validity, while the more limited the scope, other things being equal, the more likely that evidence can be marshaled to convince others. Therefore, in terms of Gottschalk's six types of generalizations, historians tend to limit themselves to the first three. Only an exceptionally brave scholar in cumulative history, convinced by much evidence, or a novice who does not know the perils, goes on to the more broad general propositions like those of Pirenne, Mahan, and Frederick Jackson Turner. (They are also occasionally presented by professional historians in the form of speculative thought in order to call attention to a viewpoint needing further consideration.) Most historians will use a generalization for only a strictly limited geographic area and time period in which enough data seem evident to establish a credible degree of probability. Even here the historian may be troubled by the uniqueness, the endless differences and gradations, when imposing regularities sensed in the data, and evaluate his or her statements as being tentative, probable, or virtually a certainty.

Even yet, an apprentice in the writing of history still tends to assume that the proper order or procedure consists in first collecting the material, then finding the generalizations and patterns in this data, and, finally, writing up the account. In practice, however, the researcher needs to know what evidence he or she is looking for in the first place, that is, a project begins with certain conjectures (not necessarily the person's own originally) about an episode that can be checked by the evidence. This material, while being collected, suggests other relationships, which compel additional investigations for affirmative or contrary evidence. Looking for data and for generalizations goes on concurrently in a shuttling process of search and re-search. Successive hypotheses may lead down blind alleys or detours. (A letter recently arrived from a colleague currently working in French archives. He writes that "the ratio of what ends up in the wastebasket, compared with the folder, is shocking.") Tentative generalizations guide the search for more evidence, serve as working hypotheses or tools for exploring the past, the road soon being strewn with abandoned suppositions.

In the making of interpretive generalizations, the process of selectivity of the evidence is of the essence. A researcher may be too limited in his or her speculations or may make judgments too soon, thereby missing relevant aspects. He or she may yield to the temptation to generalize on the basis of insufficient data, become too impressed by a certain piece of evidence, discover a few more like it, subconsciously twist several more in order to fit the picture, until, lo, a fascinating generalization emerges. Or a reasonably valid generalization may be concocted for a limited area, then enthusiastically extended too far. In both cases, the historian is trying to draw more from history than the evidence out of the past warrants.

An interpretive generalization in cumulative history sometimes may long obstruct the finding or acceptance of contrary evidence. Sir Arthur Evans's positive ideas of Minoan history delayed a major breakthrough there for several decades. Alex Hrdlicka's fixed judgment that the Indians had been in the New World for, at most, 15,000 years, blocked other interpretations there. Richard H. Tawney's ideas on the rising middle class distorted the search for contrary evidence in the history of the seventeenth-century England. Butterfield, writing about the Whig interpretation, described how specialists corrected small segments of English history, but the dominant viewpoint still blocked a thorough revision, any recasting of the larger picture based on hitherto relatively ignored evidence.

Generalizations, built on the "inferential rather than . . . demonstrative," must be "essentially loose and 'porous' " in order to respect the unique. Tenative in nature, carrying implicit mental reservations, and suggestive rather than conclusive, they are the developed tools of the historian in dealing "with a universe not of absolutes but of probabilities." To be acceptable to professional historians, generalizations must derive from the evidences out of the past, cohere to these materials directly or indirectly as verifiable parts of the context from which they arise. Imposed from external sources, they cannot be valid, whether derived from street-level, philosophical, or ideological sources.

Nevertheless, as witnessed in the chapter on interpretations, generalizations by historians are not necessarily immune to external influences. Butterfield suggests that we have "a magnet forever pulling at our minds, unless we have found the way to counteract it," a magnet that will pull out the generalizations wanted rather than a statement strictly reflecting the evidence. These prepossessions may stem from the mood and stereotypes of the times, though they may also reflect personal background and temperament.

This magnet is all too likely to produce errors in selectivity of evidence: not perceiving areas because they are taken for granted; not deeming such areas as relevant because insights about them have not been personally experienced; blocking insights out by personal feelings or ideology; overemphasizing a keenly felt area of human behavior or the outlook of the individual's loyalty groups. These sustained violations of Rankean doctrine, the obvious persistence of subjective elements in the historian's work despite the ideal of objectivity, helped precipitate the relativist revolt. Headed by Becker and Beard, the rebels concluded that these deviations from objectivity meant that history could only be relativistic. In attacking an objectivity that had become a fetish and in articulating the growing uneasiness that the concepts taken from nineteenth-century science were outmoded, Becker and Beard argued that no one could completely escape a personal point of view and that the historian must therefore be aware of his or her own subjectivism.

In a celebrated address to the American Historical Association in 1931, Becker declared that Everyman was his own historian. Woodward, many years later, suggested that Becker and Beard could in some ways be pictured as the Luther and Melanchthon of history who believed that the laity could "consult the sacred text" without aid of priesthood. By implicitly devaluing the worth of the priesthood's tools and knowledge of historical processes for comprehending the past, historical relativism seemed to challenge the professional historians' canon that generalizations must conform to the known data. Pushed to an extreme, relativism made all versions of history seem of equal validity and raised generalizations imposed by external sources to a value equivalent to those emerging from the evidence. It also implied that the true past is unknowable and that no methodology could ever divulge the true reality. In the very decade when relativist history attained the highest popularity, in the 1930s, the scourge of Hitler's and Stalin's kinds of history underlined the dangers inherent in this approach.

Practical common sense ultimately triumphed, less by rejecting than by absorbing relativism. Experience argued in favor of those insisting upon scholarly intellectual discipline; though interpretations relativistic in nature proliferate, the ongoing discussion nevertheless winnows out, judges and selects, and eventually produces better understanding of the past. The controversy brought a more flexible attitude toward objectivity coupled with a renewed faith in the "canons" and "sacred text" of cumulative history. The relativist debate formed part of the evolution of the thought processes of our age, spurred especially by the popularity of Albert Einstein's theory of relativity, and the continuing development has rendered the argument obsolete. Becker and Beard were heralds, or at least symptoms, of a change in which virtually everyone except the most literal-minded became acknowledged relativists. Much more alert to the fallibility of their individual points of view, historians deluded themselves less about their complete objectivity, became much more aware of gradations, diverse emphases, and the range of probabilities. "Freedom from point of view," wrote Howard Beale, "is not often possible," but being conscious of a personal viewpoint is not that difficult, and historians are, in this way, more likely to counteract their prepossessions by proper professional techniques, including respect for the "canons of reasonable belief."

At least part of the discussion had been conducted in the Rankean terms of subjectivist violations of the ideal of objectivity, of historians remaining a detached observer of their data. The historians' dilemma always had been that, unlike the scientists, they are participants in the human world being described. Now, however, the natural scientists have begun to realize that they, too, are participants in *their* world, that totally objective observation, in the old sense, cannot exist. The so-called Cartesian partition between observer and observed, Descartes's "splitting up of the world into the realm of matter and mind," is being removed, thereby relieving historians of intellectually impossible objectivity in favor of a more attainable goal of reporting their findings in the past with integrity.

A factor other than old-fashioned subjectivity, with its connotations of emotions and biases, may help to account for the magnet in the mind and the diversity of interpretations. Might not historical relativism have a psychological source, be rooted in how the mind itself works? Recalling Kuhn's theory of paradigms, perhaps our intellects function in much the same way with generalizations at a lower level as with universal propositions. Butterfield complained that the Whig interpretation seemed to remain dominant in general English history despite the repeated contrary evidence offered by research in various segments of that history. Major discoveries have tended to come from those individuals not yet habituated to established intellectual patterns. Perhaps the mind is intractible to treating all of the data equally for reasons other than what was formerly called subjectivism.

As the mind explores the surroundings, it files acquired knowledge in an intellectual system coherent and useful to itself. This structure seems to be ordered by a configuration of dominant insights, which on the personal level partakes of a paradigmatic quality and which in turn guides the selection of more evidence and the formulation of further generalizations. Broad summary statements then derive their convictions for their creator in part out of the evidence, but also, at least subconsciously, because they fit the already existent configuration of insights. Evidence not meshing into a personal configuration of ideas may well seem to lack cogency and thereby be disregarded. Protagonists of several interpretations, arguing at cross purposes, may not be so much separated by different external perspectives and personal feelings of the moment as by the sheer intractability of minds, each intellect having become habituated to its own structured pattern of ideas, whatever the happenstance of origin and maturation.

36

Images of the Past: Mental Constructs

For some, these last chapters may have been a Pilgrim's Progress into a Slough of Despond. Interpretations occur in kaleidoscopic variations, causality loses its motive power, facts mock the reader as the Cheshire Cat did, and generalizations lack the certainty of scientific or mathematical proof. Patterns in history—sequences, comparisons, and uniformities—become idealized schemes of relationships imposed upon the past.

Some bewildered readers may feel cheated and decide that the historians have been perpetrating a fraud. If so, a quick glance over the route traversed may be helpful and perhaps reassuring. This pilgrimage started in the mental world of the elementary-minded, where individuals require the certainty of direct, simple answers, their minds being incapable of handling anything except tangible and enduring ideas of dogmatic texture. Necessarily developed in order to cope with the nature of historical materials, the cultural tool of historical-mindedness has become, as have similar tools in the sciences or in mathematics, much too sophisticated for the untutored mind. Any advanced civilization will develop this arcanum of knowledge beyond the comprehension of the public in general.

Confronting higher forms of knowledge, the elementary-minded may assume that statements couched in terms of the tentative or the probable and propositions not magically proven potent in the laboratory or by the computer are not worth knowing. In the mental world of nonintellectuals, such ideas, which for them lack a recognizable form or substance, cannot even exist, hence can only be a form of nonsense. This confrontation must surely be a root cause for nihilism, those individuals not practiced in thought processes filling the resultant vacuum with a set of simple dogmas; they become adept at destructive criticism but remain quite incapable of formulating intellectually acceptable ideas themselves.

Developing one's personal mental faculties is an arduous and long-term affair. Reading this book will not in itself transform habitual ways of thinking, induce an easy transition or modulation from elementary historical-mindedness through the basic historical processes to the level practiced in the Mansion of History. It can, however, prepare the way by charting the route and revealing glimpses of further horizons for those with the curiosity and stamina to seek them.

Perhaps this confrontation, shattering for some, results partially from the wrong kind of education in the first place. The historian's procedures are little more than a sophisticated version of what happens naturally when the curious mind in everyday life—not being required to produce "correct" answers in the classroom—encounters a problem, suffers bewilderment, makes conjectures, tests them, produces a better hypothesis, and so on. Everyman, too, usually functions with probabilities, educated guesses, and tentative conclusions in his own career.

This, however, is only one aspect of the situation. Our age has been passing through a more agonizing odyssey, the ordeal of participating in changing intellectual concepts. The basic assumptions and thought processes with which cumulative history started this century have, with the changing spirit of the age, been transformed. The ordeal of change as the nature of historical concepts has altered is reminiscent of the intellectual distress encountered, according to Kuhn, in a paradigmatic shift from one dominant proposition to another. As described in the preceding six chapters, we have also, as participants, been glimpsing from within somewhat the kind of process of intellectual change that Butterfield described in his account of the emergence of modern science.

Having moved from causes to conditions and from facts to data, a final shift now needs to be contemplated: generalizations carry with them a tacit reservation that they could more accurately be considered Mental Constructs. Perhaps this suggestion should be whispered, since the busy workers in some of the rooms in the Mansion would protest that this is pushing matters altogether too far. Nevertheless, the word "construct" or its equivalent has bobbed up repeatedly in recent chapters. Geyl asserted that determinist causality consists of "constructions in the historian's mind," and Gerschenkron recalls Mach's reference to "arbitrary conceptual constructs" in discussing the historian's continuity. Carr believes facts to be "working models," and Gordon Leff uses the specific term "mental constructs" for ideal types. Kuhn's paradigms, in his schematic description of scientific development, are obviously constructs. Barzun has suggested that the past is an "unstable construct of the imagination," Hexter that the rise of the middle class is an "imaginary construction," and Henry Guerlac says that we "construct an image of the past" by an "act of mind."

Associating the quality of constructs with generalizations assures a more accurate and honest meaning and avoids connotations still heavily laden with the nineteenth-century belief in a final validity derived from facts by empirical methods. Constructs patently consist of idealized representations for a more complex reality, implying the tentative and the incomplete. The historian's world of the past is so complex, so largely made up of the unique, that generalizations necessarily chop off part of that reality and to that extent must be constructs, not photographic replicas of actuality. Though hoping that they capture the gist of the matter, they work, nonetheless, with a form of mental shorthand; generalizations of any scope can only be tentative, always subject to more evidence, new insights, or the possibility of greater precision.

A generalizing construct might be said to perform some of the functions in intellectual terrain that a map does for the geographic. A map depicting political Europe in 1914 will be accepted as true even though neither the political subdivisions of countries nor most cities are indicated, since clarity manifestly requires simplification. Nor will it be rejected because areas of industry, railroad systems, or population densities fail to be depicted, inasmuch as the mapmaker, being selective, deliberately limited the map only to the political. It does not represent all of the truth but is neither wrong nor unreliable as long as it is employed for the intended purpose. And so with generalizing constructs.

They serve as conceptual props to understanding, as units in our thought processes. Relevant materials must be formed into usable units in order to facilitate intellectual work, and, because reality is so packed with endless variables and modifications, the unit requires simplification in order to avoid an entangling clutter of odds and ends. As such they have what Jerome Bruner has called a "regenerative" character, a structural pattern recalling more details to the mind than their verbal expression alone indicates. Mutually intelligible constructs also serve as the means of communication, phrased in ordinary language though full of specialized shades of meanings and assumptions. They range from adjectives to cosmic generalizations, formulated into shapes capable of being transmitted and grasped by other minds, and, properly used, run the gamut from purely tentative speculation to as close to "truth" as the human mind can attain.

Certain types of constructs, those which are more commonly specifically designated as such, require further scrutiny. They include wholes, ideal types, and models. Historians constantly use wholes when talking about, for instance, the middle class or nobility, as though these were actual entities or things in themselves. Although the surface meaning seems to be that their purported behavior applies to all within the group, the historian always maintains the mental reservation that he or she is presumably only describing typical behavior in a group neither clear-cut in composition nor uniform in conduct. Similarly, to refer to "the capitalist" or "the historian" is to postulate an ideal type as reasonably representative of all who share that name; the purpose is to facilitate understanding and communication without denying in the least the existence of variety among the individuals in that category.

To borrow an illustration from Leff, the use of the ideal type by Max Weber (who originated the concept) offers a useful example of its merits and demerits. Purporting to show the influence of Protestantism (mostly Calvinism) on the emergence of capitalism, Weber's *Protestant Ethic* made a useful contribution at the time. Leff, however, points out that Weber's Protestant is a construct of an ideal type, a set of characteristics "out of an unrepresentative selection," while his capitalist, not an authentic human being either, appears as a "rationally calculating entrepreneur dedicated to profit as a calling." As a tool for isolating or identifying social forces and uniformities, it seemed reasonably convincing at the time but did so at the cost of eliminating the more representative and the contradictory. Though apparently establishing a meaningful relationship between Protestantism and capitalism, it also distorted the picture, and not least by omitting Catholic influences.

Simple models have appeared several times in the preceding chapters for purposes of conveying information in a capsule form. Thus, the description of the city-state constituted a rough model set up in order to see the similarities among many towns, subject to later modifications in individual cases. However, the social scientists are much more prone to resort to a model as an "idealized representation of reality in order to demonstrate certain of its properties." Whereas the customary working tool of the historian is the hypothetical generalization, the social scientist frequently employs models as working tools for eliciting additional information. A model is judged by its usefulness in organizing the data in order to get meaningful results; it often makes possible the use of quantitative procedures, allowing the study of deviations and the consequences of assumptions. The economists set the precedent by creating models, equilibriums, and diagrams, simplified versions of reality. Political scientists tend to see fascism in terms of a model applicable everywhere, while the historian views it primarily in terms of the varied characteristics in each specific country.

One ever-present peril in using these constructs is that they may be allowed to escape the gravitation of the data supposedly being represented and to be themselves mistaken for reality. The whole, ideal type, or model may be made to dominate the data, determine the observer's selectivity, and become a Procrustean bed into which data are crammed, whether suited or not. This tool has then fallen into the same deceptive category as the constructs devised by the mythmakers.

Reduced to its essence, the historian's intellectual universe in the preparation of his or her narrative consists of the body of evidence out of the past, a proliferating number of constructs, and two sets of powerful gravitational influences affecting the making of these constructs. One set is internal, inherent in the historian's handling of the evidence, and the other involves the external nonhistorical uses of history.

Dominating the historian's universe is the vast body of evidence that, in the process of using, he or she converts into constructs for purposes of understanding, organizing, and employing as a working tool. In this process of adaptation, of becoming a construct, the original rough image of raw reality undergoes some alteration in content and shape. Hard facts may be virtually impervious to change, while others, finally, undergo considerable modification. This careful transforming of data into constructs while retaining a faithful verisimilitude to the original data lies at the core of the historian's craft. The more the meanings are distorted in the process of being prepared, the less is their validity.

This is the universe of the scrupulous cumulative historian dealing mostly in micro history. External to it are a number of other influences, such as the uses of history by the nonhistorian and the elementary comprehension of those not matured in basic historical processes. Constructs may also be subject to these potent influences, being pulled far away from the evidence and sometimes being distorted out of all true resemblance to their origins. Careful relevancy writers may experience excruciating difficulty in formulating constructs not unduly warped by external gravitations. Popularizers are constantly tempted to use constructs primarily shaped by external sources. General or macro history occupies an anomalous position, requiring constructs for organization comprehensible to people other than historians and therefore remaining constantly subject to nonhistorical influences. Beyond these, floating free of the gravitation of the body of evidence and formulated by external agencies, exist the rudimentary constructs of the elementary-minded and the mythmakers: "Crude ideological interpretations, Marxist or nationalist, conservative or liberal, religious or agnostic, providential or progressive, cyclical or linear. . . ." For the historian, writes Plumb, these are "a violation of his discipline and an offence to his knowledge."

Constructs in macro or general history raise a number of questions to which historians do not now seem to have ready answers. To repeat, obviously macro constructs cohere much less to the evidence, to the immediate reality of the experienced past, than do the constructs in micro history, where the utmost fidelity prevails. In macro history, the large scope of the area results in the generalizing constructs nearly always appearing artificial from the perspective of the micro historian. Though supporting evidence can be found for the resultant shapes of history, their proven authenticity is apt to dwindle as their scope is enlarged.

As such, the constructs all too often are manipulated to fit other generalities in the account rather than being molded by the specific realities of what actually happened in the past. They also tend, in effect, to be imposed from outside by considerations of basic understanding and ease of organization and, therefore, become highly vulnerable to nonhistorical influences. (Consider the prospects of adhering fully to the evidence in a general American history textbook when confronted by the obstacle course imposed by outraged traditionalists, blinkered liberals, doctrinaire leftists, indignant ethnics, and neuralgic minorities.) Macro history is peculiarly vulnerable to distortions by those who use it for public purposes, relevancy seekers, ideological prophets, and philosophers seeking meanings in the past. The micro has increasingly become how the participants experience history in the making, while the macro helps them, rightly or wrongly, to make sense out of it at the time or later.

Certain questions cannot be answered here because no consensus exists among historians. Must macro constructs be totally dependent upon findings formulated at the micro level? Must macro be made up of the small segments of micro? Does sparsity of causal manifestations in the micro invalidate the use of causal factors at the macro level? Or is this kind of conclusion perhaps a surviving residue of nineteenth-century thinking that the small facts must be built up into the broader categories of generalizations. Kracauer, expounding the law of perspective in history, wondered whether the macro and micro dimensions might perhaps be mutually exclusive. Beyond the perfectly legitimate objections to crude impositions of long-term concepts upon short-term happenings, are the micro historians, just possibly, insisting that shapes and contours seen through a telescope are false if they cannot be seen in their microscope?

Contemporaries of the French Revolution knew, in their daily life, that they were living through a novel form of violent upheaval. The medieval nobility, without seeing the broad historical panorama of feudalism, took feudal ties very seriously. Protestants and Catholics experienced something distinctively different in the decades of the Reformation. Peoples entering industrial revolution encounter an innovation in their lives. In each case, the participants perceive a confusing novelty, not the whole picture. The Greeks during the Dorian invasions, says M.I. Finley in *The World of Odysseus,* saw only individual occurrences; "an infiltration over several centuries would not appear to the participants as a single connected movement at all." Though some would believe that reality can only be perceived at the micro level, a case can obviously be made for the broader perspective actually bringing into focus more effectively and quite convincingly many of the shapes of history and the processes at work in the past.

To be sure, some macro constructs have become outmoded, conventional shapes and processes in long-term history accumulated during several generations of historians. Still embedded in present-day accounts, they may reflect the relevancies of former political conflicts and developments, even though no longer persuasive; some of the uneasiness over their persistence may well derive less from the scruples of micro historians than from an eagerness to impose current relevancy patterns upon the past. A breakdown of some macro constructs may not necessarily prove that making valid generalizations is impossible, only that the professional historians need to continue to formulate new ones out of the evidence. (One interesting effort along these lines can be found in William H. McNeill's *The Shape of European History*.)

Narrative has its own forms of compulsion, beyond the strict record of the evidence, and the problem becomes not *whether* to use constructs but *which* ones to use. Beyond formulating the organization of the discourse, they must be constructs that, lying within the range of understanding by the reader, violate the sense of truth of the professional historian the least. The question of understanding has other ramifications, bearing upon the validity of constructs. Is a simplified version of general history actually a *false* history? Is it permissible, at the extreme, to offer simple constructs for Johnny in fourth grade—Stephenson and the locomotive again—constructs false for adults, but which represent, at his level of comprehension, his highest attainable form of truth?

Skill in formulating constructs in long-term history entails the ability to respond effectively to the demands of organization and the needs of various levels of human comprehension with the least loss of the gist of the relevant evidence. It requires veneration of the real past, disciplined deployment of historical processes, and scrupulous adherence to the probabilities. Constructs that are an "offense to his knowledge" cannot be tolerated, but a too rigid monopoly of history at the micro historian's own level of perception and comprehension may in time, in terms of public support, leave him with nothing much left to monopolize.

37

The Jury of Peers: Authority

Leafing through the book review section of the leading American professional historical journal, *The American Historical Review,* the reader will find that certain books may be "a welcome addition," "a sound contribution," "the first comprehensive survey since . . . ," and possibly "brilliant," "profound," or even "definitive." Perhaps an author has been "clearing new ground," or a book "fills an important gap" or offers "new perspectives." However, reviewers also serve as carnivorous vultures clearing away the debris: "an opportunity to update . . . was passed over" by some miscreant, or he seemed not to realize that "his views run directly counter to. . . ." Perhaps the author has "gone out of his way to invite criticism." He or she may lack "satisfactory documentation," be "seriously deficient in scholarship," the "prose . . . repetitious," and, indeed, the whole book may be a "rehash."

Here we have one aspect of authority at work, the Jury of Peers judging the work of its colleagues, a function constantly underway in book reviews, in scholarly monographs and books, and in the sessions of various professional associations. Though the word "authority" seems unpopular, judging by its infrequent occurrence in the index of books, the writers of history continue to be very much subject to the constraints of a scholarly authority little visible to the public.

Earlier forms of authority were likely to be much more conspicuous. An actual Sacred Text, immutable in content, provided the ultimate Word against which to measure all ideas; an ever-changing series of interpretations now furnish the Last Word, the most recent version of accepted knowledge. Explicit canons guided the search for truth in the Sacred Text, but today they combine a living process of higher skills with standards of reasonable belief. In most past societies, officially designated authorities guided people into "correct" ways of thinking with ample means to enforce the accepted views, whereas present authorities, in pluralist societies, function primarily on the level of opinion and repute.

Historians, like artists, have their own individual styles, sets of insights, and approaches that happen to be congenial to their personal background, temperament, and professional experience. Geyl once commented that in any historical work the account of the past "gets mixed up" with something else "in an almost untraceable manner," the writer's own sentiments, philosophy, and personality. Though historians develop personal styles of historical-mindedness, this does not, however, mean freedom to do whatever they please, for they are greatly constrained by their professional associates, by the Jury of Peers. Their constructs are subject to its comprehension, tolerance, and appreciation. Whatever the magnet in the mind may be, the Jury of Peers functions to balance the excesses or deficiencies, to correct the blinders imposed by personal prepossessions.

A book about historical-mindedness that does not deal with the actual methodology of historiography is likely to leave the impression that interpretations are accepted on the basis, within the contemporary mood, of persuasiveness alone. Proof consists in persuading others, however, that one's contentions have been adequately sustained, that proof has been derived from professional competency in using the sources and in devising constructs faithfully depicting the reality found in them. Obviously, each generation of historians nourishes a set of dominant insights, prevailing configurations of thought, and "canons of reasonable belief," and no doubt conforming to the "accepted history" of the times helps to win kudos within the profession. Over a period of time the viewpoint changes, amidst debate and controversy and the achievement of a new consensus, which tends to conform to the mood of a new decade. The ultimate authority, however, lies in the common standards of the craft held by the Jury of Peers, standards that subject all interpretations to the intensive coercion of the evidence and that ultimately correct the vogues and stereotypes of the decade.

This, incidentally, is also a rebuttal to Kuhn's theory of paradigms. His invaluable proposal does offer a most useful insight into the creative process of scientific theories and historical interpretations alike—how the mind works—but glosses over the concluding phase of the process, the function of the legacy of common standards in testing and judging bright, creative ideas. Much more than persuasiveness is involved.

This, too, is the professional's answer to Everyman being his own historian. For the uninitiated, the admission that generalizations actually consist of constructs may seem to allow Everyman to frame his own without consulting the clergy; if ideas are tools, then they may also be weapons at the service of party, group, or social movement, which is precisely what happens when elementary historical concepts prevail at the street level over the more sophisticated. Constructs, however, only seem to be of equal validity to a public that does not understand the other ingredients in historiography. Complete freedom to create constructs at will would mean dispensing with the entire apparatus of the scholarly handling of evidence, to operate without the techniques and skills of the trained historian. To disregard, with parochial and reckless naïveté, the cumulative experience of generations of visitors to the past would be the equivalent of abandoning scientific methodology developed in the natural sciences over the past three centuries. Amateurs lack knowledge of the Sacred Text of interpretations and its Last Word, nor are they cognizant of the canons of reasonable belief and the series of accepted judgments whereby the Jury of Peers safeguards the integrity of its craft.

The fate of a possessor of the Last Word, a scholarly authority on any area, is to be both respected and the perpetual target for attacks. Renier described the process as a "relay race of indefinite duration," and Hexter speaks of "a certain dialectic [which] requires us to augment, or modify, or partially destroy the work of our predecessors in order to advance the art."

Cumulative history, accepted history as currently known, emerges out of the many rooms in this lively workshop of the Mansion, largely invisible to the public on the street. Because of the rigorous discipline and the conscientious scrutiny, historians, in general, have confidence in the work of their peers. Authorities accepted by the public are rarely the same ones trusted by the professionals. Outside of the specialists' own areas, they depend upon other authorities because, obviously, no one can personally master all aspects of history. Historians must also rely upon experts in disciplines other than their own, must "accept much knowledge on trust."

Seen from within the family circle of professionals, the general tone or spirit may seem considerably less sacerdotal than the foregoing, since historians, naturally, possess all the usual human foibles. Like most groups, they also have their elders who, behind the scenes, run affairs. The "pecking order," based on where degrees were earned, where the person is teaching, and his or her rank and area of work, prevails to an egregious extent in all academic groups, a synthetic way of achieving status in ways other than professional achievement. Intellectuals tend strongly to snobbery, quickly consign others to the Outer Darkness.

Sundry intellectual vices include the customary assortment of weaknesses that Erasmus had fun with centuries ago, including pedestrian pedantry. The overzealous guardians of the altar may go to excess because of vested interests, or literal-mindedness, or even the pleasures of enforcing conformity; book reviewers tend to come from this group, since they cherish this way of serving the altar. Occasionally, a reviewer may be more adept at using the standard clichés than in comprehending a line of argument at variance with his or her own insights— some colorful rhetorical pyrotechnics may then bespatter the pages of a staid professional journal.

Another foible, called the "law of proprietary magnification" by the geographer J. K. Wright, states that we tend to overemphasize our own pet ideas or the viewpoints of our school of thought, generation, religion, country, or profession. Defense of prevalent insights and interpretations by those who have a vested interest in their preservation characterizes the group, which has its share of defenders of intellectual property and professional continuity because change would jeopardize status. Wright has also proposed the "law of the disparagement of the past," which consists in refuting the insights and interpretations of our predecessors, especially those of the preceding generation. Seeking to exalt ourselves at the expense of those who preceded us is part of a necessary intellectual liberation in order to clear the way for new creativeness, but loud clamor also attracts welcome attention, enabling aspirants to climb to positions of self-satisfying repute themselves. Carried to excess, this disrupts continuity, results in discrediting insights still valuable and interferes with the cumulative progression of knowledge.

An occasional impatient historian, elated at discovering a personal philosopher's stone, cannot always refrain from deploying the arguments of the cult of progress while advocating some new orthodoxy; its ahistorical thesis may broadly assert that this new discovery has rendered predecessors obsolete and that anyone who does not act accordingly is an old-fashioned has-been wandering blindly in the Outer Darkness. The unconverted stand self-convicted of inflexibility, reluctance to face fresh new viewpoints, and general stuffiness. (Usage of esoteric language, which puts others at a disadvantage, can also be intimidating.) Peter Laslett, under the rubric of "the rediscovery of what unfashionable predecessors knew," suggests that the description of the past as our generation wants to hear it is one reason why "fashions of interpretations seem to proceed as if no one knew anything until this latest and most interesting of all points of view made itself manifest." This kind of brisk interchange, fortunately, has been far less typical of history than of some of the more afflicted sister disciplines.

A mastery of the techniques of scholarship does not necessarily, then, guarantee good history, which is also a matter of the human equation, the sum total of the man or woman using the techniques. Beyond technical skill in visiting and reporting on the past must lie "sympathetic understanding" (Page Smith), honesty, judiciousness, a reverence for reality, and the humble realization of the essential arrogance in pretending to understand a segment of it. The need for these personal qualities, as well as changing intellectual currents, make the historian's task, to quote Woodward again, increasingly "a quest for wisdom instead of a quest for certainty."

38

Occasional Flak:
Always the New History

Though a dedicated social scientist might deride any claims for a *new* history, the preceding chapters have offered a glimpse of some of the continuing alterations in recent decades in response to the intellectual currents of the age. Other aspects have also undergone scrutiny, including the testing and application of new tools and techniques to the evidence.

One fairly common variation, the use of an analytical approach, largely complements the descriptive narrative. Manifestly, descriptive narrative sometimes needs to be supplemented by probing more deeply into specific explanations or into a certain historical process such as revolution or decline. Hence such works as Crane Brinton's aforementioned *Anatomy of Revolution* or Edward Fox's *History in Geographic Perspective: The Other France,* a study of maritime influences in French history.

Positivist zeal for general propositions or laws reemerged among some philosophers exploring the work of historians. Edward Cheyney had offered the last serious effort from within the profession in his presidential address to the American Historical Association in 1923, by proposing six laws: (1) the law of continuity; (2) the law of mutability; (3) the law of interdependence; (4) the law of democracy; (5) the law of the necessity for free consent; and (6) the law of moral progress. The first three are obviously truisms, and the others reflect a last glow of nineteenth-century optimism, dated by the events since then.

Earlier, Henry Adams had applied the law of entropy (degradation of energy) to history, based on the second law of thermodynamics. Carl Becker, in *Progress and Power,* wondered if a source of power, once discovered, was ever lost again, regardless of the later rise or fall of civilizations. Renier, after stressing that laws in history cannot be determined because every event or development incorporates past events and thereby makes exact repetition impossible, quite diffidently offered certain basic regularities. They included: life is reasonable, the law of change, the appointed time, the law of momentum, and political power tends to follow economic power in the community. Toynbee and Spengler, being cosmic generalizers, also offered a series of universal regularities.

For the philosophers, if scarcely for the historians, Carl Hempel's "covering law model" (1942) represented an ambitious attempt to carry the search for laws into the field of history. According to him, the laws of history should "cover" the events, explain them in ultimate terms, as scientific laws do in the physical world. Predictions would then become possible. According to Hempel, the historian's present "explanation sketches" should be progressively refined until they achieve the quality of scientific laws. Subsequently, however, Hempel reduced his covering law model to the level of a probability hypothesis.

Most historians have a "visceral reaction against it," and the subject is too recondite to be pursued further here. Historians agree that laws in their area remain empirically impossible, and any universal proposition can only apply to the one single case upon which it was based. Adequate explanations, they believe, can be provided without the use of laws, and, for that matter, historians do not concentrate that exclusively on the explanatory facet of their accounts. Samuel Beer undoubtedly voiced the consensus when he growled that no one has managed to find any laws in history yet, and it has not been for lack of trying.

It has been said that historians in certain respects have continued to function with a pre-Enlightenment mind, meaning that they antedate the search for uniformities—the classifying, labeling, and systematizing of all human knowledge—as well as the search for universal laws. They write about the past in terms of the everyday world in which people live, the concept of humanity being that of the whole person and of life being a whole, rather than dissecting for specific relationships; to scientize their actuality destroys that actuality. Physicists declare that the law of gravitation causes the apple to fall from the tree, while historians describe how someone came along and picked the fruit before it fell. Meteorologists explain why the hurricane struck, and historians graphically describe what occurred when it did. As the guardians of the collective memory of the community, they visit the past to report what happened, not to search for novel general propositions. Their constant plaint is that their critics are not paying attention to what they are trying to do or, in fact, to what they have accomplished.

History does not fit the contemporary prescriptions; it remains an irreducible discipline that refuses to be classified as either fish or fowl. Hexter has written entertainingly in *Doing History* how the philosophers have discovered that their paradigms do not work when confronted with historiography, and how, in a way reminiscent of the Ptolemaic crisis, they construct "epicycles, eccentrics, and equants" in order to make it accord with their paradigms. Inasmuch as its own basic creed has been respect for irreducible particularity, that history should itself continue to be irreducible is undoubtedly fitting.

Since World War II, the historians have both suffered and benefited from the contemporary disposition to find intellectual security in various aspects of science, and, from this point of view, virtually the entire procedure of cumulative history might seem outmoded to the public. Some social scientists regard history as a weak, underdeveloped science, a backward one still dealing with truisms and generalities, hence at the rear of the triumphant march of science. Many historians, distrusting abstract empiricists and displaying considerable obdurate insouciance about these strictures, would respond that the social scientists' prevailing paradigms and selectivity automatically exclude vast areas of objective reality, including much of the past.

History and the social sciences in the United States mutually divorced each other in the period shortly after World War II. Most historians ceased to consider themselves social scientists, and the last version of the *Encyclopedia of the Social Sciences* very nearly omits history altogether. Simultaneously, however, historians accelerated the appropriation and assimilation of insights, concepts, and techniques from the social scientists, whatever seemed acceptable within their sense of probable validity. In their very nature, historical processes as purported uniformities derive in part from the work of people other than professional historians. The cross-fertilization has gone on, both political scientists and economists having contributed stimulating and admirable history; earlier sociologists who were also partially historians, the Grand Theorists like Weber, also made a strong imprint upon history.

No complete description is intended here, only an indication of why, as disciplines, they parted company, in order to perceive the nature of history from this perspective. The ahistorical, present-minded approach of a large number of social scientists, in the interest of what they consider greater objectivity, in itself creates an unbridgeable chasm. Although social scientists focus essentially on the same area of study as historians, which involves contingencies, irregularities, innovations, and unpredictable elements, they typically eliminate these by concentrating on recurrent patterns. The human personality may be reduced to the level of a guinea pig in a laboratory, limited to its visible behavior in a given set of circumstances, which is then often depicted in a statistical form. Most historians suspect that the resultant correlations are half-truths of less validity than their own constructs and, furthermore, that events frequently do not bear out the purported recurrent patterns or possible predictability.

A certain amount of flak emerges from the community of historians, beleaguered by social scientists: "often muddled and distressingly imprecise"; "superficial generalizations"; "pretense of rigor, science, demonstrations"; "obsessive drive to classify"; "explanation through verbalization"; "restating the obvious in the most obscure fashion possible." Not that this is any more harsh than the comments of social scientists like Irving Louis Horowitz or C. Wright Mills. The latter, in *The Sociological Imagination,* fires away with such shots as "methodological pretensions," "obscurantist conceptions," "irrelevant ponderosity," "the statistical ritual," and "the curious passion for the mannerism of the non-committed."

The foregoing, however, is only one side of the picture. A more thorough survey of the interrelationships, which is not within the scope of this book, would reveal quite extensive borrowing from and experimentation with some techniques characteristic of the social sciences. No serious quarrel exists with the majority of political scientists and economists. As for the sociologists—Arthur Marwick has called this a "love-hate relationship"—some of the historical processes are essentially sociological in nature, but the historian usually finds the contemporary sociologist, now customarily adamantly ahistorical, off doing a statistical study of some minute social sector of the present. Though Comte, Marx, and Weber, among others, were both historians and sociologists, the historians now receive little help from those social scientists who deal in a shifting constellation of neologisms and abstract relationships, sermonize by means of an ostensibly scientifically proven result, and have a tendency to spend more time worrying the methodology along than letting the reader observe the substantive material of a study.

Amidst a certain amount of internecine sniping, the professional historians have experimented with, and to some degree absorbed, quantification, behaviorism, and psychohistory. Far from being novel in the profession, quantification goes back to the 1870s and 1880s, but the recent emphasis on statistics and the computer has greatly extended its usage. Where data are available it can be enormously exciting and valuable in reconstructing an accurate picture of an earlier environment. Such data can provide reasonably accurate knowledge of occupational and cultural groups, the social structure of a community, and population mobility. Quantification has been successfully used with electoral and legislative voting patterns, shipping and commerce statistics, and the incidence of violence and strikes. Primary sources include census records, election returns, roll-call votes, banking records, court archives, import and export statistics, records of towns and counties, and biographical data.

Quantification can be a highly useful method of getting at the "grass roots" and seeing hitherto unsuspected patterns at the mass level, when adequate data are available, which they rarely are prior to the nineteenth centry. One expert, William O. Aydelotte, has warned, however, that the procedure also involves two nonstatistical steps: collecting data on the basis of certain assumptions and making inferences at the conclusion. The raw data frequently suffers from inexactitude and incomparability, and "neat and watertight compartments" usually are not available for purposes of classification. These conclusions may also reflect the nature of prior speculation or, in computer language, "GIGO—Garbage in, Garbage out." However beloved by the public at the present time, quantification has weaknesses, including, oftentimes, a false precision. Also, those things that count the best do not necessarily count the most in history. The end product is only as good as the individual practitioner of quantification may happen to be, the use of statistics in themselves offering no guarantee of validity.

The behavioral sciences grew rapidly in popularity during the 1950s and 1960s. As the name implies, they deal with the behavior of individuals and groups in various political, social, and economic situations, answering the question of why people behave as they do. The behaviorists consider the typical historian's handling of motivation to be based on much too simplistic psychology and offer a method for more precise evaluation. Behaviorism also, as mentioned earlier, rescues the historian from multicausal explanation and its weaknesses in connecting the causal factors with the actual motivations of the historical figure.

Approaching the explanation from the individual's rather than from the broad, causal side of the problem sets up a "dynamic interrelationship of factors" existing in the specific circumstances being investigated. The resultant explanation of the nexus between events is, according to behaviorists, much more specific and credible. In expert hands, some excellent history resulted from this approach. It offered the assistance of psychology where long needed, and it did get away from the overemphasis on economic motivations. It also generated much acrimonious discussion, especially in political science, which was polarized into behaviorists and nonbehaviorists by the controversy. In fully developed versions, behaviorism boldly challenged some of the truths whose validity had been repeatedly experienced by historians, and some of the old errors in truth-telling seemed to reappear in a new guise in some of its more extreme advocates.

Behaviorists by no means agree among themselves, nor is there any consensus about them among professional historians. Some of the general objections, however, run as follows. To begin with, a reliance on any single method rouses unease, a feeling that while the selectivity will undoubtedly reveal a set of data perhaps otherwise missed, this particular focusing of attention will omit equally valid evidence. A false sense of precision veils the "profoundly incomplete" nature of the findings. Elements not quantifiable tend to be eliminated, the human personality being reduced to "tropisms" because only overt external behavior is studied. As Isaiah Berlin expressed it, behaviorism deals with "human beings purely as material objects in space—must, in short, be behaviorist."

To use behavioral data effectively requires a thorough knowledge of the historical context, but does this approach ensure a more intimate grasp of what actually was there? The suspicion remains that current psychological theories of behavior may not actually explain human beings in other times and places, that these theories mostly depict the mid-twentieth-century, Western type of individual. For the historian, these theories of behavior are acceptable only as working hypotheses, but in behaviorist thinking they tend to be used in dogmatized form as conclusive proof. Do historical figures actually behave in this schematized way, or are the limitations on conduct less than assumed, as, for instance, in the role of sheer opportunism?

When the behaviorist starts working with ideal types, the value of behaviorist techniques in eliciting motivations and explanations seems vitiated. Or is their use necessary because not enough convincing evidence (or evidence too complexly interwoven) can be uncovered to achieve the presumed principal benefit from the procedure? That is, for many historians the procedure seems too schematized, the element of determinism too strong, the implicit patterns of behavior too limiting, and the assumption that human beings "react in a similar fashion under similar conditions" too ahistorical. The use of behaviorist constructs as working hypotheses may be perfectly valid when properly used, but the conclusions, often offered as a superior form of construct because they are produced by scientific methods, sometimes seem to have a much lower probability rating than historical constructs should have. As in the case of the quantifier, a useful technique is being assimilated in which the results are only as good as the practitioner; no single tool or technique can in itself be the measure of historical validity.

An increasing development of so-called psychohistory derives from the historian's need for psychological explanations, as well as from the well-known displays of the irrational in our times. Though attempts to blend psychological elements into descriptions of the past go back at least to Wilhelm Dilthey, Lucien Febvre, and Karl Lamprecht at the beginning of this century, the problem of which of the several schools of psychology to rely upon has persisted. Beyond this, the historian distrusts several other aspects, including criteria for the selection of evidence and too much reliance on monocausal explanations exclusively psychological in nature. The use of analogies also makes the historian unhappy, as does the imposition of general theories upon the evidence, patterns that are essentially imposed from sources external to the evidence. Helen Merrill Lynd, criticizing the "reductionism" of psychoanalytical theory, objects to reducing the complex to the simple or to one basic principle, the whole to its parts, the qualitative to the quantitative, human development to rewards and punishments, and human society to the here and now. This does not obviate the pressing need for the psychological aspects of historical processes, testified to by the increasing assimilation of psychological terminology and explanations as these attain common acceptance and understanding; only the use of social psychology, however, has won general approval. It has also been suggested that if historical-mindedness ever undergoes a paradigmatic transformation, the likeliest source of change would seem to be the psychological.

The negative aspects have been accentuated in the foregoing pages as a means of bringing the methods of cumulative history into stronger relief, and only in rare exceptions has the discussion within the ranks of historians reached the intensity of a major confrontation. It has all been a part of the assimilation of tools and techniques seldom altogether new to the historian but now being offered in more sophisticated forms; the experimenting continues before the Jury of Peers, which sometimes seems to worry too much.

Thus, historians adapt the useful without also accepting those procedures that the long experiences of their craft warn them are faulty. While historians are accused of being outmoded and obtusely backward social scientists, they themselves tend to see their former clumsiness being repeated: the assumption that piling up more and more data will eventually produce broad, valid theory; the earlier awkwardness of their own profession in selecting evidence and handling constructs; the confusion between working hypotheses and definitive conclusions; and the heedless creation of popular myths. They still deeply suspect the scientific paraphernalia of being in part merely a response to this generation's sense of truth, reject the arrogant presumption that this is the only avenue to truth-telling and wisdom, and believe that those inebriated by their contemporary popular acceptance as prophets will live to encounter the fate of the historian as a prophet and mythmaker in an earlier day. Historians, maturing historical-mindedness as a way of thinking and as a cultural tool, have benefited from and refined their techniques in each scholarly conflict since the Enlightenment, and the current phase is no exception.

VI

EVERYMAN'S HISTORY

39

Cosmic Meanings: The Prophet

For the general public in the middle of the twentieth century, *the* great historian was Arnold Toynbee, who donned the ancient vestments of the historian-prophet and fulfilled the ancient—and not so ancient—purpose of unveiling for the people profound meanings in human affairs. While the people acclaimed this modern St. Augustine, few praises came from professional historians, some of whom nourished for him all the admiration that an astronomer feels for an astrologer. That professional historians would not accept his work as history in itself is one indication that present-day history resembles its earlier versions as much as modern physics resembles that of Archimedes.

A long lineage precedes Toynbee. The cosmic generalizers, or metahistorians, go back to Plato, Lucretius, St. Augustine, and the Bible itself. The fertile nineteenth century produced Hegel, Comte, Spencer, Buckle, and Marx, and also the racist Count Joseph Arthur de Gobineau; the work of another racist, Houston Stewart Chamberlain, foreshadowed some of the Nazi theories. Next to Marx, the positivist sociologist, Comte, may have exerted the most enduring influence with his vision of a technocratic millennium, to be made possible by the discovery of laws in social science and their implementation by an elite of scientist-technocrats. Though Comte, like Marx, called his history scientific, he forced his facts into a preconceived system of progress through successive theological, metaphysical, and positive ages. His work, along with that of Darwin, Buckle, and Marx, is characteristic of the mid-nineteenth century, with its exciting discoveries of new vistas.

Pitirim A. Sorokin, also a sociologist, tried to find cosmic generalizations by the statistical approach. Using many tables and graphs, Sorokin purported to show historical patterns based on the ideational, the idealistic, and the sensate. On the surface vastly impressive for a statistically minded age, his data concealed the subjective selectivity whereby he produced the statistics in the first place and which, for the historian, invalidated the whole procedure.

Oswald Spengler published *The Decline of the West* in 1918, timed perfectly to offer answers for Europeans shattered by the experience of World War I. He presented a cyclical history in which self-contained cultures inevitably passed through successive stages of youth, maturity, and old age, each culture going through the same parallel phases. For Europeans, the book offered the consolation that what had happened could not be helped, no responsibility devolving upon them because the catastrophe had been determined by the cycle itself.

His scheme involved essentially five cultures—the Egyptian, Babylonian, classical, Arabic, or "Magian," and Western, or "Faustian"—each of which followed the same sequence without interacting upon each other or displaying any cumulative growth in world culture. Following the traditional and hierarchical forms of society came the imperialistic and socialistic stages, Europe being in its imperialistic phase when Spengler was writing. The first great war, he asserted, would be followed by a series of them, plebeian Caesars would arise, and a "rootless" urban civilization would lose touch with the natural organic processes. Spengler's account did have certain fascinating insights, drew some suggestive parallels, and bore just enough resemblance to subsequent events, including the appearance of Mussolini, Hitler, and Stalin and the obsessive, monumental style of building by their regimes, to give an aura of successful prediction to his work. Though Spengler temporarily restored some public faith in history, the historians themselves totally rejected his work.

Spengler was not educated as an historian, and he lacked previous experience with historical materials and methodology. His shapes of history were imposed from outside, based on biological analogy, and he had little genuine success in making them conform to the evidences of the real past. He ignored contrary data and the infinite variations in the human scene while often distorting supporting evidence to fit his patterns, thereby indulging in a "wild, reckless, uncontrolled construction of hypotheses." The cycle itself was based on only the Western and the classical cultures (the two Spengler knew something about), causality being derived from a biological determinism, while his concept of change and continuity reflected his notion of preordained life durations. In sum, the entire apparatus used by the present-day historian for assuring a reasonable approximation of the constructs according to the authentic past is missing in Spengler's work, which typically presents a form of historical-mindedness bereft of the cultural tool being developed in cumulative history.

Arnold Toynbee's *A Study of History,* the first volume appearing in 1934, required twenty-seven years of labor for its completion. Already a well-known historian before he started his master work, no one could possibly be more intensely historically minded than Toynbee. His work conveys a powerful, inspired vision. Tidily compartmentalized, a joy to read for those who know enough history, its profuse illustrations infinitely satisfying, the historians have nevertheless not accepted it as history. A more detailed analysis will reveal, broadly, the objections to all cosmic generalizers, the "system-mongers," to use Trevor-Roper's epithet.

In superficial appearance, Toynbee's earlier volumes seem

empirical enough, give the impression of being solidly based on scientific methodology through the building up of generalizations by an elaborate collecting and weighing of the evidence. Much talk of regularities, laws, norms, and historical processes bolsters his claims. Closer examination, however, reveals the series of examples that buttress his conclusions, and which convince all except the expert, to be illustrations, not proofs. The examples have been carefully selected and arranged to fit the concepts, "marshalled in accordance with the writer's preconceived conclusions" (Geyl), the result being, at best, a half-truth. Under a barrage of criticism, Toynbee virtually abandoned the empirical pose in the later volumes, where he increasingly emerges as an historian turned prophet, one seeking the Hand of God in human history while writing a theodicy under the inspiration of faith.

Toynbee applies his patterns, drawn largely from Graeco-Roman history, to all ages of history, patterns that may be utterly alien to the spirit, values, and particular genius of these other eras. His own moral judgments, writes Henri Frankfort, are peculiarly nineteenth-century Western European, as witness his belief that the Polynesians and the Zuni, societies that had achieved enduring harmony, should be considered "arrested" in development because they were not pursuing the characteristic goals of recent Western society.

Toynbee posits twenty-one civilizations, plus several more that he considered abortive or arrested, which he treats as wholes, an especially dangerous kind of historical construct if applied literally. Alfred Kroeber, an anthropologist, wondered why he stopped with twenty-one, thereby omitting such others as the Pueblos, the Northwest Indians, and the Congo–West African complex. In this breathtaking classification, can these twenty-one, stretching over all of recorded history, actually be comparable as civilizations, identifiable as similar entities, and amenable to such comparative methods? In an unconvincing analogy with biology, they are compared to representatives of a species, primitive societies being another species in this genus. Not approving of the national state, that supreme reality of our age, Toynbee glosses over it to talk instead about civilizations, but nevertheless he frequently selects examples from national history to illustrate the evolution of that larger entity, a civilization.

Part of the pleasure in reading Toynbee derives from watching him develop his shapes of history, including his choices of historical processes. Some of these manifestations almost any historian vaguely senses as possible shapes or regularities, and here they appear in a fully articulated form. Initially, at least, the slow and seemingly secure construction of these patterns induces a certain comforting confidence in the writer. A reader may sometimes even strengthen Toynbee's case by thinking of additional corroborating evidence. Whatever the validity of his work, Toynbee undoubtedly displays a creative, original, and imaginative mind.

A comprehensive set of shapes and processes appears in these volumes, a few of them already in common usage: challenge and response, withdrawal and return, the creative minority, the dominant majority, the internal and external proletariat, etherealization, the Golden Means, a time of troubles, the universal state, the universal church, and historical fossils. These constructs are beautifully meshed together by an expert artistry that inspires both admiration and aesthetic pleasure to scrutinize. *A Study of History* constitutes a brilliant exercise, a major achievement, and if sheer symmetry and balance of structure alone offered proof, it would be formidably convincing.

Merely as working hypotheses for exploring evidence, these constructs are admirably suggestive and might even be tolerated as cosmic generalizations if plainly intended to be only speculative. If serving as conclusions, they should not be presented more strongly than in a tentative form—a very modest tentative. Apparently Toynbee, convinced by his own constructs, became trapped in his own set of historical processes and made them claim too much. He succumbs to the temptation to universalize his admittedly brilliant generalizations and sometimes even refers to them as laws. Though Toynbee pretends that they have been formulated by means of scientific methodology, they amount to descriptions of historical processes, most of them highly useful if limited to a probabilistic range.

For the critic, the selectivity of the data helps to test the reliability. Toynbee frequently chooses corroborating phenomena while, like Spengler, ignoring or rearranging contradictory evidence. The most startlingly conspicuous omission is his rejection of much of the whole modern era—science, technology, the Enlightenment, and his presenting only the obverse side of modern democracy, industrialization, and materialism—because this does not fit his theses. Koestler points out in *The Sleepwalkers* that the index to Toynbee's abridged volume of his *Study* contains no mention of Copernicus, Galileo, Descartes, or Newton. In the complete work, there are three allusions to Copernicus, two to Galileo, three to Newton, and none to Kepler, all the comments being asides. Naturally, a lopsided view of history results. Toynbee believes that Western civilization has been declining ever since the sixteenth century, and he demonstrates this decline by an unbelievably obtuse neglect of the conquest of nature's forces and by the virtual omission of other major achievements of Western civilization.

Experts in the topics he uses often consider his data dubious, that is, they suspect his treatment of the basic evidence. Factual material often comes suffused with the quality of generalizations not carefully tested. He frequently claims to have established proof, thereafter employing this data in establishing proof elsewhere. Consequently, he does not seem interested in the actual past, which is only "grist to Toynbee's mill" (Geyl). The unique, the variations, the contradictions to his uniformities do not greatly concern him, the parts only deriving their importance and meaning from the whole.

Frankfort calls attention to how Toynbee insists on inserting a "time of troubles" into Egyptian history and a "life in death" after that because his scheme requires them. His use of the "far stretched generalization" becomes equally flagrant when he applies his patterns to the little-known Minoan civilization. Toynbee also uses the "bold analogical argument" (Walsh), as, for instance, in employing "chrysalis" as an analogy for a universal church gestating a civilization. Analogies may be highly useful for purposes of communicating an image to another mind, and they may be used as working hypotheses in probing the evidence, but they do not, in themselves, constitute proof. He constantly uses monocausal explanations, utilizing one single cause in a large number of instances by choosing the one that fits the pattern and ignoring the remainder. While the impact of causal illustrations may be cumulatively impressive, an expert in any one of them will find the explanations superficial; apply independent criticism, and his scheme collapses.

Toynbee makes civilizations break down internally, treating external attacks and conquests much too cavalierly in an a priori assumption that a civilization must first be vitiated internally because his system requires this. Quite correct in some instances, but *always*? Geyl, the most devastating of his critics, cites his listing of Holland as a country becoming successful through challenge and response—the challenge of the sea—but points out his omission of good harbors and good soil as favorable factors. Toynbee also uses New England as a "hard country" successfully responding to challenge but does not bring in the decisive role of the mother country or of sea power in the English victories on the North American continent.

As for his concepts of change and continuity, could so many civilizations in various places and times actually follow the same sequence of development, or does he only superimpose chosen contours upon materials that more closely examined indicate discrete patterns? Each civilization contains within itself various areas of human endeavor—political, social, artistic, technological—surely all do not parallel this pattern? Does he leave enough room for sudden changes within a civilization or for those periods of crisis or creativity when a mold seems to be made that will long endure, as in very early Egypt? The great Englishman, however, provides ample opportunity for chance, as well he might, considering that a chance attack of dysentery in Greece prevented him from serving in a war in which half of his colleagues died.

Arnold Toynbee has many illuminating insights and instructive juxtapositions of materials; despite the foregoing, he is a true genius who created what must surely be one of the greatest intellectual achievements of this century. Even Geyl exclaims: "What learning, what brilliance!" Elsewhere, paraphrasing General Bosquet's immortal exclamation about the charge of the Light Brigade, Geyl writes, "C'est magnifique, mais ce n'est pas l'histoire." Renier believed his great work to be based upon "misleading arguments, intellectually dangerous, and totally false. . . ." Walsh remarks rather sadly that Toynbee could have escaped much criticism, mostly about his historical methods, if he had only admitted to not operating as an historian throughout this masterpiece; this work has the wrong label, inasmuch as historical materials are being used for philosophical or religious purposes.

Badly hurt by the reception of his first volumes, Toynbee did indirectly admit the truth later by becoming more avowedly religious, less the historian. The most savage of his critics, Trevor-Roper, who is as adept with historical processes as any contemporary, referred to Toynbee's Old Testament (the first six volumes) and his New Testament (the remainder) and suspected him of a messiah complex. Many historians would evict him from the Mansion of History entirely for yielding to the temptation to create sweeping patterns in the past and for trying to enunciate a series of ultimate insights as the keys to all of history.

Toynbee, more fairly assessed, is a St. Augustine caught in the twentieth century, who apparently felt obliged to use its terminology and thought processes in order to be heard. More accurately, however, his work presents a cross section of the aspirations and concepts of the later nineteenth century, including much pseudoscientific terminology. It stands in glaring contrast to the disciplined product of the cumulative historians, which, even as Toynbee was working, continued to diverge ever more sharply from its nineteenth-century origins. The sharp criticism of his work measures the width of the divergence.

By no means all would exclude him from one of the many rooms of the Mansion. Page Smith suggests that the great thinker be judged against our contemporary background of minute specialization, of erudite monographs covering small areas in time and place. Stern adds that at least Toynbee did what historians did not *dare* to do, and his reception by the public indicated a genuine need: Everyman still wants meaning in history. Not given it, he turns elsewhere and especially to the ahistorical heirs of the positivists.

40

A Political Tool: Marxism

In 1935, the Soviet regime ceased putting out the collected works of Karl Marx, with over thirty volumes left to go, because the founder was not sufficiently Marxist for Stalinist Communists. Since his opinions sometimes changed, later writings might contradict earlier ones, and supporting evidence for many points of view could be found. Consequently, any short sketch of Marxism, quite aside from the divergences of a number of rival schools of thought, tends to be oversimplified into a caricature. Used as a political tool on the mass level, to which the following sketch is limited, Marxism necessarily appears in an elementary guise; the following comments do not apply to numerous scholars, Marxist or using Marxists insights, who have made indispensable contributions to a better understanding of the past.

In many respects Marx can be compared to such other cosmic generalizers as Toynbee, the difference being that, having become a political tool, his scheme has been implemented in the living world of human beings. Within the intellectual context of its original creation, the work of Marx remains a monumental achievement, one of the greatest in the Century of History. Having focused on the economic aspects of society, on the reality of existent social and economic phenomena, and having traced out in suggestive detail some of its social energies, Karl Marx would still be remembered as a founder of the economic interpretation of history had he never been apotheosized by a political movement. Marxism opened the door to a whole new approach, though it subsequently continued to incorporate within itself the long-obsolete, nineteenth-century devices of causality, change and continuity, and pseudoscientific procedure and terminology.

For serious students first beginning to sense something more to history than a frame of reference, Marxism offers one entry to a higher level of historical processes and uniformities, providing the mental tools for articulating a growing historical-mindedness in a satisfying and intellectually exciting way. The sharply delineated shapes and regularities facilitate groping efforts in learning how to think historically, and tangible entities, the social classes, replace the confusing wilderness of individuals, groups, and happenings, thereby making the past more comprehensible. Facts occur largely in a concrete, materialistic form, making them easy to handle, while simple, comprehensible "laws" provide the conceptual tools for dealing effectively with the informational material. Marxism features movement, sequence and development, a clearly perceptible framework of change and continuity. Causality is clear, specific, and functioning with reassuring determinist power.

Altogether an intellectual package coherent and congenial, it offers a satisfying, if erroneous, sense of using the mental tools of our age for a modern mind striving to penetrate beyond elementary concepts. Used in this way, Marxism generates a feeling of intellectual achievement, of having won the way to great personal insights. It can also serve as a highly successful introduction, a way station, to the basic historical processes of cumulative history; those who come to history through Marxism are, in a sense, recapitulating a portion of the process whereby nineteenth-century history evolved into the present version.

Though legitimate enough in terms of his own time and the conceptual tools then available, the Marxist approach has long since become intellectually outmoded. Marx claimed to be founding a "scientific socialism," but, with the passage of time and the changing nature of science, the "scientific" now has about as much validity as the "socialism" in Hitler's National Socialism. Although denying that theory could be imposed upon the facts of history, Marx nevertheless did so quite flagrantly in his own work. Trying to use empirical evidence to explain the new phenomenon of industrialization, he, in effect, universalized the situation observed in the 1840s through the 1870s, an image that soon went out of joint with reality. The methodology consists in imposing a series of constructs, extracted from a certain historical situation, upon the entire past and projecting it into the future.

Where civilizations served Toynbee as wholes, Marx's sweeping generalizations scooped capitalists and factory workers, feudal lords and serfs, slave owners and slaves into fixed social-class entities. Marx's caricature of a 1850 capitalist became the permanent ideal type of the capitalist, whether in 1550 or in 1950. Bankers, manufacturers, and all the other so-called middle-class elements lumped together became a single archetype. How accurate is it to posit capitalist domination in England in 1750, when the dominant class still derived much of its revenue and power from the land rather than from control of industrial and trading capital? Where do landed gentry and landowning peasants fit into these archetypes?

Once accepted as axiomatic, these wholes can be postulated in various eras and societies, like Toynbee's with regard to Egypt or Minoan Crete, merely because according to the system they *must* be there. Thus, Boris Grekov, a distinguished Russian historian, could, in writing of the early history of the Ukraine, impose the scheme upon sparse archaeological and documentary evidence and fill in gaps with surmises conforming to the system. Russian historians have been obliged to compartmentalize their history in Marxist terms for an area and society where, with Asiatic influences, the pattern reflects the evidence even less faithfully than in Western Europe.

The less an individual knows about an era of society, the more persuasive the Marxist scheme. For the last two centuries, the Marxist constructs, measured against the evidence, have achieved the level of half-truths, symbolizing certain existent social forces in an overdrawn, schematic manner that violates the likelihood of probability. In some other eras, the facile application of terms and shapes has little relevance to actuality, nor do the older cultures document the kind of data the Marxists need.

If the evidence backs up the Marxist constructs anywhere, it should be in the 1848 street fighting in Paris, where Marx himself thought he saw class struggle in full display. Peter Amman has depicted the drama largely in terms of unrest caused by the coming of industrial revolution. On one side of the barricades, he finds manual laborers, but also retail merchants, small employers, and various nondescripts who should not have been there according to the Marxist formula. However, "a very substantial minority" of manual workers also participated on the other side, in the National Guard. Gordon Wright comments that some of the Marxist version is attractive, though "more plausible than convincing."

Seen only from within its narrow frame of reference, Marxism is seductive and intellectually fascinating, like Toynbee's or Spengler's theories. But how much validity can a system have that flagrantly ignores the influences of religion, nationalism, bureaucracy, and the rural countryside? Religion, with its perpetually pervasive influence on humanity, is brushed aside as an old-fashioned superstition, thereby reflecting the simplistic beliefs of nineteenth-century dogmatic materialism. An urban, political movement, Marxism has often appeared hopelessly irrelevant to the countryside, and Marx's own comment about the "idiocy of rural life," spoken by someone who had not lived on the land, reveals the attitudes that would eventually lead to the war of the city against the rural areas in Communist countries. Its consequences, under Communist rule, have been the blighting of agrarian productivity and the unnecessarily low living standards in the cities.

In a century of burgeoning nationalism, the Marxists also originally chose to ignore the whole set of factors generating national feeling. Perhaps the most devastating result of Marxist selectivity, however, remains the disregard of the institutional forces in history. Lenin, to be sure, understood very well how to use institutional power, but in setting up a monolithic party, run from the top, he opened the way to an unrestrained institutional drive, which in Stalinism, if not earlier, would corrode and distort the original movement. Max Weber declared that the ultimate consequence would be the dictatorship of officialdom, not of the workers, and believed that the Marxist mistake lay in failing to ask who would run the socialized industry: the technocrats, the managers, and the intelligentsia wielders of paper forms.

Again as with Toynbee's concept, Marxist causality at first acquaintance seems fascinating and reassuring, though in fact it is now a nineteenth-century museum piece. Standing at the graveside of Marx on March 14, 1883, Friedrich Engels said that "just as Darwin discovered the law of development of organic nature, so Marx discovered the law of development of human history. . . ." According to Marx, material needs and the means of production provide the preponderant motive power in human history, a basically monocausal source of historical forces. At the time, this was a most salutary proposal, one of the most fecund in the history of history, and which in turn led to economic interpretations of the past. Profoundly useful as a construct among other constructs, does it actually exercise such overwhelming hegemony over all other kinds of social energies? Marx goes on to push otherwise illuminating generalizations too far: "The history of all hitherto existing society is the history of class struggles." Rivalries among economic groups may be a constant in history, but "struggle" would usually be too strong a word. Then, using the Hegelian dialectic of thesis and antithesis, he places the conflict between only two classes at any one point in history, each one oversimplified and the conflict, in most cases, exaggerated: "Oppressor and oppressed stood in constant opposition to one another," and now, in the bourgeois age, he saw society "more and more splitting up into two great hostile camps."

Even if, possibly, economic considerations tended to predominate in the nineteenth century, one may legitimately question their equally decisive importance in most eras, this being one more projection of a contemporary scene upon a decidedly different past, the reading of history backwards. This, too, may be magnificent, but, again, it is scarcely history!

Studying the early Industrial Revolution, Marx claimed to have discovered laws derived from economic relationships operating in human society, an inner mechanism beyond the volition of the individual. These forces—steadfast, constant uniformities—prevail throughout history, must prevail, he thought, because they have all the operative power of natural laws in science. Though an element of chance exists and the personality may be of influence, thereby retarding or accelerating developments, nevertheless an economic Hidden Hand determines the ultimate outcome. Marx thus elevated otherwise useful constructs to the level of ultimate scientific truth.

Spelled out further, causality derives its motive power from Economic Man, the other elements of the human personality being grossly subordinated. In the case of the factory workers, he postulated laborers who, stripped of their traditions and not even interested in improving their immediate working or living conditions, were chiefly devoted to overthrowing capitalism. Causes operate with astonishing immediacy here: the behavior of individuals is inexorably determined by the wholes of which they are members, and these wholes, in turn, are propelled in a preordained direction by a deterministic historical evolution. An individual laborer as a member of the working class obeys the automatic impulses of this whole, and the workers as a group thereby generate certain social energies; these, in the class struggle, inevitably help determine a specific sequence of developments in history. Extracted from a more complex reality and rounded out into depicting supposedly autonomous forces, the constructs are grossly overdrawn, intellectual diagrams rather than genuine representations out of the real world.

If Marx had discovered laws, his predictions should have been accurate. But instead of the poor becoming poorer, as he foresaw, the standard of living went up, and, though control of capital did become increasingly centralized, the range of private property continued to expand. Governments learned to control to some extent the economic crises, and capitalism developed planned production. Rather than modern society dividing into two camps, additional groups attained importance, such as the lower middle class, the service groups, and the technicians. Finally, with the growth of service facilities and automation, the actual proportion of factory workers began to decline. Novel, unforeseen developments upset the predicted course of events, which is precisely why the historian normally refuses to project past patterns into the future. When the Communist Revolution came, it happened in Russia rather than in industrialized states as Marx had predicted, due to largely non-Marxist reasons—a transitional stage in industrial revolution coupled with defeat in World War I and the Great Man qualities of Lenin and Trotsky.

These sweeping uniformities, the impression of great and effective causality, the discovery of laws in society, all typify the time of Marx, Darwin, Buckle, and Comte. Applying the concepts of nineteenth-century natural science to the human community was a perfectly natural procedure in terms of Marx's own era. So was the borrowing of the Hegelian pattern of change and continuity, which quickly became antiquated. Marxism was a product of the age, brilliant in terms of the intellectual milieu and the tools then available for historical comprehension, but it became outmoded and obsolete as the historian's tools developed further. Marxism has long since ceased, in any scientific sense, to derive validity from the evidences out of the past. Its successes have their sources elsewhere.

It will be recalled that, according to Ulam, Marx made the mistake of seeing the "death throes of capitalism" in the "birth pains of modern industrial society." Marxism has remained powerful, in part, because it couples the worship of science and technology with protests against the social consequences of the machine age. Losing support where industrialization has been achieved, it survives as a potent political tool in developing countries by reproducing "to a remarkable degree . . . the social psychology of the period of transition from a pre-industrial to an industrial society" (Ulam). As a tool for comprehending history and society, Marxism has always been more effective in non-Marxist countries than in areas where, being dominant, this ideology becomes sacred dogma.

Much of the Marxist appeal lies in its clear explanations for the bewildering changes brought by industrial revolution and in its foretelling of the enchanted shapes of the future. When these predictions, says Camus, failed to come true, the Marxists fell back, like the Christians and their Second Coming, upon the ultimate prophecy of an apocalyptic world revolution some time in the future. Leftist ideology became a successor to Christian millenarianism, appealing to the mood of the apocalyptic in the pseudoscientific language popular with the modern masses and offering the intense moralizing of the millenarianists (or, indeed, of a new Manichaeanism), rooted in the long ages when one family's wealth in the midst of limited resources meant poverty for others. Still obsessed with the ancient conviction that affluence proves a propertied person wicked, Marxism missed, because of ideological blinkers, some of the essential lessons of industrial and technological revolutions, the methods whereby poverty might be eliminated by rapid creation of more wealth.

In organized form, the Communist party took on the contours of a church, with party meetings as chapel attendance, the scriptures of Marxism-Leninism, didactic applications to daily life, and the quibbling by scholars over "theological" details. So pervasive is this phenomenon that an observer might be tempted to wonder if certain elements in the parts of the world that missed the training of these forms of Christianity now have a compulsive psychological need to go through that experience. A Westerner reared in fundamentalist Christianity can almost feel nostalgia for the parallel to the old-fashioned spectacle of earnest, moralistic Christians fervently believing in the Hand of God.

As for the ideological use of the past, the Western professional historians, facing the orthodox Marxist historians, feel that in some ways they are confronting their prophet-predecessors of the last century. With them, history still reigns supreme, the historian, following the party line, serving as the dispenser of ultimate meanings to the populace. Nor do the Marxists suffer from the constant anxieties of their Western colleagues about historical processes. Like earlier Christian writers about the past, they possess a final authority, a rigid pattern of historical development and a strictly delimited body of evidence whereby to prove their conclusions.

Wherever political uses predominate, Marxism tends to reveal most of the defects of very bad history, of those who only visit the past in order to utilize it for purposes of the present. Like a scientific paradigm, this ideology owes much success to the simplicity, neatness, and suitability to the age of its well-integrated body of thought. Marxism functions as a superb political tool for convincing and guiding people by the usage of the elementary historical concepts. At this elementary level, it comes equipped with a driving sense of progress, a full conviction of suffering humanity in these evil days, of the noble savages in the exploited working class, an impending apocalypse of world revolution, and the Golden Age of a classless society. For the adolescent, it provides a special package: justification for restlessness and a craving for change, a political articulation for normal teen-age rebellion, a Plot theory and scapegoats to satisfy frustrations and hatreds, and the élan of the righteous marching out on crusade. For more intellectual types, Marxism offers a ready arsenal of terminology and adds the false assurance of being progressive, sufficiently avant-garde intellectually to possess "advanced" ideas not yet understood by the benighted in the Outer Darkness.

Marxism, as a survival from nineteenth-century history, functions as a rival form of history. It has successfully combined an alluring cluster of street-level concepts with a superficially convincing set of historical processes of a higher order, hence the perennially exciting attraction for the sophomoric mind. Marxist constructs seem all the more convincing because historians all too often neglect to put their own well-developed cultural tool of historical-mindedness at the service of Everyman as an alternative.

41

The Voice of Posterity: Let History Judge!

Alexander Solzhenitsyn in *August 1914* raised the question of the meaning of Russian history in this century; a commentator voiced the queries implicit in this work: "What has it all been for? Need it have been like this? Why did tens of millions have to die, where did it go wrong? Is there any sense in our history?" *Let History Judge* cried another Russian, Roy A. Medvedev, in the title of a book about the Stalinist repression. Former Prime Minister Hideki Tojo of Japan, when sentenced to death for his role in World War II, also appealed to the ultimate earthly supreme court: "Let history judge!"

The public assumes that a major function of the historian is to serve as judge. He or she supposedly officiates as that voice of posterity to which leaders appeal, playing God by sending names to Heaven or Hell, conferring immortality in the community's collective memory while most of humanity goes, nameless, to oblivion. Throughout most of the past, historians usually did perform this role, sometimes telling the story with considerable relish as a morality tale. Morality itself was assumed to be a form of causality, wickedness bringing divine judgment and punishment.

Nietzsche, we recall, early protested the emerging cult of objectivity, saying that by escaping to the past the historians avoided the moral burdens of their own age. At the beginning of this century, Lord Acton insisted on the utter necessity of the historian serving as judge. This seer of the later Victorian Age wanted to "try others by the final maxim that governs your own lives," and claimed that it was "the office of historical science to maintain morality as the sole impartial criterion of men and things." History should be the seat of judgment, inflicting the "undying penalty" of condemnation on wrongdoers.

Everyman, at the street level, continues to make moral judgments in history, blithely substituting moralizing for historical processes and often preferring the Bad King John and Good Queen Bess kind of history. To become an Immortal is to become public property, forevermore the subject of discussion on the level of small-town gossip.

Meantime, the historians, in learning how to visit the authentic past, had become keenly aware of the parochialism and unfairness in this approach. In historicism, they developed an appreciation for the individual manifestation of the human spirit through the ages, as well as for the manifest differences of each age from any other. The becoming of things, the developmental nature of the past in its infinite variety, scarcely made possible any permanently valid judgment at any stage of the transitory events. With every age equal in the eyes of God, how judge historical figures *now*? To impose a certain standard upon a past age or individual would not be to apply absolute truth, as Acton thought, but simply our own equally transitory values and outlook. An age can be judged only from within, thought the historicists, by its own standards of morality.

Out of the requirements of narration, an historian can scarcely avoid certain types of judgment, some at least verging on moral assessments. Pontius Pilate had the excruciatingly bad luck to intrude on the stage of history for one brief hour and to be shown, in the full glare of 2,000 years of enduring memory, in a most unfavorable light. Like a sportswriter telling about the athlete, ordinarily competent enough but who just happens to become the goat in the big game, an historian must narrate this kind of story as best as he or she can, knowing that vanished evidence might have done much to balance the indictment. And, like Pontius Pilate himself, historians wash their hands of the judgment, all the while suspecting the unfairness of fate.

In selecting data to narrate, the historian, like the journalist, constantly plays judge, though not necessarily in a moral sense. By what the writer chooses to tell and, perhaps even more importantly, by what is left out, the historian determines the image of each figure.

Another frequent type of judgment, overt or implicit, revolves about the idea of natural punishment, that certain kinds of behavior by individuals, groups, or nations bring their own chastisement. History offers many possible examples: Hitler's evils caused his ultimate defeat; the Communist seizure of power as a small minority resulted in permanent dictatorship; the weaknesses of the democracies in the 1930s brought on World War II; French failure to begin decolonization soon enough precipitated the wars in Vietnam and Algeria; the Germans going to total war suffered total retaliation. This can be perfectly legitimate at one level, while being only simplistic lessons of history at the other.

Nor can the historians entirely avoid the Big Battalions form of history, viewing the past from the standpoint of the victors. The triumphs of the Big Battalions help mold the shapes of the future, and thereafter the perspective of the historians may cause them to depict the Good Guys emerging triumphant. Another theme, to be sure, dwells on the losers, the romanticized "casualties of history." Power, however, invents its own past when historians become camp followers of the winners in an historical struggle. National unifications in Europe were not necessarily carried out by the most moral or most civilized; it was generally the Tough Guys, seemingly, in Prussia, Muscovy, and medieval Paris who won out, not to forget the Macedonians unifying Greece, the Ch'in conquering the China of that day, and the Romans becoming masters of the Mediterranean basin.

"Every successful act of violence is evil, and at the very least a dangerous example," wrote Jakob Burckhardt, and yet a worldly wise historian, contemplating the long succession of successful violence in the past, may suspect that this is not all of the story. Although the historians give respectability to the victors, perhaps they also contribute to inducing the victors to behave respectably.

If the winners are not necessarily righteous, they triumph because they are the best adapted to the historical circumstances of the time, so runs a common nineteenth- and twentieth-century judgment in several variants. Whatever happens is the product of history; the survival of the fittest ensures that whatever emerges must be historically right. The sheer circumstances of operative historical forces, whether all visible to an observer or not, creates this result out of the sum total of the situation. Conservatives cherish the argument that if something exists there must be good reasons for its continuing survival. Any drastic change may also seem to its supporters to be rooted in history and thereby derive its justification. For the Marxists, the existent is the product of the dialectic, and the victories of socialism the inevitable result of historical processes.

As Berlin has vehemently argued, a belief in these deterministic historical processes eliminates the possibility of moral responsibility or judgments. Any guilt rests on the group rather than on the person because the individual cannot help but act as a member of it, hence individual responsibility ceases. As for the group, its actions are ineluctably determined by historical circumstances, so runs the rationale, and therefore it has no moral responsibility either. Berlin reminds us that the historian deals with real life in a real world where people constantly make judgments and insists that eliminating such judgments in history "is one of the greatest and most destructive fallacies" of the last century.

Certainly we encounter here the core of a moral dilemma of the century, the moral code expected of the individual versus the imperatives and compulsions of the politicians as these are rationalized by mythical versions of the historical processes. The historicists insisted upon the incongruity of imposing righteous judgment on a person behaving within the context of his or her milieu, such as a politician in eighteenth-century England or a successful practitioner of *Realpolitik,* like Bismarck. With what we now know about the irrational and with the multiplicity of other extenuating circumstances, moral judgments may even seem to have an antiquated quality about them. Does this mean that no moral judgments can be made on crematoriums, on Aztecs sacrificing their prisoners, or on slavery? Solzhenitsyn, in his Nobel lecture, protested the application of standards based only on time and place, therein reflecting the perspective of a free soul long embattled with an unrestrained institutional drive and its resultant institutional barbarism, a perspective rarely now experienced by a Western historian. At this extremity of human existence, Lord Acton's austere moral mood reappears, demanding absolute standards beyond the cultural norms of any given era. Watching this spectacle from afar—and recognizing other Solzhenitsyns trapped in other contemporary milieus— does the historian have a duty to defend the civilized aspects of that Western civilization which the sophisticated tool of historical-mindedness reflects and upon whose survival it depends? Or does he or she serve that civilization most effectively by adhering to the role of a dispassionate observer?

Historians offer diverse opinions on the making of moral judgments. Rowse wants us to judge within the standards of the times being described, but Geyl feels an historicism that "acknowledges no standards outside the object" to be "abhorrent." Commager thinks the question probably insoluble, that historians do judge and they might as well admit it; perhaps the best recourse, he thinks, is to provide an accurate account and let the reader do the judging. Butterfield suspected that moral judgments often are political ones in disguise, used on behalf of various causes and accentuating the antagonisms; as a Christian, he sets the whole question within the framework of the "human predicament."

Butterfield did offer a clue to one possible answer in talking about "muddy" moral judgments, a low level of moral observation. Everyman frequently uses a double standard, seeks to pin the blame on someone, employs moral observations to smear one side of an issue, and judges others according to the viewpoint espoused. All this is standard operating procedure by human beings enjoying "the luxury and pleasing sensuousness of moral indignation" while moralizing on the basis of a misapprehension or manipulation of the facts.

"The amateur in history plunges instinctively and often rashly into moral criticism," concludes John Higham, in urging that the historian use a more subtle critique based upon "skilled and patient historical study." Not deploying any set hierarchy of values or ethical absolutes, the writer explores "a spectrum of human potentialities and achievements" with disciplined sensitivity. Keenly aware of the moral standards of the age being discussed, the historian observes what people might have done, *should* have done within that milieu. Most of the historian's judgments do not focus on morality; they consist of commenting on the competency of public leaders, on the caliber of their decisions and their capacity to carry them out. He or she offers explanations, describes the circumstances under which deeds occurred, in place of simplistic judgments; if fairly and adequately presented, the explanations, as Commager suggested, permit readers their own conclusions. Hannah Arendt, in her description of the Nazi concentration camps and their background, provided an excellent example, by amplifying the details of an evil beyond indignation—banal, tawdry, tedious, and bureaucratic.

42

Those Lessons of History

Of course, there are lessons of history. Government leaders use them constantly in the form of habitual conduct, precedences, and repetition of whatever has proven effective before. Here, on a day-by-day level, any high government official must have a very high batting average of success in consulting the past. Most crucial decisions, involving a consideration of numerous factors, necessarily entail the recollection of how similar situations were formerly handled. In this sense, the lessons of history are as constantly in use as the lessons of experience in Everyman's daily life.

This term, however, carries another meaning for the public, which desires an oracle to enunciate broad generalizations, often moralistic and essentially taken from folklore, that will reflect the wisdom and meaning of the ages. Or a succinct axiom providing reliable guidance in a certain set of circumstances. Since history does not repeat itself exactly, lessons cannot be applicable exactly. Since history often broadly repeats itself, lessons may be quite relevant—so broadly and in such numbers that any pronouncement can only be as ambiguous as the Oracle of Delphi; a broad range of past experience in a complex situation conveys many messages whose comparative value for a complex present must be carefully assayed. Lessons undoubtedly exist in profusion, but this wisdom requires circumspect handling, much skill in estimating a series of probabilities. If the world cannot be saved by history, it can perhaps be saved from those who, using bad history, would try to save it.

One of the rich rewards for being historically minded is the development of the ability to perceive comparisons, parallels, and differences between past events and the present. These personal lessons form part of an individual's style of historical-mindedness, and, though all too likely to be at the service of subjective preferences, it would be a pity to eliminate them from the thought processes. Such facile constructs ensure neither reliable proof nor accurate prediction, but an individual does nevertheless gain a greater depth of perception and understanding of the contemporary scene through their persistent usage.

A comprehension of the nature of the politician's simplistic constructs offers another type of lesson. Persons in public life apparently must express themselves in common-denominator vernacular, must use political caricatures in order to convey meanings to all, and much too often this is the only level of communication the mass media will transmit. The individual is enabled to surmount the environment intellectually, attains a clearer understanding of what really goes on, once liberated from a belief in the elementary constructs used by various manipulators of power. Equally helpful is a knowledge of the pedigrees and fallacies of the cosmic systems; these "Idols of the Theatre," as that oddly prescient man, Sir Francis Bacon, called them centuries ago, were refuted by him as "so many stageplays, representing worlds of their own creation after an unreal and scenic fashion. . . ."

Most valuable of all are the lessons emerging out of cumulative history, the wisdom of how things usually happen in the basic historical processes. Because they reflect the real world in which we live, where scarcely anything is totally certain, they lack the surety of predictability, but, compared to elementary constructs and cosmic schemes, their sources in the everyday world of probabilities make them profoundly relevant in confronting the problems of the present. The knowledge of a history more in accordance with reality emancipates us; ceasing to be an animate particle of one or more tyrannical social forces, the individual becomes an autonomous human being.

Consider, by contrast, those volatile particles of social energy, the True Believers. They often serve as the active carriers of elementary historical-mindedness at its most crass, the instrumentality for that *active* ignorance that Goethe once called the most dangerous thing in the world.

To a special degree, Marcel Proust's words apply here: "The facts of life do not penetrate to the sphere in which our beliefs are cherished." The overpowering persuasion of a particular insight, so characteristic of the intellectual novice, obliterates all evidence to the contrary. Obsessed by their own beliefs and energized by emotional intensity, fanatics remain obdurately resistant to observed reality. Greedily absorbing that which accords with their views in a selectivity of very narrow scope, they block out contradictory evidence by an expedient moralism and by thrusting opponents into an Outer Darkness beyond reach of reason or morality.

Manifestly, ideas depict veritable truth for them, hence cannot be mental constructs or tools for dealing with reality. The more subtle thought processes of any mature civilization do not satisfy, and that true wisdom may be doled out in tentative and provisional doses escapes their comprehension. Possessing the intellectual philosopher's stone that will turn the future into a Golden Age, the spirit and texture of their ideas contrast starkly with the cumulative historian's use of constructs.

Some individuals seem doomed, at least for a brief period in their lives, to be part of an elect living on their chosen battleground between Heaven and Hell. They universalize their own ills and project them upon otherwise prevalent beliefs and symbols in the community, whether religious, nationalist, or twentieth-century social creed, and consequently their images of the environment do not reflect the real world as much as measure the intensity of their own inner suffering. Their portrayal of the external world should be taken seriously only as an indication of inner states of mind and feeling. Though the mass media customarily depict such people as an integral part of the community, as leaders or representatives of one side or the other in public controversies, in truth they live in another dimension, explicable only within a psychological framework; normalizing the clinical details as news, the contagion spreads, as did such earlier manifestations of collective irrationality as the witchcraft mania.

History as a cultural tool liberates the individual from the dogmas of the True Believer by depicting realistically the full array of social energies and the tangible contours of the community. It teaches that salutary lesson—what does *not* happen, what, despite the exalted visions of fanatics, cannot be successfully achieved, and that the True Believers usually sacrifice themselves for mundane purposes quite beyond their psychological ability to suspect it at the time. Historical-mindedness rescues those who can rescue themselves, helps them to be more than overheated particles of social energy. As for the rest, in the words of Max Weber, with this kind of crusader "no peace can be made, one can only render them harmless."

To depict the True Believer by means of an ideal-type description may convey a proximate truth, but not so Everyman. He runs the gamut from the True Believer through Becker's Everyman worrying about his coal bill to the professional working at a high intellectual level in his or her own area of endeavor. In the division of labor in the community, the business people, housewives, clerks, factory workers, farmers, doctors, and others have their own preoccupations, can scarcely be expected to mature historical-mindedness as a way of thought any more than an historian is likely to be versed in their areas. Though the historian is the guardian of the past, it is not his or her property; the past belongs to all humanity, and the public is scarcely poaching when using history for various purposes. An historian's neighbors, whose past is often an ever-present dimension in their lives too, do not deserve to be relegated to the Outer Darkness.

The most striking feature of Becker's Everyman address, read decades later, is Becker's recognition that Everyman obviously *is* his own historian, rather than that he *should* be. Beyond the personal uses of the individual for his or her own day, the past also belongs to families, local communities, and traditional affiliations. Nations, churches, associations, and political movements inculcate loyalties, sometimes eventually rendered more intellectually respectable by the historians' influences, sometimes not. The historical dimension is automatically appropriated in order to ensure group cohesion and to expedite cooperative effort in the resolution of public problems. Elementary constructs, however much they distort the realities, continue to serve as part of the living fabric of society in the form of common-denominator communications. History's authentic lessons go unheeded by those who, in often the most well-meaning way and guided by their preferences, offer answers derived from faulty political mathematics, leaving out of the equation what they do not like or find inconvenient or do not realize exists.

Meantime, concentrating on the discipline of cumulative history, the historians have been caught up in the intellectual momentum of their profession, the intensification of the characteristic thought processes of their own group. Their typical response to the public could well seem to the outsider to take the form of trying to turn everybody into historians, rather like Joachim of Fiore wanting to save the world by converting everyone into contemplative monks. As witnessed in these last four chapters, Everyman is denied the use of history for ultimate meanings, political creeds, moral judgments, and axiomatic lessons. It may seem to many that the historian, as a guide to the past, has wandered out of sight of those who might wish to follow him or her. The layperson now seldom consults the professional historian for practical purposes, and the historian rarely effectively meets the civic needs of the forum, thereby virtually relinquishing the entire area to elementary constructs or truncated ahistorical doctrines. A profession that neglects to cultivate its grass roots would seem to risk vitiating its own vitality.

Confronted with this essentially insoluble dilemma, the historian—and especially students planning to teach—would do well to reconsider the historian's immemorial skills as both storyteller and schoolteacher and to recall how priesthoods, always faced with this same dilemma of knowledge at more than one level, have handled the problem in the past. In one form or another, they presented knowledge at several stages of comprehension, starting with stories and pageants and ranging up to abstract theology at the intellectual level.

We have worried about little Johnny and the invention of the locomotive before. Should he be told that Stephenson invented it, or is this bad history? Especially since the scholar's account would pass him by completely. Obviously, this would be poor history in high school and totally unacceptable at a university, but, as a storyteller and as a schoolteacher, the historian knows that knowledge comes in a hierarchy of levels of constructs according to the mental capacities and experiences of the audience. The telling of the story must be gauged according to the readers' or listeners' understanding. Scholarly history is incomprehensible at some levels, conveys no genuine knowledge whatsoever, whereas simplified accounts, conscientiously devised, will impart credible knowledge *at that level* without committing a falsehood. The simple question of an inquiring mind requires a simplified answer, and prematurely answering questions not yet formulated leads to more bewilderment than wisdom.

Historians sometimes behave like parents who, living in the intellectual flatlands of the overly literal-minded, cheat their children of Santa Claus and today's equivalent of fairy tales because these are not strictly true at the adult level, however real they may be in the world in which the small child lives. The human mind needs to be nurtured through the successive phases of its development. It commences to learn about the past by living through many stories, then quite naturally progresses to the elementary concepts that have been repeatedly scourged in these pages, concepts that often automatically spring from the story and serve as obvious explanations for the untutored mind. Students spontaneously resort to these mental tools at the level where the historian commonly commences his or her teaching.

Unless the instructor begins by meeting students' minds at that level, the more advanced concepts may be only memorized for a test, not appropriated as personal insights, and the habitual elementary devices may then remain the credible workaday tools. The task becomes *remedial* by striving to substitute the usage of basic historical processes as these become comprehensible. Elementary concepts, natural at one stage, become ignorance if retained beyond the ability to understand more. Historians are apt to be poor teachers of survey courses if they do not first engage their students at the elementary level and remiss in their duties if they leave them there.

If they want an audience, they necessarily have to develop skills in devising constructs suited to its understanding while simultaneously ensuring that, honestly and with integrity, these cohere as much as possible to the evidences out of the authentic past. Whatever may go on in their minds while visiting the past and producing scholarly accounts of the findings, historians still return, in their more public role, to the duress of composing narratives comprehensible to that public.

As schoolteachers they should, while providing the informational frame of reference of substantive general history, also be encouraging the mental skills of historical-mindedness by something more positive than customary osmosis or imitation of the teacher in the classroom. Historical episodes offer an almost infinite number of opportunities to mature such skills. These skills include an ability to recognize the contours of the authentic past and present, to winnow out the elementary and the fraudulent, an awareness of various social forces, an empathy for interacting change and continuity, some sensitivity for the selectivity of evidence and the tentative nature of constructs as working hypotheses and conclusions, and some sureness in probability reasoning.

Plus, of course, the beginnings of wisdom about how things usually do happen in historical processes. Some acquaintance with both micro and macro perspective is essential. In short-term history, the learner is taken into the present of an earlier generation and vicariously lives through, in unfamiliar surroundings, many experiences familiar to all generations. The macro concepts of long-term history are necessary because the human mind "finds intelligible only what is orderly" (Nowell-

Smith), and they help us make sense out of both past and present. Never fully satisfactory and gradually changing with each generation, they only seem wholly adequate when measured against elementary and rival forms of history.

Charles A. Beard, warning his colleagues a generation ago about the growing gap between the public uses of history and the professional, suggested that plans and schemes based on other criteria are tested in history. More recently, Trevor-Roper wrote that history is "sociology in movement: the empirical evidence of societies in action, and tested by action over a long period of time." Whatever specific practical uses of history may be deemed necessary for justification, the original axiom of the historicists that the nature of things is best comprehended by a knowledge of their development remains at the core of its contemporary relevancy. Though modified by an awareness of the long intricate path between the present and the world of even a century ago, an understanding of the present nevertheless requires the time dimension, a detailed knowledge of how elements in the present have functioned over a period of time. History tells the origins of the present, how things have come to be as they are now, and indicates trends and tendencies, correcting and often virtually nullifying static images of the present based upon only a cross section of the contemporary.

"Without knowledge of the past, the way into the thickets of the future is desperate and unclear," declared Loren Eiseley in *The Unexpected Universe*. Fear of the future is fear of the unknown, but those familiar with the continuum between past, present, and future in earlier historical episodes should rarely feel such terror. In almost any conceivable contemporary situation, the mature traveler to the past experiences a sense of *déjà vu*, that we have stood here before. Sometimes many times. The way into the future appears less desperate and unclear if an individual can recognize familiar contours and recall ancient responses.

Those who lose their nerve are the ahistorical, those suffering dysfunction from the excessive, disjointed stimuli of the perpetually high-decibel mass media and who are unable to reduce events, often ripped out of the context of even the last few years, to proper proportions. The wave of the future is unlikely to be heralded by the crest of the highest visible wave— the extremes of a current vogue; it may come silently and unannounced, like a great swell in the ocean. Watching past generations move into their future instills a certain "feel" for historical processes, a sense of factors relevant for the future, especially those likely to be missed by the present-minded. The historically minded will have their bearings in the thickets of the future, will usually be able to distinguish the significant pathfinding elements from the irrelevant. They will miss some, especially the beginnings of innovations, but will know the probabilities, will know *enough*. If we are living through a "Great Mutation," a sense of history becomes more imperative, not less.

Six generations of historians have been participants in the world of Everyman while simultaneously devising the cultural tool of historical-mindedness. The storytellers of the Heroic Ages responded with tales of bravery, and the chroniclers of earlier mature civilizations stressed the morality necessary for the maintenance of their communities. Cumulative history essentially developed as the product of the democratic, pluralistic community, its attributes reflecting intellectual qualities required for the survival of this form of society. The historians have created an image of a world composed of the unique but which, because only the orderly is intelligible, also possesses visible shapes, identifiable energies, and modes of probable conduct. In each era, the human consciousness—and the conscious intelligence of the living must surely be the ultimate creation of our universe—imprints a characteristic version of the human story upon the scroll of Time. The skills of mature historical-mindedness as a form of thought are inextricably interwoven into the texture of our civilization, and to the extent that they are indispensable for its survival, the ultimate relevancy for the historian is the sustaining of civilization itself.

Bibliographical Notes

Anyone attempting to serve as a reporter of professional wisdom must necessarily articulate the insights, responses, and phrases that have become the common property of the craft; some of the sources are no longer readily identifiable, while the complete pedigrees of others would require lengthy documentation. The basic citations are listed below according to the pages where the material appears.

(Abbreviations: *AHR, The American Historical Review; HT, History and Theory; Studies in the Philosophy of History*; SCTH, Service Center for Teachers of History of the American Historical Association.)

PART I

(5–6, China)   Joseph Needham doubts this commonly accepted story. *Science and Civilisation in China*, vol. I (Cambridge, England: Cambridge University Press, 1965), 101.

(7)   Paul Valéry, *The Collected Works of Paul Valéry*, vol. X, in *History and Politics*, ed. Jackson Mathews, trans. Denise Folliot & Jackson Mathews (New York: Random House, 1962), 114. Sanche de Gramont says that history is the national vice of the French in *The French: Portrait of a People* (New York: G. P. Putnam, 1969), 329.

(7)   C. V. Wedgwood, quoted by Ved Mehta in *Fly and the Fly-Bottle: Encounters with British Intellectuals* (Boston: Little Brown & Co., 1962), 200. Similar comments by Crane Brinton: "There are . . . many mansions in Clio's house," in "Many Mansions," *AHR*, LXIX: 2 (January 1964), 311; by Arthur Marwick: "In the mansion of history are many chambers," in *The Nature of History* (London: Macmillan, 1970), 87; and by Peter Gay: "The house of history has many apartments," in *AHR*, LXXIX:1 (February 1974), 103.

(12)   Jacques Barzun, "History: The Muse and Her Doctors," *AHR*, LXXVII: 1 (February 1972), 61.

(24)   Arnold Toynbee, *A Study of History*, vol. X (London: Oxford University Press, 1954), 139.

(24)   Hugh Trevor-Roper, "Arnold Toynbee's Millennium," *Encounter*, 8:6 (June 1957), 24–25.

(26)   John Lukacs, *Historical Consciousness; or, The Remembered Past* (New York: Harper & Row, 1968), 247.

(27)   Loren Eiseley, *The Immense Journey* (New York: Random House, 1957), 5,11.

(27)   Charles Breasted, *Pioneer to the Past: The Story of James Henry Breasted* (New York: C. Scribner's Sons, 1943), 335–339.

(28, Schliemann)   An alternative version: "Today I have looked upon the face of Agamemnon."

(28, statue)   Kenan T. Erim, "Aphrodisias, Awakened City of Ancient Art," *National Geographic*, 141:6 (June 1972), 782.

(29)   Others who have used the analogy of history to travel include, among others, Butterfield, Kracauer, Marwick, and W. H. Walsh.

(30)   Herbert Butterfield, *The Whig Interpretation of History* (London: G. Bell & Sons, 1951), 17.

(31)   Frederic W. Maitland, *Domesday Book and Beyond* (Cambridge, England: Cambridge University Press, 1921), 356.

(36)   V. H. Galbraith, *An Introduction to the Study of History* (London: C. A. Watts, 1964), 79.

(37, Beard)   William H. Nelson, "The Revolutionary Character of the American Revolution," *AHR*, LXX:4 (July 1965), 999.

PART II

Material and insights borrowed from the following: Elias J. Bickerman, *Chronology of the Ancient World* (Ithaca, N.Y.: Cornell University Press, 1968); Norman Cohn, *The Pursuit of the Millennium* (Fairlawn, N.J.: Essential Books, 1957); William S. Haas, *The Destiny of the Mind, East and West* (London: Faber & Faber, 1956); Julius T. Fraser, ed., *The Voices of Time* (New York: G. Braziller, 1966); Samuel N. Kramer, *History Begins at Sumer* (Garden City, N.Y.: Doubleday, 1959); John B. Priestley, *Man and Time* (Garden City, N.Y.: Doubleday, 1964); *A History of Technology*, vols. I & II, ed. Charles Singer, E. J. Holmyard, & A.

R. Hall (Oxford: Clarendon Press, 1954–1958); Jan Vansina, *Oral Tradition: A Study in Historical Methodology*, trans. H. M. Wright (Chicago: Aldine, 1965); essays by Elizabeth Eisenstein, Arnaldo Momigliano, & Chester Starr in *"History and the Concept of Time," HT*, 6 (1967).

(44) Howard La Fay, "Leningrad, Russia's Window on the West," *National Geographic*, 139:5 (May 1971), 669.

(51) Eisenstein, "History and the Concept of Time," 51.

(52) Irene Nicholson, *Mexican and Central American Mythology* (London: Paul Hamlyn, 1967), 37–38.

(62) Jordanes borrowed the "mistake" from Cassiodorus.

(62) For one detailed analysis of the historical value of legends and king lists, see David P. Henige, *The Chronology of Oral Tradition: Quest for a Chimera* (Oxford: Clarendon Press, 1974).

(81) Herbert J. Muller, *The Uses of the Past: Profiles of Former Societies* (New York: Oxford University Press, 1957), 201.

(83) Mark Twain (Samuel Clemens), *Life on the Mississippi* (New York: Harper & Brothers, 1902), 414.

(89) Butterfield, *Whig Interpretation*, 17.

(91) Raphael Demos, "The Language of History," *Ideas in History*, vol. II, ed. Ronald H. Nash, (New York: E. P. Dutton, 1969), 280.

(94) Pieter Geyl, *Debates with Historians* (New York: Philosophical Library, 1956), 237.

PART III

(For Chapter 12) *A History of Technology*, vols. I & II; Lynn White, *Medieval Technology and Social Change* (Oxford: Clarendon Press, 1962); William H. McNeill, *The Rise of the West: A History of the Human Community* (Chicago: University of Chicago Press, 1963); Russel B. Nye, *The Unembarrassed Muse* (New York: Dial Press, 1970); Geoffrey Barraclough, *History in a Changing World* (Oxford: Basil Blackwell, 1957).

(106) G. M. Young, quoted by Wedgwood, *The Sense of the*

Past: Thirteen Studies in the Theory and Practice of History (New York: Collier Books, 1960), 95.

(107) *The Anglo-Saxon Chronicle*, trans. G. N. Garmonsway (New York: Dutton, 1965), 47.

(109–112) For the most commonly accepted version of feudalism see Marc Bloch, *Feudal Society*, trans. L. A. Manyon (Chicago: University of Chicago Press, 1961). But also see Elizabeth A. R. Brown, who believes that the concept of feudalism should be eliminated, in "The Tyranny of a Construct: Feudalism and Historians of Medieval Europe," *AHR*, LXXIX:4 (October 1974), 1063–1088.

(109) Joseph R. Strayer, *Western Europe in the Middle Ages* (New York: Appleton-Century-Crofts, 1955), 60.

(136–137, witchcraft) Trevor-Roper, *The Crisis of the Seventeenth Century: Religion, the Reformation and Social Change* (New York: Harper & Row, 1968), 90–192.

(145) *Ibid.*, 24.

(145) John Jewkes, David Sowers, & Richard Stillerman, *The Sources of Invention,* 2nd ed. (New York: W. W. Norton, 1969), 183.

(151) Donald Kagan, ed., *Decline and Fall of the Roman Empire: Why Did It Collapse?* (Boston: D. C. Heath, 1962).

(152) Carlo M. Cipolla, ed., *The Economic Decline of Empires* (London: Methuen, 1967), 4.

(162) J. B. Bury, *Selected Essays of J. B. Bury*, ed. Harold Temperley (Cambridge, England: Cambridge University Press, 1930), 60–69.

(163) Geoffrey Marcus, *The Maiden Voyage* (New York: Viking Press, 1969), 288–296.

(164) Butterfield, *Whig Interpretation*, 66.

(171) Barbara Tuchman, *The Zimmermann Telegram* (New York: Bantam Books, 1971), 108.

(171) George Kubler, *The Shape of Time: Remarks on the History of Things* (New Haven, Conn.: Yale University Press, 1962), 87–92.

(172) Morton White, *Foundations of Historical Knowledge* (New York: Harper & Row, 1965), 141.

(175, Kissinger) *Time*, 103:5 (February 4, 1974), 24.

PART IV

(179)   *Time*, 98:15 (October 12, 1970), 16.

(182)   Trevor-Roper, *The Rise of Christian Europe* (New York: Harcourt, Brace & World, 1965), 131.

(190)   Eric Hoffer, *The True Believer* (New York: Mentor Books, 1951), 17.

(For Chapter 22) Robert Redfield, *Peasant Society and Culture: An Anthropological Approach to Civilization* (Chicago: University of Chicago Press, 1969); Marc Bloch, *Land and Work in Medieval Europe*, trans. J. E. Anderson (Berkeley, Calif.: University of California Press, 1967); Michel Crozier, *The Bureaucratic Phenomenon* (Chicago: University of Chicago Press, 1964); Alvin W. Gouldner, *Patterns of Industrial Bureaucracy* (Glencoe, Ill.: Free Press, 1954).

(194)   Lynn White, *Medieval Technology*, 39.

(198)   Jacques Barzun & Henry F. Graff, *The Modern Researcher*, rev. ed. (New York: Harcourt, Brace & World, 1970), 143.

(199)   Lukacs, *Historical Consciousness*, 147.

(201)   Richard Herr in *Ideas in History: Essays Presented to Louis Gottschalk by His Former Students*, ed. Richard Herr & Harold T. Parker (Durham, N.C.: Duke University Press, 1965), 368.

(201)   Gerhard Ritter, "Scientific History, Contemporary History, and Political Science," *HT*, 1:3 (1961), 269.

(202)   Bernard Norling, *Timeless Problems in History* (Notre Dame, Ind.: University of Notre Dame Press, 1970), 200.

(203)   Hoffer, *Ordeal of Change* (New York: Harper & Row, 1964), 66–71.

(209)   David T. Pottinger, *The French Book Trade in the Ancien Régime*, 1500–1791 (Cambridge, Mass.: Harvard University Press, 1958), 23.

(209)   Hans J. Hillerbrand, "The Spread of the Protestant Reformation of the Sixteenth Century," in *The Transfer of Ideas: Historical Essays*, ed. C. D. W. Goodwin & I. B. Holley, Jr. (Durham, N.C.: South Atlantic Quarterly, 1968), 75.

(209–210) Paul Hazard, *European Thought in the Eighteenth Century from Montesquieu to Lessing*, trans. J. Lewis May (New Haven, Conn.: Yale University Press, 1954), xvii.

(For Chapter 25) Butterfield, *The Origins of Modern Science, 1300–1800* (London: G. Bell & Sons, 1950); Eiseley, *Darwin's Century: Evolution and the Men Who Discovered It* (New York: Doubleday, 1958); Thomas S. Kuhn, *The Structure of Scientific Revolutions* (Chicago: University of Chicago Press, 1962). For further illustrations see Elting E. Morison, *Men, Machines, and Modern Times* (Cambridge, Mass.: M. I. T. Press, 1966) 17–44, 123–205.

(215) Edmundo O'Gorman, *The Invention of America* (Bloomington: Indiana University Press, 1961).

(218) Arthur Koestler, *The Sleepwalkers: A History of Man's Changing Vision of the Universe* (New York: Grosset & Dunlap, 1963), 124.

(228) Adam B. Ulam, *The Unfinished Revolution* (New York: Random House, 1964), 6.

(229) A. Rupert Hall in *The Cambridge Economic History of Europe*, vol. IV, ed. E. E. Rich & C. H. Wilson, (Cambridge, England: Cambridge University Press, 1967), 102–106.

(230) Eric E. Lampard, *Industrial Revolution: Interpretations and Perspectives* (Washington, D.C.: SCTH, 1957), 17.

(230) Jonathan Hughes, *Industrialization and Economic History: Theses and Conjectures* (New York: McGraw-Hill, 1970), 57.

(230, China) For an explanation very different from this conventional interpretation see Mark Elvin, *The Pattern of the Chinese Past* (Stanford, Calif.: Stanford University Press, 1973), 285–316.

(232–234) Jewkes *et al.*, *The Sources of Invention*, 62, 45, 27, 96, 82.

(233) Heinz Gartmann, *Rings Around the World: Man's Progress from Steam Engine to Satellite*, trans. Alan G. Readett (New York: William Morrow, 1959), 147.

(237) John H. Elliott, *Europe Divided, 1559–1598* (New York: Harper & Row, 1969), 375.

(238) Lynn White, *Medieval Technology*, 37.

(240)   Cipolla, *The Economic Decline of Empires*, 1–11.

(242)   Kubler, *The Shape of Time*, 33–36, 54.

(246)   Lu Ting-yi, quoted by Klaus Mehnert, *Peking and Moscow*, trans. Leila Vennewitz (New York: Mentor Books, 1964), 381.

(247)   Brinton *The Anatomy of Revolution* (New York: W. W. Norton, 1938).

(248)   Harry Eckstein, "On the Etiology of Internal Wars," *HT*, 4:2 (1965), 133–163.

(250)   Eugene Kamenka, "The Concept of a Political Revolution," in *Revolution* (Nomos VIII), ed. Carl J. Friedrich, (New York: Atherton, 1966), 126–127.

(251, Calvert)   Carl Leiden & Karl M. Schmidt, eds., *The Politics of Violence: Revolution in the Modern World* (Englewood Cliffs, N. J.: Prentice-Hall, 1968), 9.

(251, Johnson)   *Ibid.*, 8.

(254)   George V. Taylor, "Noncapitalist Wealth and the Origins of the French Revolution," *AHR*, LXII:2 (January 1967), 469–491.

PART V

(257)   Friedrich Meinecke, *Historism, The Rise of a New Historical Outlook*, trans. J. E. Anderson (London: Routledge & Kegan Paul, 1972), liv.

(258)   Stephen Toulmin & June Goodfield, *The Discovery of Time* (London: Harper & Row, 1965).

(258)   Fritz Stern, ed., *The Varieties of History: From Voltaire to the Present* (London: Macmillan, 1970), 19.

(261)   Galbraith, *An Introduction to the Study of History*, 77.

(264)   Stern, *The Varieties of History*, 12.

(265, Fustel de Coulanges)   "Ne m'applaudissez pas; ce n'est pas moi qui vous parle; c'est histoire qui parle par ma bouche" in *Revue Historique*, XLI (September–December, 1889), 278.

(266)   Lukacs, *Historical Consciousness*, 22.

(267)   John H. Plumb, *The Death of the Past* (Boston: Houghton-Mifflin, 1970), 108.

(268)   Friedrich Nietzsche, *The Use and Abuse of History*, trans. Adrian Collins in *Thoughts Out of Season*, Part II (London: T. N. Foulis, 1909), 16, 49, 84.

(268)   Julian Benda, *The Treason of the Intellectuals*, trans. Richard Aldington (New York: W. W. Norton, 1969), 75.

(269)   Theodore H. White, *The Making of the President 1972* (New York: Bantam Books, 1973), 498.

(272)   H. A. L. Fisher, *A History of Europe* (New York: Houghton-Mifflin, 1935–1936), vii.

(272–273)   Siegfried Kracauer, *History: The Last Things before the Last* (New York: Oxford University Press, 1969), 114–132.

(276–277)   Butterfield, *Whig Interpretation*, *34*–63.

(277)   Henry Cord Meyer, *Five Images of Germany: Half a Century of American Views on German History* (Washington, D.C.; SCTH, 1960).

(278, Ritter)   Marwick, *The Nature of History* (London: Macmillan, 1970), 176–177.

(279)   Theodore S. Hamerow, ed., *Otto von Bismarck: A Historical Assessment* (Boston: D. C. Heath, 1962), xiv.

(279)   Brison D. Gooch, ed., *The Origins of the Crimean War* (Lexington, Mass.: D. C. Heath, 1969), vii.

(280)   Edward Carr, *What Is History?* (New York: Random House, 1967), 35.

(280)   Cyril E. Black, ed., *Rewriting Russian History*, 2nd ed. rev. (New York: Random House, 1962).

(For Chapter 31)   Peter Amman, ed., *The Eighteenth-Century Revolution: French or Western?* (Boston: D. C. Heath, 1963); Ralph W. Greenlaw, ed., *The Economic Origins of the French Revolution: Poverty or Prosperity?* (Boston: D. C. Heath, 1958); John Hall Stewart, *The French Revolution: Some Trends in Historical Writing, 1945–1965* (Washington, D.C.: SCTH, 1967); George Rudé, *Interpretations of the French Revolution* (London: Cox & Wyman, 1961).

(282)   Rudé, *Interpretations*, 25.

(282–283)   Stewart, *The French Revolution*, 21.

(285–286)   Barraclough, *History in a Changing World*, 7.

(286)   Eisenstein, "History and the Concept of Time," 38.

(287)   Plumb, *The Growth of Political Stability in England, 1675–1725* (London: MacMillan, 1967), xvi–xvii.

(287–288)   Kubler, *The Shape of Time*, 12, 13, 64, 92–93.

(288)   Robert F. Berkhofer, Jr., *A Behavioral Approach to Historical Analysis* (New York: The Free Press, 1969), 229–230.

(288–289)   Alexander Gerschenkron, *Continuity in History and Other Essays* (Cambridge, Mass.: Harvard University Press, 1968), 11–39.

(292)   Jack Hexter, *Reappraisals in History* (Evanston, Ill.: Northwestern University Press, 1961), 71–116.

(295–296)   Gordon Wright, *France in Modern Times: 1760 to the Present* (Chicago: Rand McNally, 1968), 161.

(297)   Lynn White in *Scientific Change . . .* , ed. A. C. Crombie (New York: Basic Books, 1963), 280.

(298)   Hexter, *The History Primer* (New York: Basic Books, 1971), 198.

(299)   Albert Camus, *The Rebel: An Essay on Man in Revolt*, trans. Anthony Bower (New York: Knopf, 1956), 221.

(300)   Barzun, "History: The Muse and Her Doctors," 60.

(303)   Henry Steele Commager, *The Nature and the Study of History* (Columbus, Ohio: Charles E Merrill, 1965), 48.

(303)   Louis Gottschalk, ed., *Generalization in the Writing of History* (Chicago: University of Chicago Press, 1963), 116.

(305–306)   Carr, *What is History?*, 24; W. H. Walsh, *Philosophy of History: An Introduction* (New York: Harper & Row, 1960), 18; G. J. Renier, *History: Its Purpose and Method* (New York: Harper & Row, 1965), 97–98; Barzun & Graff, *The Modern Researcher*, 303; Bloch, *The Historian's Craft*, trans. Peter Putnam (New York: Random House, 1953), 64.

(308)   David H. Pinckney, "The Myth of the French Revolution of 1830," in *A Festschrift for Frederick B. Artz,* ed. David H. Pinckney & Theodore Ropp (Durham, N.C.: Duke University Press, 1964), 52–71.

(308)   Isaiah Berlin, *Historical Inevitability* (London: Oxford University Press, 1954), 61.

(312)   Gottschalk, *Generalization in the Writing of History*, 113.

(314, "inferential") Gordon Leff, *History and Social Theory* (University, Alabama: University of Alabama Press), 80; ("porous") Patrick Gardiner, *The Nature of Historical Explanation* (London: Oxford University Press, 1952), 93; ("probabilities") William Aydelotte, "Notes on the Problem of Historical Generalization," in Gottschalk, *Generalization in the Writing of History,* 175.

(314) Butterfield, *Whig Interpretation,* 6–7.

(315) Carl Becker, "Everyman His Own Historian," *AHR,* XXXVII:2 (January 1932), 221–236.

(315) C. Vann Woodward, *American Attitudes toward History* (Oxford: Clarendon Press, 1955), 20.

(316) Howard Beale, "What Historians Have Said about the Causes of the Civil War," *Theory and Practice in Historical Study: A Report of the Committee on Historiography,* Bulletin No. 54 (New York: Social Science Research Council, 1946), 91.

(317) Not irrelevant to the field of history is Sheldon S. Wolin's essay on paradigms and political theories in *Politics and Experience: Essays Presented to Professor Michael Oakeshott. . . ,* ed. Preston King & B. C. Parekh (Cambridge, England: Cambridge University Press, 1968), 125–152.

(321) Geyl, *Debates with Historians,* 239; Carr, *What is History?,* 136; Leff, *History and Social Theory,* 132; Barzun, "History: The Muse and Her Doctors," 60–61; Hexter, *Reappraisals,* 39; Henry Guerlac in A. C. Crombie, *Scientific Change,* 797.

(322) Jerome Bruner, *The Process of Education* (Cambridge, Mass.: Harvard University Press, 1960), 24.

(323) Leff, *History and Social Theory,* 47; Max Weber, *The Protestant Ethnic and the Spirit of Capitalism,* trans. Talcott Parsons (New York: Charles Scribner's Sons, 1930).

(325) Plumb, *Death of the Past,* 138.

(326) Moses I. Finley, *The World of Odysseus* (New York: Viking Press, 1954), 5.

(326) For one detailed presentation of the micro viewpoint, see the previously cited *AHR* article by Elizabeth A. R. Brown on the concept of feudalism.

(327) William H. McNeill, *The Shape of European History* (New York: Oxford Press, 1974).

(330) Geyl, *Debates with Historians,* 1.

(332)   Renier, *History: Its Purpose and Method*, 88.

(332)   Hexter, *Reappraisals*, 28.

(333)   John Kirtland Wright, *Human Nature in Geography: Fourteen Papers, 1926–1965*, (Cambridge, Mass.: Harvard University Press, 1966), 161–65.

(333)   Peter Laslett in Crombie, *Scientific Change*, 861.

(335–336)   Edward P. Cheyney, "Law in History," *AHR*, XXIX:2 (January 1924), 231–248.

(336)   Carl Hempel, "The Function of General Laws in History," *The Journal of Philosophy*, XXXIX:1 (January 1, 1942), 35–48.

(336–337)   Samuel Beer, "Causal Explanation and Imaginative Re-enactment," *HT*, 3:1 (1964), 8.

(337, pre-Enlightenment mind)   Among others, Alan Donagan, "Can Philosophers Learn from Historians?" in *Mind, Science, and History*, ed. Howard E. Kiefer & Milton K. Munitz (Albany, N.Y.: State University of New York Press, 1970), 242–243.

(337)   Hexter, *Doing History* (Bloomington: Indiana University Press, 1971), 73–75.

(339)   Phrases by Page Smith, Barzun, and Marwick.

(339)   C. Wright Mills, *The Sociological Imagination* (New York: Oxford University Press, 1959), 20, 26, 72, 79.

(340)   Aydelotte, "Quantification in History," *AHR*, LXXI:3 (April 1966), 803–825. Also see Robert W. Fogel, "The Limits of Quantitative Methods in History," *AHR*, LXXX:2 (April 1975), 329–350.

(341)   Berlin, *Historical Inevitability*, 53.

(341–342)   Robert A. Dahl, "The Behavioral Approach in Political Science . . . ," *The American Political Science Review*, LV:4 (December 1961), 763–772.

(342)   A useful introduction to Lucien Febvre, not well known in North America, can be found in *A New Kind of History, From the Writings of Febvre*, ed. Peter Burke, trans. K. Folca (New York: Harper & Row, 1973).

(343)   Helen Merrill Lynd, quoted by Page Smith in *The Historian and History* (New York: Random House, 1966), footnote 129–130.

PART VI

(349, "wild, reckless")   Erich Brandenburg, quoted by H. Stuart Hughes in *Oswald Spengler, A Critical Estimate* (New York: Charles Scribner's Sons, 1952), 91.

(350)   Geyl, *Debates with Historians*, 161.

(350)   Henri Frankfort, *The Birth of Civilization in the Near East* (London: Barnes and Noble, 1968), 28.

(350)   Alfred Kroeber, *American Anthropologist*, 45:2 N.S. (April–June, 1943), 298.

(352)   Koestler, *The Sleepwalkers*, 13, 547.

(354)   Geyl, *Debates with Historians*, 170; Walsh, *Philosophy of History*, 165; Geyl, *Debates with Historians*, 113; Renier, *History: It's Purpose and Method*, 216.

(354)   Trevor-Roper, "Arnold Toynbee's Millennium, 14.

(360)   Amman, "The Changing Outlines of 1848," *AHR*, LXVIII:4 (July 1963), 938–953.

(360)   Gordon Wright, *France in Modern Times*, 170.

(361)   Weber, *Der Sozialismus* in *Max Weber, Werk und Person*, ed. Eduard Baumgarten (Tübingen: J. C. B. Mohr, 1964), 259. (Translation mine.)

(361)   Friedrich Engels in *The Marx-Engels Reader*, ed. Robert C. Tucker (New York: W. W. Norton, 1972), 603.

(363)   Ulam, *The Unfinished Revolution*, 7–8, 29–30.

(364)   Camus, *The Rebel*, 193f.

(367)   Michael Glenny, "Solzhenitsyn's 'August 1914'," *Survey* 18:2 (Spring 1972), 121; Alexander Solzhenitsyn, *August 1914*, trans. Michael Glenny (New York: Farrar, Strauss & Giroux, 1972).

(368)   John Acton, *English Historical Review*, 2:7 (July 1887), 578; Acton, "Inaugural Lecture on the Study of History," in *Lectures on Modern History*, ed. John Neville Figgis & Reginald Vere Laurence (London: Macmillan, 1956), 24.

(370)   Jakob Burckhardt, "On Fortune and Misfortune in History," in *Force and Freedom: Reflections in History*, ed. James Hastings Nichols (New York: Random House, 1943), 362.

(370)   Berlin, *Historical Inevitability*, 47–53,

(371)   Geyl, *Debates with Historians*, 18; Commager, *The Nature and the Study of History*, 60–71; Butterfield, *Whig Interpretation*, 128.

(372)   John Higham, "Beyond Consensus: The Historian as Moral Critic," *AHR*, LXVII:3 (April 1962), 623–624.

(372)   Hannah Arendt, *Eichmann in Jerusalem: A Report on the Banality of Evil* (New York: Viking Press, 1963).

(376)   Weber, *Der Sozalismus*, 267.

(379–380)   P. H. Nowell-Smith, "Historical Explanation," in *Mind, Science, and History*, 228.

(380)   Charles A. Beard, "Grounds for a Reconsideration of Historiography," *Social Science Research Council*, Bulletin No. 54, 10–11.

(380)   Trevor-Roper, "What is Historical Knowledge for Us Today?" *Survey*, 17:3 (Summer 1971), 10.

(381)   Eiseley, *The Unexpected Universe* (New York: Harcourt, Brace & World, 1969), 230.

Index